Nov 14, 1976

To Goldie,
　　With warm & cordial
good wishes for a successful
Convention filled with information
and inspiration and for a very
Happy Birthday.
　　　　Fondly,
　　　　Selma Rapaport

Living
Thoughts

Living Thoughts

Inspiration, insight, and wisdom from sources throughout the ages

Edited by
Bernard S. Raskas

HARTMORE HOUSE
NEW YORK & BRIDGEPORT

Copyright © 1976, by
HARTMORE HOUSE, Inc.
1363 Fairfield Avenue
Bridgeport, Conn. 06605

All Rights Reserved
Manufactured in the United States of America

LIBRARY OF CONGRESS CATALOGING IN PUBLICATION DATA

Living thoughts.

   1. Quotations, English.   I. Raskas, Bernard S.
PN6331.L37   808.88'2   76-22418
ISBN 0-87677-145-2

Acknowledgments

    The quotations included in this anthology were collected over a period of twenty-five years. Every effort has been made to trace materials used in this book. If there is any copyrighted material which has not been acknowledged, its inclusion was inadvertent.
    The editor wishes to thank the following for their kind permission to use copyrighted material:

Abingdon Press—for selection from *When Crisis Comes* by T. Cecil Myers; and for selections from *A Lamp Unto My Feet* and *Devotions For Adult Groups* by Wallace Fridy.

Beacon Press—for selection from *Man's Search for Meaning* by Viktor E. Frankl. Copyright 1959, 1962 by Viktor E. Frankl.

Ruth F. Brin—for selections from *A Time to Search* published by Lerner Publications; and for selections from *Interpretations* published by Jonathan David Company.

Coward-McCann, Inc.—for selections from *Lonely Americans* by Rollo Walter Brown.

Doubleday & Company, Inc.—for selection from *The Substance of Man* by Jean Rostand.

Droke House Publishing, Inc.—for selection from *The Quotable Fulton J. Sheen* by Fulton J. Sheen; for selection from *The Quotable American Rabbis* edited by Samuel M. Silver; and for selection from *Grief's Slow Wisdom* by Cort R. Flint.

William B. Eerdmans Publishing Co.—for selection from *A Touch of Greatness* by Harold E. Kohn.

Hawthorn Books, Inc.—for selection from *Victory Over Suffering* by A. Graham Ikin.

D. C. Heath & Company—for selection from *The Hill Top* by R. M. Lucey.

Holt, Rinehart & Winston, Inc.—for selection from *The Gates of the Forest* by Elie Wiesel.

Houghton Mifflin Company—for selection from *Pleasure and Palaces* by Lester Warner.

Alfred A. Knopf, Inc.—for selection from *The Second Sex* by Simone De Beauvoir.

J. B. Lippincott Company—for selection from the book *Parnassus On Wheels* by Christopher Morley. Copyright 1917, 1945 by Christopher Morley.

Little, Brown & Company—for selection from *As I Remember Him* by Hans Zinsser.

McGraw-Hill Book Company—for selection from *Life Is Worth Living* by Fulton J. Sheen.

Prentice-Hall, Inc.—for selection from *Winning Personal Recognition* by Charles B. Roth; and for selection from *Distilled Wisdom* by Phillips Brooks, edited by A. A. Montapert.

G. P. Putnam's Sons—for selection from *The Path to Leadership* by Field-Marshall Viscount Montgomery; and for selection from *The Need for Roots* by Simone Weil.

Schocken Books, Inc.—for selection from *Art and Society* by Herbert Read.

Simon & Schuster, Inc.—for selection from *How to Stop Worrying and Start Living* by Dale Carnegie; for selections from *Everything But Money* by Sam Levenson; for selection from *The Torch of Life* by Rene Dubos; and for selection from *Human Resources: The Wealth of a Nation* by Eli Ginzberg.

World Publishing Company—for selection from *The Will to Meaning* by Viktor E. Frankl; and for selection from *Search For Love* by Lucy Freeman.

Gratitude is also extended to the following magazines, journals, and newspapers for making available passages which are included in this book:

About Face / Alliance Witness / American Mercury / Arkansas Baptist / Arkansas Methodist / Armstrong Journal / Atlantic News Telegram / Atlas Way

Balance Sheet / Beam / The Blue Jacket / Bulletin, North Lake Tahoe / Burbank News

Capper's Weekly / The Catholic Digest / The Catholic Layman / Catholic Quote / Cheer / Cherryvale Republican / The Christian Athlete / Christian Century / Christianity Today / Cincinnati Enquirer / Civil Service Journal / Clayton "Spokesman" / The Colonel Says / Columbia Record / Construction Digest / The County Parson

Daily Telegraph / Dallas Morning News / Defender / Des Moines Register

Eagle / Ethical Outlook / Everyday Saint

Friendly Chats / Future

Galilee / Good Impressions / Good Reading / Grit

Highways of Happiness / Houston Times / Humor Variety / Humour

Illustrated London News / Indianapolis Star / The International Teamster / Instrumentalist

The Jerusalem Post / The Jewish Press / Jobber Topics / Journal of American Association of University Women / Journal of American Insurance

Locomotive / Look Editorial / The Lookout

Medical Scientist / Megiddo Message / Milwaukee Journal / Modern Maturity / The Mongolian Steppe

National Association of Mental Health / Nation's Business / New Century Leader / New York Post / The New York Times / North Vernon Sun / Nuggets / NYLIC Review

Personnel / Personnel Administration / Personnel Journal / Powerfax / Presbyterian Life / The Proof Sheet

Revue / Rotarian / Royal Neighbor / Royale Forum

San Angelo Rotary Brand / Saturday Review / Science of Mind / Selected / Shield / Sikh Review / Star Reporter / Sunday Guardian / Sunday School Times / Sunshine Magazine / Survey Bulletin / Swedish Newspaper

This Day / Thoughts For Today / Time Magazine / Tit-Bits / Topeka Daily Capitol / Treasures

UNESCO Courier / Uplift

Visitor

Weirton Steel Employees Bulletin / Wesleyan Methodist / Western Recorder

Quote Magazine, issued weekly by Public Speakers Press, Inc., Anderson, S. C., has been an excellent source of materials.

Dedicated to

Ruth and Louis Raskas
Bessie and Rabbi Abraham Halpern

whose memories will always be for a blessing

The publication of this volume

was made possible by grants from the

Phillips Foundation

and the

Elmer L. & Eleanor J. Andersen Foundation

Introduction

THOUGHTS SHAPE our minds and direct our actions; in this sense they are *"living* thoughts." This insight was first stated in the Hebrew Scriptures; it was expressed in the classic tradition by Marcus Aurelius, and it was then reaffirmed in the more modern words of Ralph Waldo Emerson. There is hardly anything new in this observation, even though we tend to overlook its daily as well as long-range implications.

Columbus thought about the sea and became a sailor, eventually touching a new world. Madame Curie thought about chemistry and eventually discovered radioactivity, which in turn laid the foundation for nuclear energy. Charles Goddard thought about outer space and it was his concept that eventually moved men to the moon. In short, we *live* as we *think*.

If this is so in the long-range, it is even more correct about our daily lives. Our best friends and our worst enemies are our thoughts. Thoughts shape what we say, what we are, and how we live. At times, thought can do us more good than a doctor or a friend. On the other hand, destructive thoughts can do us more harm than a blow, an insult, or even an illness. As we *think* so do we *relate* to ourselves, to others, to the wider world.

It is in this spirit that this anthology, *Living Thoughts,* has been created. Its purpose is to assemble some of the greatest thoughts ever set down in writing and to make them available in a systematic way. While *Living Thoughts* is intended for the general reader as an inspirational source of guidance, comfort, and reflection, it can also serve as a source book for public speakers who wish to find ideas for a given occasion, and for editors seeking a facile expression of a specific trend of thought. This collection embraces many thought systems; and thus, what is collected here may reflect some ideas which may not ordinarily be available to individuals who usually work and think in a particular cultural pattern.

Most importantly, it is our hope that *Living Thoughts* will be helpful to every reader who must cope with the perplexing situations in life that we must all face. It has been wisely observed, "The more things change the more they stay the same." Techniques change, programs change, and plans change. But people are still people. Love and hate, joy and sorrow, pain and progress are still part of our lives.

What happens to us is not nearly as important as *what we think and feel* about what happens to us. If we can cope with our feelings, we can cope with almost any situation; for we are as we think.

Thanks are due to Cecilia Rose Waldman whose counsel and practical help enabled this book to see the light of day and to Sheila Edelstein Kaufman whose efforts were most useful in the final editing.

Finally, I express my profound gratitude to those who shaped my thoughts: my teachers, my family, and my friends—and all who have helped me by sharing thoughts on the path of life.

BERNARD S. RASKAS

Contents

1. Thoughts shape the inner world   17

1. Thoughts Are Things
2. Who Is Content?
3. To Create Anew
4. The Wise Use of Wealth
5. Patience Pays Off
6. With Charity Toward All
7. A Sense of Ethics
8. The Pursuit of Happiness
9. Confidence Is Crucial
10. What Is the Idea?

2. Life is with people   34

11. To Crown Our Good With Brotherhood
12. Caring Is a Form of Sharing
13. Peace — The Greatest of All Blessings
14. Born Free
15. Significance of Silence
16. A Matter of Attitude
17. Culture and Commitment
18. Friends and Enemies
19. Love Still Makes the World Go 'Round
20. Universal Is Over All

3. The world around us   50

21. The Greatness of the Outdoors
22. Science — Servant of Humanity
23. The Wages of War
24. Art Endures
25. The Melody Lingers On
26. Action and Passion
27. On Taking a Chance
28. A Thing of Beauty
29. The Natural Law and the Universe
30. Inner Space and Outer Space

4. The function of faith   67

31. A Faith for Living
32. The Bible Is Basic
33. Pathways to God
34. Prayer Has a Purpose
35. Theologies Are Many But God Is One
36. For God's Sake
37. Between the Individual and God
38. Deeds Not Creeds
39. The Grandeur of God
40. Religion Is a Requirement

5. Each age is a stage   84

41. Train a Child
42. Youth Is a Part of You
43. The Middle Years Can Be Marvelous
44. The Time of Your Life
45. The Golden Years
46. To Hallow This Day
47. The Life Cycle
48. From Generation to Generation
49. Death Is a Part of Life
50. The Meaning of Our Memories

6. Learning for living   101

51. What Is Past Is Prologue
52. Teaching Is Reaching
53. The Benevolence of Books
54. The Influence of Inspiration
55. Study Is a Form of Worship
56. The Only Constant Is Change
57. The Good Society
58. Laugh and the World Laughs With You
59. When Trouble Comes
60. Worship Is Worthwhile

7. The family   *119*

61. The Art of Loving
62. A Man and a Woman
63. Marriages Are Made on Earth
64. Parenthood Is Pain, Privilege, and Pride
65. The Family That Stays Together
66. Home Is More than a House
67. Habit and Discipline
68. Margin for Error
69. The Importance of Little Things
70. Making a Life

8. Character is the key   *136*

71. The Greatest Ability Is Responsibility
72. Integrity Is Integral
73. To Tell the Truth
74. To Walk Humbly
75. The Right Kindness
76. Conscience — The Still Small Voice
77. Thankfulness — The Greatest of All Virtues
78. Honest to God
79. Beliefs That Matter
80. Compassion Means Involvement

9. The values in our lives   *153*

81. Dealing In Ideals
82. Understanding Is Essential
83. That Which Is Eternal
84. The Measure of a Man
85. Goals To Strive For
86. Life Is Worth Living
87. A Standard Is Something to Stand By
88. Good for Something
89. The Importance of Giving While Living
90. Growing and Glowing

10. The better part of wisdom   *169*

91. The Use of Judgment
92. Knowledge Is Basic
93. The Very Best
94. Together and Alone
95. The Eyes of the Wise
96. Caution: Mind at Work
97. The Practical Approach
98. The Heart of the Matter
99. Whistle While You Work
100. A Joy Forever

11. Government is for the people   *185*

101. Politics Is People
102. This Land Is Mine
103. Every Day Is Law Day
104. The Enlightened Citizen
105. America, God Shed His Grace on Thee
106. The Democratic Way of Life
107. Power Is As Power Does
108. Discontent Can Be Divine
109. The Just Cause
110. Points of View

12. The meaning of each person   *201*

111. You Can Make a Difference
112. The Duties of the Heart
113. The Fullness of Human Experience
114. Feelings Are Real
115. To Be Aware of One's Self
116. Your Neighbor as Yourself
117. Personal and Private
118. Our Real Needs
119. Achievement That Matters
120. Choose Life

13. Improving the quality of life — 219

    121. With Liberty for All
    122. By Teachers We Are Taught
    123. For the Sake of Humanity
    124. Training Ourselves for Sensitivity
    125. Rest and Recreation
    126. The Power of Speech
    127. Balm for the Suffering
    128. The Open Mind
    129. Worry Wears One Down
    130. Growing a Soul

14. Marks of maturity — 237

    131. According to the Effort So Is the Reward
    132. Health and the Art of Healing
    133. Serenity in the Face of Sorrow
    134. Mentally Awake
    135. The Vital Balance
    136. The High Price of Hate
    137. Problems Must be Seen in Perspective
    138. Pathways to Spirituality
    139. Loyalty Is More Than an Oath
    140. The Calm Within the Storm

15. Toward the future — 255

    141. Hope Springs Eternal
    142. Improving Our Vision
    143. Thoughts on Immortality
    144. The Possible Dream
    145. This, Too, Shall Pass
    146. Mystery and Wonder
    147. The Quest for Meaning
    148. Be Strong and of Good Courage
    149. Moving Toward Tomorrow
    150. A Rendezvous With Destiny

1 Thoughts shape the inner world

1 Thoughts are things

Show me a man's philosophy and I'll show you the man.
G. K. Chesterton

The divinity that shapes our ends is in ourselves. All that a man achieves or fails to achieve is the direct result of his own thoughts.
James Lane Allen

The soul is dyed the color of its leisure thoughts.
Dean Inge

Set aside a little time once a year, at least, to decide where you are going, where are your priorities, ambitions, aspirations—not just in your business alone, but also in the personal things—your own free evenings, your own feelings of status and worthwhileness in life, and your own dignity, your own integrity, your family.
William C. Menninger

A man without a plan for the day is lost before he starts.
Lewis E. Bendele

A man can stand a lot as long as he can stand himself. He can live without hope, without books, without friends, without music, as long as he can listen to his own thoughts.
Axel Munthe

I conceive of God as a verb, not a noun. Intellect manifest in man is to some extent God. God is part of the thinking process of every man.
R. Buckminster Fuller

The greatest revolution in my generation was the discovery that human beings can alter the outer aspects of their lives by changing their inner attitudes of mind.
William James

If we spend 16 hours a day dealing with tangible things and only five minutes a day dealing with God, is it any wonder that tangible things are two hundred times more real to us than God?
William R. Inge

Among the students at a well-known college was a young man on crutches. A homely fellow, he had a talent for friendliness and optimism. He won many scholastic honors and the respect of his classmates. One day a classmate asked the cause of his deformity.

When the fellow said briefly, "Infantile paralysis," the friend questioned further.

"With a misfortune like that, how can you face the world so confidently?

"Oh," he replied, smiling, "the disease never touched my heart."
Pentecostal Evangelical

Mind is the foundation of man. If the foundation is solid, the building is secure. By the same token if a man's mind is filled with holy thoughts, his action will be sound. But if his mind is occupied with selfish thoughts, even his good actions are unsound, being built on a weak foundation.
Baal Shem Tov

A man is what he thinks about all day long.
Ralph Waldo Emerson

Prejudice is thinking ill of others without sufficient warrant.
Gordon Allport

We are not mere sponges of plankton afloat on the tide. We are rational beings, capable of charting the tide and navigating it, and even directing it.
A. Whitney Griswald

The reading which counts is the reading which, in making a man think, stirs and exercises and polishes the edge of his mind.
Leon Gutterman

Capacity to survive is directly proportional to high morale. Cultivate cheerfulness, hope, confidence, optimism, buoyancy and reassurance. Invite anger because it is a healthier reaction than depression or apathy. Curse your circumstances, but not yourself. Never allow frustration to become apathy, apathy to become depression, depression to sink into despair and despair to allow you to accept death. People who fight to live, live. Those who accept death, die.
Eileen Crimmin

The miracle of mind is that it can transmute quantity into quality. This property of mind is something given: it is just so. It cannot be explained: it can only be accepted.
Julian Huxley

2 Who is content?

Blessed is the man or woman who goes through life easily, not irritable, touchy, impatient. It's wonderful how helpful this way of life is to the nervous system; and it is wonderful how much energy it leaves free for useful work.
Walter Alvarez

The most valuable things in life are not measured in monetary terms. The really important things are not houses and lands, stocks and bonds, automobiles and real estate, but friendships, trust, confidence, sympathy, mercy, love and faith.
Russell V. Delong

He who smiles rather than rages is always the stronger.
Japanese Wisdom

Happiness consists in being happy with what we have got and with what we haven't got.
Charles H. Spurgeon

The deed is everything.
The glory is naught.
Goethe

Those who possess gifts must not be possessed by these gifts.
Jas Paul Kennedy

A pedestrian is a man in danger of his life; a walker is a man in possession of his soul.
David McCord

He who understands others is learned.
He who knows himself is wise.
He who conquers others has muscular strength.
He who subdues himself is strong.
He who is content is wealthy,
He who does not lose his soul will endure.
Lao Tse

There are nine requisites for contented living: health enough to make work a pleasure; wealth enough to support your needs; strength enough to battle with difficulties and overcome them; patience enough to toil until some good is accomplished; charity enough to see some good in your neighbor; love enough to move you to be useful and helpful to others; faith enough to make real the things of God; hope enough to remove all anxious fears concerning the future.
Goethe

Lives based on having are less free than lives based either on doing or on being.
William James

There are two tragedies in life. One is not to get your heart's desire. The other is to get it.
George Bernard Shaw

He is richest who is content with the least, for content is the wealth of nature.
Socrates

An old farmer in an Alabama hamlet remained cheerful despite a variety of afflictions that would have shattered an ordinary mortal.

"How do you manage to keep so happy and serene?" marveled a friend.

"I'll tell you," grinned the old man. "I've just learned to cooperate with the inevitable."

Bennett Cerf

We seldom think of what we have but always of what we lack.

Arthur Schopenhauer

Many years ago Rudyard Kipling gave an address at McGill University in Montreal. He said one striking thing which deserves to be remembered. Warning the students against an over-concern for money, or position, or glory, he said: "Some day you will meet a man who cares for none of these things. Then you will know how poor you are."

Halford E. Luccock

For every ailment under the sun,
There is a remedy, or there
   is none;
If there be one, try to find it;
If there be none, never mind it.

Dale Carnegie

It is of great advantage that man should know his station, and not erroneously imagine that the whole universe exists only for him.

Maimonides

---

3   To create anew

Albert Einstein was once asked what he would most like to say to the science students in American schools. Without hesitation he replied: "I would ask them to spend an hour every day rejecting the ideas of others and thinking things out for themselves. This will be a hard thing to do but it will be rewarding."

Oscar Schisgall

Down under the conscious mind is the subconscious mind . . . It is the mental fireless cooker where our ideas simmer and develop, while we are loafing. Newton was loafing under an apple tree when he saw an apple fall and got the gravitation idea. While loafing and finding peace for his soul, Galileo watched the great swinging lamp. It gave him the idea of a pendulum swinging to and fro as a means of measuring the passage of time. Watt was loafing in the kitchen when he noticed the steam lifting the top of the teakettle and conceived the idea of a steam engine. . . . Many times we will get more ideas and better ideas in two hours of creative loafing than in eight hours at a desk.

Wilfred A. Peterson

From all that we know of the creative individual—and we now know a good deal—he thrives on freedom. Recent research shows that he is not the capricious and disorderly spirit some romantics have imagined him to be. He may be

quite conventional with respect to all the trivial customs and niceties of life, but in the area of his creative work he must be free to believe or doubt, agree or disagree.
John W. Gardner

Curiosity is, in great and generous minds, the first passion and the last.
Samuel Johnson

Imagination disposes of everything. It creates beauty, justice and happiness, which is everything in the world.
Blaise Pascal

A book can give greater riches than any other form of recreation but it cannot provide the last answers. They must be found in the loneliness of a man's own mind. Books can help a man be ready for those moments. But neither books nor teachers can provide the answers.
Carl Sandburg

Nothing in the universe reaches its perfection without some dependence on or relation to the external. Not even the coal will give light and heat without first a fire being applied to it; even then it releases the energy the sun stored up in it centuries before. The grain of wheat will not send forth the green stalk without contact with the environment of another world than itself. Why then does man think his basic worries, fears and inner unhappiness can be cured by himself and within himself? The best violin and bow in the world will produce no harmonies without an outside hand endowed with talent.
Fulton J. Sheen

In the Book of Elijah we read: Everyone of Israel is duty bound to say: When will my works approach the works of my fathers, Abraham, Isaac and Jacob? How are we to understand this? How could we ever venture to think that we could do what our fathers did?

Just as our fathers invented new ways of serving, each a new service according to his own character; one, the service of love, another, the service of justice; a third, the service of beauty; so each one of us in his own way should devise something new, in the light of the teaching and of service and do what has not yet been done.
Martin Buber

Creativity is not dulled by age, only by disuse.
O. Aldrich Wakeford

On several occasions men have been likened to sheep, and so far as lack of initiative is concerned, the simile appears to be remarkably appropriate. Most of us spend our lives in getting through gaps made by others. It requires great effort to be original and to avoid the habit of slavish imitation.
R. M. Lucey

It is an erroneous impression, fostered by sensational popular biography, that scientific discovery is often made by inspiration—a sort of coup de foudre—from on high. This rarely the case. Even Archimede's sudden inspiration in the bathtub; Newton's experience in the apple orchard; Descartes' geometrical discoveries in his bed; Darwin's flash of lucidity on reading

a passage of Malthus; Kekule's vision of the closed carbon ring which came to him on top of a London bus, and Einstein's brilliant solution of the Michelson puzzle in the patent office in Berne, were not messages out of the blue. They were the final coordinations, by minds of genius, of innumerable accumulated facts and impressions which lesser men could grasp only in their uncorrelated isolation, but which—by them—were seen in entirety and integrated into general principles.
Hans Zinsser

We learn to do neither by thinking nor by doing; we learn to do by thinking about what we are doing.
George D. Stoddard

Copy nature and you infringe on the work of our Lord. Interpret nature and you are an artist.
Jacques Lipchitz

A famous psychologist once pointed out to me that creative thinking is the reassociation of old ideas in new ways.
Lloyd V. Berkner

---

4 The wise use of wealth

A great fortune is a great servitude.
Lucius Annaeus Seneca

During a depression we lose our houses; during prosperity we lose our homes.
Sterling Price

One day a farmer came to pay his rent to a man whose love of money was very great. After settling the account, the farmer said, "I will give you a shilling if you will let me go down to the vault and have a look at your money."

The farmer was permitted to see the piles of gold and silver in the miser's big chest. After gazing for a while the farmer said, "Now I am as well off as you are."

"How can that be?" asked the man.

"Why, sir" said the farmer, "you never use any of this money. All you do with it is look at it. I have looked at it, too; so I am just as rich as you are."
New Century Leader

Who is wealthy? He who is content with his lot.
The Talmud

At rainbow's end, long journey's close,
One man when he was very old
Found the fabled treasure pot
Then wept that it held only gold.
Anonymous

If all the gold in the world were melted down into a solid cube it would be about the size of an eight-room house. If a man got possession of all that gold—billions of dollars' worth—he could not buy

The wise use of wealth

a friend, character, peace of mind, clear conscience or a sense of eternity.
Charles F. Banning

How easy it is for a poor man to depend on God! What else has he to depend on? And how hard it is for a rich man to depend on God! All his possessions call out to him: "Depend on us!"
Moshe Leib of Sassov

Money solves any problem except for them that's got it!
Edna Ferber

It is good to have the things that money can buy, but it is also good to check up once in a while and be sure we have the things that money cannot buy.
George Horace Lorimer

If a man has a lot of money and doesn't use it, then it means that he hasn't money. It means that money has him.
Albert D. Lasker

For every one hundred men who can withstand adversity there is only one who can withstand prosperity.
Thomas Carlyle

An Anchorage school teacher was taking a shower in her apartment when the quake hit. Terrified, she rushed out into the hall and went scrambling down the stairs, pausing for nothing, not even a bathrobe. One of the calmer neighbors stopped her. "Haven't you," he hinted "forgotten something?"

"Ye gods, yes!" she shrieked, dashing back to her apartment. "My purse!"
Ross Wood

What money can and cannot buy—

A bed, but not sleep;
Books but not brains;
Food but not appetite;
Finery but not beauty;
A house but not a home;
Medicine but not health;
Luxuries but not culture;
Amusements but not happiness;
Boon-companions but not friends;
Flattery but not respect.

Author Unknown

Sooner or later every man has to come to terms with his money, either as its slave or as its master.
Arkansas Methodist

If we command our wealth, we shall be rich and free. If our wealth commands us, we are poor indeed.
Edmund Burke

On one occasion a painter asked Einstein to sit for a portrait, and was told, "No, no, no, I do not have time."

"But I need the money I'll get for the picture," the painter said candidly.

"Well, that's different," Einstein replied. "Of course I'll sit."
Thomas Lee Bucky

5 Patience pays off

If I miss practicing on the piano one day, I can tell the difference in my playing. If I miss practicing on the piano for two days, my friends can tell the difference. But if I miss the practice for three days, my audience can tell the difference.
Jan Paderewski

When Roosevelt was asked after a long campaign how he kept it up, he replied: "I spent two years learning to wiggle my big toe. Nothing is impossible for me now."
The New York Post

My son, observe the postage stamp! Its usefulness depends upon its ability to stick to one thing until it gets there.
Henry Wheeler Shaw

Grover Cleveland once gave some good advice to George Rice, an oil refiner and financier, who despised the Standard Oil group. He wrote to Grover Cleveland: "I want to ask you one point-blank question: What if you were in my place, a real oil refiner, and had it in, justly had it in for John Rockefeller and William Rockefeller—just what would *you* do? Tell me that!"

The answer was prompt and specific. Mr. Cleveland wrote at the bottom of the note: "I'd keep refining."
Atlas Way

One moment of patience may ward off great disaster, one moment of impatience may ruin a whole life.
Chinese Wisdom

Wait! Wait! To children it seems this is all they hear. Yet the very act of waiting is valuable training, for waiting is something they will have to do all their lives. The youth must wait for his right to drive a car, the student for his diploma, the lawyer for his degree, the worker for the salary increase, the married couple for the home they want. Teaching a child to wait is just as important as the training in manners and morals that he receives at his mother's knee.
Dorothy Brant Warrick

To work without complaining; to be tolerant, tender and forgiving with someone who may be a little slower than we; to wait with calmness when someone does the right thing the wrong way, or the wrong thing the long way—this is patience.
Megiddo Message

While attempting to invent the incandescent lamp, Thomas Edison remarked after the 187th failure:

"We are making progress. Now, at least, we know 187 things that won't work."
Source Unknown

Have you ever watched a stonecutter at work? He will hammer away at a rock perhaps 100 times without a crack showing in it. Then at the 101st blow, it will split in two.

It is not alone that blow which accomplishes the result, but the hundred others that went before it as well.
Benjamin Disraeli

Plant patience in the garden of thy soul!
The roots are bitter, but the fruit is sweet:
And when at last it stands a tree complete,
Beneath its tender shade the burning heat
And burden of the day shall lose control—
Plant patience in the garden of thy soul!

Henry Austin

A small boy was learning to skate. His frequent mishaps awakened the pity of a bystander. "Sonny, you're getting all banged up," he said. "Why don't you stop for a while and just watch the others?" With tears still rolling down his cheeks from the last downfall, he looked from his adviser to the shining steel on his feet and answered: "Mister, I didn't get these skates to give up with; I got 'em to learn how with!"

Arkansas Baptist

O yesterday our little troop
  was ridden through and through
Our swaying, tattered pennons fled,
  a broken beaten few,
And all the summer afternoon they
  hunted us and slew;
But tomorrow
By the living God, we'll try the game
  anew.

John Masefield

The man who tries to work for the good, believing in its eventual victory, while he may suffer setback and even disaster, will never know defeat. The only deadly sin I know is cynicism.

Henry L. Stimson

---

6   With charity toward all

Someone asked Dr. Menninger—the great psychiatrist—"Suppose a nervous breakdown is imminent. What are you to do?" He suggested a simple thing: "Turn the key in your door, walk out across the tracks, find some people, and do something for them. You'll probably ward off a nervous breakdown." Get interested in something other than yourself.

Author Unknown

A family is not sufficient unto itself. Home ties are not safe unless the members of the family have larger interests in causes outside themselves.

Ralph W. Sockman

Even God dare not approach a hungry man except in the form of bread.

Mohandas Gandhi

He who gives alms to the poor is rewarded with six blessings; he who speaks kindly to him is rewarded with eleven blessings.

The Talmud

Our charity may seem to be
More than our equal part
But goodness true depends upon
Sincerity of heart.

No special glory is deserved
For generosity
When contributions large or small
Are made begrudgingly

Or when a gift is prompted by
Desire to attain
A public recognition or
To make some other gain.

Whether our charity we can
Or we cannot afford
It must be done sincerely to
Deserve the least reward.

God does not judge us by our gifts
No matter what they be
He measures and He weighs our souls
By our sincerity.
James J. Metcalfe

'Tis not enough to help the feeble up,
But to support him after.
William Shakespeare

The wife of a rabbi said to him: "Your prayer was lengthy today. Have you succeeded in bringing it about that the rich should be more generous in their gifts to the poor?" The rabbi replied: "Half of my prayer I have accomplished. The poor are willing to accept them."
Hasidic Lore

We make a living by what we get, but we make a life by what we give.
Royle Forum

The old doctor never had refused a call from anyone, whether rich or poor, but now he was tired.

"Have you any money?" he asked the midnight caller.

"Certainly!" was the reply.

"Then go to the new doctor. I'm too old to get out of bed for anybody who can pay for it."
Mrs. Ernest Miller

The word "alms" has no singular, as if to teach us that a solitary act of charity scarcely deserves the name.
Anonymous

The act of charity is measured by the loving-kindness with which it is administered.
The Talmud

A young man applying for a police job in London, England, was asked what he'd do to break up a hostile crowd. "Take up a collection," he replied.
The International Teamster

A bone given to a dog is not charity. Charity is the bone shared with the dog when you are just as hungry as the dog.
Uplift

Nowadays we think of a philanthropist as someone who donates big sums of money, yet the word is derived from two Greek words, *philos* (loving) and *anthropos* (man): loving man. All of us are capable of being philanthropists. We can give of ourselves.
Edward Lindsey

7 A sense of ethics

It is more and more apparent that the biggest question before the human race is whether man will be able to establish an ethic for the whole world in time to save the world from destroying itself.
Harold L. Taylor

I've read about women in underdeveloped countries who walk half a mile for a gallon of water; I turn on a faucet and get all the water I want. These other women spend two hours a day pounding corn into meal; I buy my cornmeal already ground. If the conveniences in my life do not give me a few hours to study and take action on social problems, then I'm wasting my time somewhere.
Rosemary Thielke

Respect for life is the highest ethical law. Ethics is the uncircumscribed responsibility toward all living things.
Albert Schweitzer

In the end, the problems we face and shall face are not first of technology but of ethical value, not first of controlling machines but of controlling ourselves, not first of devising ingenious techniques of conveying instructions into pupils' heads but of setting before ourselves a clear standard of what they should carry with them through their lives in mind and heart and character.
Thomas J. Watson, Jr.

Always do right. This will gratify some people and astonish the rest.
Mark Twain

In the wonderful dialogue written by Plato, we are told that when Socrates' friend told him that he would help him escape from prison to a neighboring state, Socrates answered: "I can leave the prison; I can escape into the next state; but on the way someone will meet me—Justice, Law, Righteousness . . . Righteousness in the name of the deity—and will say to me: 'What did you do?'"
Source Unknown

I was eyes to the blind, and feet to the lame, I was a father to the poor; and I searched out the cause of him whom I did not know. I broke the fangs of the unrighteous, and made him drop his prey from his teeth.
Job 29:15-17

Build me a World, said God,
Out of man's fairest dreams;
Heaven must be its dome,
Lighted by prophet-gleams;
Justice shall be the stones
On which my world shall rise;
Truth and love its arches,
Gripping my ageless skies,
Out of dreams in the earthy sod,
Build me a World,
Said God.
Thomas Curtis Clark

Virtue will have naught to do with ease. It seeks a rough and thorny path.
Montaigne

One man with courage is a majority.
Andrew Jackson

What a man has been is history, what he does is law, what he is is philosophy, what he ought to be is ethics.
Eugene P. Bertin

No man can be right all of the time in his actions or decisions, but he can be himself, willing to recognize his identity as a thinking individual and to risk his reputation and compensation on his honesty with himself first and with his fellow man afterward. Managing one's self is a primary exercise in personal ethics with the stranger at our side, a man we ought to know better.
A. M. Sullivan

They are slaves most base
Whose love of right is for themselves, and not
For all their race.
James Russell Lowell

We are the decent people of the world;
We are the great majority, for most people are decent;
There are almost two billion of us on the earth;
We live in all nations; we live under many flags . . .
We want to live quietly and enjoy life's simple pleasures;
We want a chance to think our own thoughts, live our own lives;
We want our sons to save, not to slaughter;
We want our children to grow up without the fear of death;
We believe that this is a beautiful universe and that it is meant for love and not for hate;
The only things we desire to conquer are disease and poverty and failure and unhappiness;
We believe that, if a man is decent and highminded, the language he speaks and the color of his skin do not matter;
We, the decent people in every corner of the world, must wage an eternal battle against hate, intolerance, greed and all the other mental poisons that create wars;
Guns and bombs only destroy what we, the decent people, must build up again;
The time has come to speak up for human decency!
Wilfred A. Peterson

---

8 The pursuit of happiness

The door to happiness opens outwards.
Soren Kierkegaard

Only those who get joy out of their work know what real happiness is.
William Feather

To do great work one must fall in love with his task. Cellini, the goldsmith, pouring his whole soul into his creations, achieved masterpieces and the love he thus liberated brought him the praise of kings. You've seen the designer of a piece of machinery pat it with pride, as he might pat the head of a son. It is part of him. He has built his personality into it. That's why it is such a fine machine. Work that is done in a spirit of love glows with a mystic quality no one can explain. And the worker feels as did Robert Louis Stevenson, who said, "I know what happiness is, for I have done good work."

Author Unknown

You cannot be happy doing something which you know to be wrong.

John Osborn

Spring is a happiness so beautiful, so unique, so unexpected, that I don't know what to do with my heart.

Emily Dickinson

Happiness eludes the individual who uses his talents destructively. A law of nature cannot be broken with impunity. No one can be forced to be happy. This simple lesson has eluded the father who bemoans his family's ingratitude, "I've done everything to make my children happy, and I can't understand why they don't appreciate it." This parent has done everything except recognize that the happiness of each individual depends upon engaging in and fulfilling some useful productive task.

Stanley Yankus

Happiness is no easy matter; 'tis very hard to find it within ourselves, and impossible to find it anywhere else.

Sebastian Roch Chamfort

Plenty of people miss their share of happiness, not because they never found it, but because they didn't stop to enjoy it.

William Feather

There's an Oriental story about two friends who stood on a bridge watching the fish in a stream below. "How happy the fishes are," observed one. "You're not a fish," said his friend. "How can you know whether they're happy or not?" "You're not me," the first man replied. "How can you know whether I know whether fish are happy or not?"

Edwin Way Teale

Tolerance is letting other people find happiness in their way instead of in your way.

Construction Digest

Happiness at its deepest and best is not the portion of a cushioned life which never struggled, overpassed obstacles, bore hardships, or adventured in sacrifice for costly aims. A heart of joy is never found in luxuriously coddled lives, but in men and women who achieve and dare, who have tried their powers against antagonisms, who have met even sickness and bereavement and have tempered their souls in fire. Joy is begotten not chiefly from the impression of happy circumstances, but from the expression of overcoming power. If we were set upon making a happy world, then we could not leave struggle out nor make adversity impossible. The unhappiest world conceivable by man would be a world with nothing hard to do, no conflicts to wage for

ends worth while; a world where courage was not needed and sacrifice was a superfluity.
Harry Emerson Fosdick

The foolish man seeks happiness in the distance; the wise grows it under his feet.
James Oppenheim

People who are running frantically after happiness remind me of those who are peering everywhere for the spectacles that are perched on their foreheads.
Sidney J. Harris

Happy are they that are upright in the way.
Psalms 119:1

Happy is the man that hath not walked in the counsel of the wicked.
Psalms 1:1

Happy is the man that findeth wisdom.
Proverbs 3:13

Happy are they who dwell in Thy house, O Lord.
Psalms 84:5

Happy are they who keep justice.
Psalms 106:3

Happiness is a perfume you cannot pour on others without getting a few drops on yourself.
Ralph Waldo Emerson

9 Confidence is crucial

The world is all of us, and if we do not collapse, it will not.
Booth Tarkington

There are two days in the week upon which and about which I never worry—two carefree days kept sacredly free from worry and apprehension. One of these days is yesterday. Yesterday with its cares and frets and all its pains and aches, all its faults, its mistakes and blunders has passed forever beyond recall. It was mine; it is God's. And the other day that I do not worry about is tomorrow. Tomorrow with all its possible adversities, its burdens, its perils, its large promise and poor performance, its failures and mistakes, is as far beyond my mastery as its dead sister, yesterday. Tomorrow is God's day; it will be mine.

There is left for myself, then, but one day in the week—today.
Robert J. Burdette

A friend one day asked Mary Pickford how she had been able to maintain her poise and good cheer when she had faced so many heartaches and disappointments in her life. Miss Pickford replied, "All the water in the world can't sink a ship unless it gets on the inside."
Max Merritt Morrison

A man having only one leg and supporting himself on crutches makes his way slowly to a sacred shrine. A passerby watches and asks a companion, "Do you think that fellow believes the Lord will give him another leg if he prays hard enough?" Overhearing the comment, the cripple says, "I don't expect the Lord to give me another leg; but I do expect Him to answer my prayer to help me make the best use of the one I have."
Theodore F. Adams

When the going gets tough, let the tough get going.
Frank Leahy

A woman suffered a stroke that paralyzed the left side of her body. After some months, she was taken to the office of a psychiatrist in her wheel chair. There was definite paralysis of her left arm and leg. When asked to rise and walk, she leaned toward her left side. Helplessly she fell back. Gently prodding her right shoulder, the doctor suggested: "Now instead of testing your weaker side, why not try the stronger one? Make your first step with the right foot." Gingerly she put that foot forward, leaning toward the right. She rose, and this time she took a step or two. She simply shifted from her weakness to her strength.
Louis Binstock

A little boy came home in high excitement. "Daddy! Mother!" he shouted, "I jumped off the high diving board!" "But, son," his parents interjected, "that's what you told us last week."

The boy answered quickly, "But this time no one pushed me!"
Source Unknown

If you think you are best, you are;
If you think you dare not, you don't
If you'd like to win, but think you can't,
It's almost a cinch you won't.

If you think you'll lose, you're lost,
For out in the world we find
Success begins with a fellow's will
It's all in the state of mind.

Life's battles don't always go
To the stronger or faster man;
But soon or late the man who wins
Is the one who thinks he can.
Walter D. Wintle

A celebrated French painter, Daumier, once defended his way of painting by saying: "One must be of one's time." Another notable French painter, Ingres, replied by asking a question: "What if one's time is wrong?"
Halford E. and Robert E. Luccock

"I think I can" are four magic words that create success; four magic words that when woven into the fiber of our human thoughts can make all the difference in the world as to whether we succeed or fail.
Gertrude Cramer Williams

A friend once took his fine Swiss watch to a jeweler for adjustment. The jeweler asked, "When do you wind your watch?" "Why, at night, before I retire," replied my friend. "Oh," said the jeweler, "a watch as fine as that should be wound in the morning, so that it can start the day

on a strong spring. It would then be prepared against the bumps and shocks of the day." What is good for the watch is good for the human spirit. We should start our days and our careers on a strong spring.
Ralph W. Sockman

The most fearful unbelief is unbelief in yourself.
Thomas Carlyle

Youth is a time of developing fidelity which, when fully matured, is the strength of disciplined devotion. This fidelity involves a commitment on the part of the individual, commitment to a set of values, to a goal, to a way of life. Such a commitment must add relevance and meaning to one's life if it is to endure.
Erik H. Erikson

A friend watched a little girl pull out a big weed and, patting her on the head, remarked, "My what a strong girl you are!"

"Yep, I know it," the child agreed, "and the whole world was hangin' on the other end of it."
Burbank News

---

10 What is the idea?

Sometimes a new idea so stretches a man's mind that it never quite shrinks back to its former dimensions.
Oliver Wendell Holmes

Ideals have value. They are the means by which we prepare ourselves to overcome the limitations of our imperfection. If it were not for ideals, man would have nothing toward which he could direct his attempt to improve the future for himself and others.
Cecil A. Poole

All the intelligence in the world is of no avail to a man who has none of his own. If he has no ideas he cannot profit from those of other people.
Jean de La Bruyere

Whoever shrinks from ideas ends by having nothing but sensations.
Goethe

Ideas are funny little things. They won't work unless you do.
Columbia Record

Great ideas come into the world as gently as doves. Perhaps then, if we live attentively enough we shall hear, amid the uproar of empires and nations, the faint flutter of wings—the gentle stirring of life and hope.
Albert Camus

To live in the Idea means to treat the impossible as though it were possible.
Goethe

New ideas can be good or bad, just the same as old ones.
Franklin Delano Roosevelt

The story is told of a preacher who was chided for borrowing ideas from other sources. He explained himself as follows: Look at the spider and the bee. The spider uses only original materials to spin its web. The bee, on the other hand, takes nectar from a multitude of flowers.
Source Unknown

Ideas come from exposure. If you're in the rain long enough, you're bound to get good and wet.
Melanie Kahane

There is nothing in the world more powerful than an idea. No weapon can destroy it; no power can conquer it except the power of another idea.
James Roy Smith

A proud parent congratulated Harvard President Charles W. Eliot on all he had done to make Harvard a great storehouse of knowledge. President Eliot answered that Harvard might be a great storehouse of knowledge, but "only because our freshman bring so much knowledge in and our seniors take so little out."
Carl T. Rowan

A tired-looking man dragged himself through his front door and slumped into a chair. His wife came out of the kitchen and looked at him with misgivings.
"Busy day at the office, dear?" she asked sympathetically.
"Terrible," he answered with a heavy sigh. "The computer broke down in the middle of the afternoon and we all had to think."
Clarence Roeser

Great discoveries or ideas have one characteristic in common. Before they are achived they are considered incredible and not worth the effort deemed necessary to make them real. After they are achieved, it seems incredible that we should be without them.
M. Stanton Evans

To know the taste of wine, it is not necessary to drink the whole barrel.
Hayyim Nahman Bialik

2

Life is with people

11 To crown our good with brotherhood

Human brotherhood is not just a goal. It is a condition on which our way of life depends. The question for our time is not whether all men are brothers. That question has been answered by the God who placed us on this earth together. The question is whether we have the strength and the will to make the Brotherhood of man the guiding principle of our daily lives.
John F. Kennedy

The most fundamental kind of love, which underlies all types of love, is brotherly love. By this I mean the sense of responsibility, care, respect, knowledge of any other human being, the wish to further his life. This is the kind of love the Bible speaks of when it says: love thy neighbor as thyself. Brotherly love is love for all human beings; it is characterized by its very lack of exclusiveness. If I have developed the capacity for love, then I cannot help loving my brothers.
Erich Fromm

To see the earth as it truly is, small and blue and beautiful where it floats, is to see ourselves as riders on the earth together, brothers on that bright loveliness in the eternal cold —brothers who know they are truly brothers.
Archibald MacLeish

The world has become too dangerous for anything but Truth, and too small for anything but Brotherhood.
A. Powell Davies

Brotherly love is a love that brings acceptance. It says, I love you for what you are and for what you can be. It says, I understand, and, I care. It says, try again, when failure is evidenced. It is an acceptance of the man, not necessarily what the man does.
C. Neil Strait

Brotherhood is common sense saying: "Get rid of your prejudices in order to live peacefully with yourself and your neighbors."

Brotherhood is good sportsmanship saying: "Do not make another person or another group the scapegoat for your own shortcomings and frustrations."

Brotherhood is education saying: "Beyond the development of skills, and the acquiring of knowledge, we must learn to live together."

Brotherhood is science saying: "Humanity is one; there is no such thing as a superior or an inferior race."

Brotherhood is American democracy saying: "We hold these truths to be self-evident, that all men are created equal, that they are endowed with certain inalienable rights."
L.E. Metcalf

Until you have become really, in actual fact, a brother to everyone, brotherhood will not come to pass. No sort of scientific teaching, no kind of common interest, will ever teach men to share property and privileges with equal consideration for all.
Feodor Dostoevski

May the day come when all men shall invoke Thy name, when corruption and evil shall give way to purity and goodness, when superstition shall no longer enslave the mind, nor idolatry blind the eye! O may all men recognize that they are brethren, so that one in spirit and one in fellowship they may be forever united before Thee. Then shall Thy kingdom be established on earth and the word of Thine ancient seer be fulfilled . . . On that day the Lord shall be One, and His name shall be One!
Jewish Prayer Book

A Buddhist saint one time was asked whether he would want to go to heaven or hell. His answer was unequivocal. He wanted to go to hell, because there his help and compassion were needed.
Frederick Mayer

We can all use the lesson of the little boy who was to have a birthday party. He was making up his guest list and reading it to his mother. She stopped him at one point and asked, "Isn't that a little boy who is colored?"

"I don't know," he replied, "but the next time I see him I'll look."
Mrs. Paul Brown

Almighty God, the time has passed for long sentences. The time has passed for rich, full oratory. Please, dear God, help us to get to the heart of the matter and help us to get there fast.
Donald J. Curran

12 Caring is a form of sharing

My piece of bread only belongs to me when I know that everyone else has a share and that no one starves while I eat.
Leo Tolstoy

This capacity for caring is something that can be cultivated. All of us come into this world with a certain amount of it, but whether we expand this capacity or let it diminish is largely up to us. Caring is not always a spontaneous thing, any more than love is always at first sight. Many great artists have served long and difficult apprenticeships before they learned to love what they were doing. Many people have had to work at a friendship before it amounted to much.
Arthur Gordon

Strange is our situation here upon earth. Each of us comes for a short visit, not knowing why, yet sometimes seeming to divine a purpose. From the standpoint of daily life, however, there is one thing we do know: That Man Is Here for the Sake of Other Men . . . Above all, for those upon whose smile and well-being our own happiness depends, and also for the countless unknown souls with whose fate we are connected by a bond of sympathy. Many times a day I realize how much my outer and inner life is built upon the labors of my fellow men, both living and dead, and how earnestly I must exert myself in order to give in return as much as I have received and am still receiving.
Albert Einstein

What you keep is lost—what you give is forever yours.
Shota Rustaveli

The will to live is animal; the will to let live is human; the will to help others is divine.
Mordecai M. Kaplan

A man may give liberally, and yet because he gives unlovingly and wounds the heart of the poor, his gift is in vain, for it has lost the attribute of charity; a man may give little, but because his heart goes with it his deed and himself are blessed.
The Talmud

I believe that every person must act according to the dictates of his conscience. I feel that the capacity to care is the thing that gives life its deepest significance and meaning.
Pablo Casals

It is not enough merely to exist. It's not enough to say, "I'm earning enough to live and support my family. I do my work well. I'm a good father. I'm a good husband. I'm a good churchgoer."

That's all very well. But you must do something more. Seek always to do some good, somewhere. Every man has to seek in his own way to make his own self more noble and to realize his own true worth.

You must give some time to your fellow man. Even if it's a little thing, do something for those who have need of a man's help, something for which you get no pay but the

privilege of doing it. For remember, you don't live in a world all your own. Your brothers are here, too.
Albert Schweitzer

Music I heard with you was more than music, and bread I broke with you was more than bread.
Conrad Aiken

When he has more than he can eat
To feed a stranger's not a feat.

When he has more than he can spend
It isn't hard to give or lend.

Who gives but what he'll never miss
Will never know what giving is.
Edgar A. Guest

Heaven forming each on other to depend,
A master, or a servant, or a friend,
Bids each on other for assistance call,
Till one man's weakness grows the strength of all.
Alexander Pope

To know the needs of men and to help them bear the burden of their sorrows, that is the true love of men.
Moshe Leib of Sassov

The true opposite of love is not hate but indifference. Hate, bad as it is, at least treats the neighbor as a thou, whereas indifference turns the neighbor into an it, a thing. This is why we may say there is actually one thing worse than evil itself, and this is indifference to evil. In human relations the nadir of morality, the lowest point as far as ethics is concerned, is manifest in the phrase, "I couldn't care less."
Joseph Fletcher

13 Peace—the greatest of all blessings

Great is peace; all the benedictions end with peace, because benedictions are worthless unless they are attended by peace.
The Talmud

The time has come when we should take some risks in the name of peace, rather than continue the greater nuclear gamble in the name of security.
Hubert H. Humphrey

No man is so foolish as to desire war more than peace; for in peace sons bury their fathers, but in war fathers bury their sons.
Herodotus

I am looking for peace. I am looking for a way to stop war, but you will not stop it by pious sentiments and appeals. You will only stop it by making practical arrangements.
Winston Churchill

Closer to the truth than he meant to be was the schoolboy who wrote on an exam paper: "The Armistice was signed on the 11th of November in 1918, and since then every year there has been two minutes of peace."
Shield

The world will never be the dwelling place of peace until peace has found a home in the heart of each and every man.
Christian Century

May it be Thy will, O God, to extend peace, great and wondrous, in the Universe. Let all the peoples of the earth recognize and know the innermost truth; that we are not come into this world for quarrel and division, nor for hate and jealousy, contrariness and bloodshed; but we are come into this world to recognize and know Thee.
Nahman of Bratzlav

Peace must made. Like bread, it must be made daily.
G. Bromley Oxnam

We've learned how to destroy, but not to create; how to waste, but not how to build; how to kill men, but not how to save them; how to die but seldom how to live.
Omar Bradley

We must acknowledge that mere absence of war cannot be a stable state; that true peace requires more than mere co-existence of basically antagonistic camps. It requires extensive cooperation of nations and social systems in the pursuit of universal common strivings of humanity.
Eugene Rabinowitch

Times have changed since diplomats could sit around a table and divide up the world for a hundred years to come. Peace is not the product of a single conference, but rather of continuous conversation.
Adlai E. Stevenson

Disarmament of minds and hearts must precede disarmament of the hands.
Dominique Georges Pire

For centuries now we've tried everything else; the powers of wealth, of mighty armies and navies, and combinations of nations, machinations of diplomats. All have failed. Before it's too late, and time is running out, let us turn from trust in the chain reactions of exploding atoms to faith in the chain reaction of God's love. Love—love of God and fellow men, that is God's formula for peace. Peace on earth to men of good will.
Richard Cardinal Cushing

Nothing has ever been decided by war that could not be decided without it; and if decided after war, why not before?
Ulysses S. Grant

Trying to explain the reason for worldwide disagreement, an Indian said, "When nations smoke pipe of peace, no one inhale."
Locomotive

14 Born free

Let us discard all this quibbling about this man and the other man, this race and the other race being inferior and therefore they must be placed in an inferior position. Let us discard all these things, and unite as one people throughout this land, until we shall once more stand up declaring that all men are created equal.

Abraham Lincoln

A three year old girl was riding in a taxi with her mother when she pointed to the Negro driver and asked "Mommie, why is he so black?" The mother, seeing the man's shoulders tense, hastily searched for the right words to satisfy both her companions. She said "God makes people as He makes flower gardens, so the world will be more colorful. Some of us are white, some brown, some black, some yellow—and there are variations of all these shades. That makes us all the more interesting to look at, don't you agree?" The little girl nodded, and as they left the cab the driver said, "Ma'am, when my little girl gets big enough to ask me why some people are so white, I'll be happy to know what to tell her."

Dawn Crowell Norman

To deny human beings their rights is to set the stage for political and social unrest—wars, hostility between nations and between groups within a nation—and leads to urgent demands for a better life in larger freedom. Human rights, far from being an abstract subject for philosophers and lawyers, affects the daily lives of everyone—man, woman and child.

UNESCO Courier

Along the Mississippi River and particularly in sections where cotton was king, some ruthless slaveholders were more concerned with profits than with human feelings. With utter disregard for human ties, many slaves were sold down the river and their family groups broken up. This possibility was regarded with tragic awe by Negroes and abolitionists and has come into the language as a phrase referring to that which is done without consulting the wishes of the individual affected.

David T. Armstrong

The Nation who loses her liberty is not aware of her misfortune at the time, any more than the patient is, who receives a paralytic stroke.

Francesco Petrarch

He who believes that a country can be free while legally withholding human rights from a single resident knows nothing of the essence of liberty.

Leipzig Orient

There is no such thing as equality. No one is exactly the equal of anyone else. These things we know. But what we do embrace in our country is an idea that everyone should have a chance— if you will, an equal chance—to become equal!

Monroe E. Spaght

They that can give up essential liberty to obtain a little temporary safety deserve neither liberty nor safety.
Benjamin Franklin

If the voice of liberty be silenced in the university, and the intolerance that now prevails in church and in state be permitted to invade the precincts of the universities of the world, then, indeed, must we be permitted to enter upon a new and dismal dark age that will cast the thoughts and activities of man in common and uniform molds, there to remain until such time as the unquenchable thirst for liberty shall again effectively manifest itself among men.
Nicholas Murray Butler

The God who gave us life, gave us liberty at the same time.
Thomas Jefferson

Freedom threatens to degenerate into mere arbitrariness unless it is lived in terms of responsibleness. I like to say that the Statue of Liberty on the East Coast should be supplemented by a Statue of Responsibility on the West Coast.
Viktor E. Frankl

Liberty lies in the hearts of men and women, When it dies there, no constitution, no law, no court can save it.
Learned Hand

I have a dream, and when it happens, when we allow freedom to ring, when we let it ring from every village and every hamlet, from every state and every city, we will be able to speed up that day when all of God's children, black men and white men, Jews and Gentiles, Protestants and Catholics, will be able to join hands and sing in the words of the old Negro spiritual: "Free at last, free at last. Thank God Almighty, we're free at last."
Martin Luther King

During the summer, I read a remarkable evaluation of German education in the 1920's. "The thousands of alumni of German gymnasia did not let the cultivated humanism of their intellectual formation prevent them from stamping out people like ants. One is so busy looking up to the sky that one does not watch the streets."
Seymour J. Cohen

I know the Negro race has a long road to go. I believe the life of the Negro race has been a life of tragedy, of injustice, of oppression.

The law made him equal, but man has not. And, after all, the last analysis is, what has man done? And not what has the law done.
Clarence Darrow

I must study politics and war that my sons may have liberty to study mathematics and philosophy. My sons ought to study mathematics and philosophy, geography, natural history . . . navigation, commerce and agriculture in order to give their children the right to study painting, poetry, music, architecture.
John Adams

15 Significance of silence

Silence is the element in which great things fashion themselves together, that at length they may emerge full-formed and majestic into the daylight of life which they are thenceforth to rule.
Thomas Carlyle

Let us be silent that we may hear the whisper of the gods.
Ralph Waldo Emerson

The moment a man can really do his work he becomes speechless about it. All words become idle to him. Does a bird need to theorize about building its nest, or boast of it when built?
John Ruskin

Carl Sandburg was once persuaded to attend a rehearsal of a play by a very serious young dramatist, but unfortunately slept through the greater part of the performance. Later the outraged dramatist chided him, "How could you sleep when you knew how much I wanted your opinion?"
　"Young man," Sandburg reminded him, "sleep is an opinion."
Edgar Chrisemer

I have often said that all the misfortunes of men spring from their not knowing how to live quietly in their own rooms.
Blaise Pascal

If people did as much as they said they did, there would be no time to talk about it.
Virginia B. Leckie

Words can sting like anything
But silence breaks the heart.
Source Unknown

A saintly woman who was greatly loved in her community was asked how she made and kept so many friends. She replied, "I stop and taste my words before I let them pass my teeth."
Claude A. Ries

The water is shallowest where it babbles.
Welsh Proverb

Lord, I have shut my door
Shut out life's busy cares and fretting noise;
Here in this silence they intrude not more:
Speak Thou, and heavenly joys
Shall fill my heart with music sweet and calm
A holy Psalm.
Author Unknown

To be outspoken is easy when you do not want to speak the complete truth.
Rabindranath Tagore

Speaking the truth in love may mean, at times, keeping silence.
Willard L. Sperry

The joy derived from meditation will strain off the bitter dregs from the cup of life.
Megiddo Message

All beauty whispers to the listening heart.

Love does not shout, and ecstasy is still!
The friendly silence of infinity
Forever broods above a lifted hill.

A flower leaps to life, the quiet clod
Has uttered music!
Noiselessly a tree flings forth green song.
The snow breathes soundless prayers,
And stars are vocal with tranquility.
Mary Hallett

Silence is golden when someone is playing Chopin, or when the thrush is singing. But when there is really cause for something to say, silence is sheer stupidity.
Bruce Marble

Some people speak from experience and others, from experience, don't speak.
Author Unknown

The tragedy of today is not so much the noisiness of the bad people, but the silence of the good people.
Grit

16 A matter of attitude

Einstein dictated a definition for his secretary to use in her replies about relativity: "When you sit with a nice girl for two hours you think it's only a minute, but when you sit on a hot stove for a minute you think it's two hours. That's relativity."
Mary Alkus

Early one morning after a bombing attack upon London, a boy about twelve years old stood by the ruins of his home in which he had lost everything. When someone tried to commiserate with him upon his loss, he replied: "I've got my life, haven't I?"
Frederick G. Pearson

Uncle Ezra had lived with the couple over 40 years, being as cantankerous and as difficult as can be. When the old man died, the husband returning from the funeral said to his wife, "If I didn't love you so much, I couldn't have taken your Uncle Ezra all these years. What an ordeal it was!" His wife looked up with surprise and said: "What? My Uncle Ezra? I thought he was your Uncle Ezra!!"
Author Unknown

Everything has been said before—our task is to think it anew.
Goethe

Any book that is at all important ought to be at once read through twice; partly because on a second reading the connection of its parts will be better understood, and partly because we are not in the same temper and dispositon on both readings.
Arthur Schopenhauer

If it's a halo you have to wear,
Don't let it get in others' hair.
Author Unknown

Our five year old came home from school one afternoon announcing that he had a new friend on the big yellow school bus which stopped for him each day. The friend turned out to be a new bus driver, an important person in a kindergartener's life—his adult link between home and school. "I like him," he announced. "He treats me like I'm a people!"
Gladys M. Hunt

It is never too late to give up your prejudices.
Henry David Thoreau

Said the lady, shaking hands with the preacher after the service: "Wonderful sermon! Everything you said applied to somebody or other I know."
Source Unknown

Booth Tarkington, past master of the art of compliment, seemed always to know how to say the right thing at the proper time. Returning to his early home after an extensive absence, he was greeted very warmly by a lovely girl whom he did not recognize.

Eyeing the black-eyed beauty with open admiration, he remarked, "I suppose you're still living at home with your parents?"

"No, sir," corrected the girl. "Papa and mamma are both in heaven. And I'm married now and live with my husband."

Tarkington smiled knowingly. "Then your husband is in heaven too!"
Webb B. Garrison

A little science estranges men from God; much science leads them back to Him.
Louis Pasteur

The minister inquired of his visitor to cite the reasons he is seeking to divorce his wife. The man declined, claiming that it is wrong to talk about one's wife, since this is an area of inviolable privacy. This logic seemed unassailable. After the divorce was given, the minister asked, "Well, now she's not your wife and you can tell me the reasons." "What?" was the reply. "Do you expect me to talk about strange women?"
Source Unknown

A housewife one day was particularly sharp in rebuking her maid. "The house was not cleaned and dusted properly," she complained. The maid was flushed with amazement, for all looked immaculate. Finally, someone turned to the housewife and said, "Madam, I think the dust you see is on your own glasses." The woman removed her glasses and sure enough, the lenses were covered with dust.
Source Unknown

Riots are evil, but so are the conditions that produce them.
Michael Hamilton

17 *Culture and commitment*

To know how to read is to light a lamp in the wind, to release the soul from prison, to open a gate to the universe.
Pearl Buck

An educated man is one who can entertain a new idea, another person and himself.
Sidney Herbert Wood

In the plurality and mutual tolerance of American culture lies the secret of our strength and of the freedom which we so proudly profess to the rest of the world.
Arthur J. Goldberg

Once a simple German peasant discovered the treasures of the mind. Over his doorway he wrote, "Dante, Moliere and Shakespeare live here." He lived in a crude house, but remarkable guests came there to abide.
Source Unknown

After a big college football game on the West Coast a visiting easterner said to his host, the head of the chemistry department:

"What a plant you have here! What a campus! How many students would you say you have?"

"About one in a thousand," was the answer.
Kenneth Wertz

The greatest thing a human soul ever does in this world is to see something, and tell what it saw in a plain way. Hundreds of people can talk for one who can think, but thousands can think for one who can see. To see clearly is poetry, prophecy, and religion, all in one.
John Ruskin

Values are not inborn and absolute traits in people, although the capacity to acquire values depends on available psychic structures in each individual. Values can only be learned, no one is born with them.
Rudolf Ekstein

While showing color slides of a recent trip, our friend Bill commented, "The next time I go West, I'm leaving the camera home."

"Why?" we asked.

Bill explained, "Rita and I have decided we get so involved collecting photographs we forget to take in the real picture with our eyes."
Eleanor Kolker

I like to pay taxes, That's the way I buy civilization.
Oliver Wendell Holmes

Paul Dore, the great French artist was wandering through the Swiss Alps and was stopped by a government official demanding to see his passport papers. Dore tried to explain who he was and said that he had left his passport at the hotel. The official was skeptical and finally said, "If you are Paul Dore you can readily demonstrate it by painting a picture of this landscape." Whereupon Dore unpacked his equipment and proceeded to paint a beautiful scene. On observing the great skill with which Dore painted,

the official said, "Indeed, it is plain to see that you are Paul Dore. It is not by what you say about yourself that demonstrates what and who you are. It is by what you do that you prove it."
Whitfield W. Johnson

The way a people use language reveals a great deal about the way they look at the world around them.
Morton T. Kelsey

Any culture that robs most of its people of traditional faith must supply them with substitutes for mystical experience. Ours supplies everything from pot and television to mass spectator sports and something called the cultural explosion.
John Canaday

Civilization is a race between education and catastrophe.
H. G. Wells

Society needs more than anything else to be reminded that neither the pressure of events nor the exigencies of diplomacy can warrant the final debasement of man. We need a resurgence of the humanities, a rebirth of spirit.
Ben Shahn

The triumph of culture is to overpower nationality.
Ralph Waldo Emerson

If thou hast two pennies, spend one for bread. With the other, buy hyacinths for thy soul.
Ancient Persian Poet

18 Friends and enemies

How cramped becomes a spacious land—
Where two enemies try to stand.
Just as a tiny span of space
Is ample where a thousand friends embrace!
Judah Al Harizi

To have a friend you must be a friend.
Ralph Waldo Emerson

Georges Clemenceau, noted French statesman, was in the habit of bluntly speaking his mind, to the dismay of his political advisers.

"You must be more tactful," they urged him. "Your strong language only makes you enemies."

Clemenceau couldn't see it that way.

"It also makes me friends," he argued. "I have as my supporters all the enemies of my enemies."
Milwaukee Journal

The world is a great child and tires easily. You cannot make friends for long with all the world.
Fritz Kreisler

You can't hold a man down without staying down with him.
Booker T. Washington

Friendship is a priceless gift that
  cannot be bought or sold,
But its value is far greater than a
  mountain made of gold—
For gold is cold and lifeless, it can
  neither see nor hear,
And in the time of trouble it is
  powerless to cheer—
It has no ears to listen, no heart to
  understand,
It cannot bring you comfort or reach
  out a helping hand—
So when you ask God for a gift, be
  thankful if He sends
Not diamonds, pearls or riches, but
  the love of real true friends.
Helen Steiner Rice

Comprehension must be the soil in which grow all the fruits of friendship.
Woodrow Wilson

Friendship endures; the lesser
  things may pass;
The little sorrows, trifling discontent;
The petty troubles that amass,
These go! But friendship is a
  sacrament,
Ending when life ends only—even
  more
It goes ahead to open Heaven's door.
Author Unknown

Scavenging the beach after a crowded holiday weekend is always an exciting adventure for my three youngsters. We live on a cliff overlooking a small cove, and after one such weekend my two boys burst into the kitchen with grins from ear to ear. "Look what I found, Mom!" shouted John, holding up one wet swim fin.

"I found a volleyball!" shrieked my ten-year-old.

My six-year-old daughter was late, and came in quietly. "And what did you find, honey," I encouraged. "A ring? A bracelet?"

"No, Mommy," she smiled as another girl followed her in. "I found a friend."
Mrs. B. J. Newman

Better is a dinner of herbs where love is, than a fatted ox and hatred therewith.
Proverbs 15-17

Not to hate with those who hate, but to love with those who love, I live.
Antigone

The only people to get even with are those who have helped you.
William R. Link

Let me live in a house by the side of
  the road
Where the race of men go by—
They are good and they are bad,
  they are weak, they are strong,
Wise, foolish—so am I.
Then why should I sit in a scorner's
  seat,
Or hurl the cynic's ban?
Let me live in a house by the side of
  the road
And be a friend to man.
Sam Walter Foss

A friend loves at all times, and a brother is born for adversity.
Proverbs 17:17

19 Love still makes the world go 'round

When the satisfaction or the security of another person becomes as significant as is one's own satisfaction or security, then the state of love exists. So far as I know, under no other circumstances is a state of love present, regardless of the popular usage of the word.
Harry Stack Sullivan

The ability to love is at the basis of all true religion.
Abraham Blau

We receive love—from our children as well as others—not in proportion to our demands or sacrifices or needs, but roughly in proportion to our own capacity to love.
Rollo May

If we could love our neighbors as ourselves we could have Utopia. In fact, the hope of the world rests on our capacity to love because it is the only way to neutralize the hate within us that comes from the deepest layers of our personality.
William C. Menninger

He who cares to do good knocks at the gate; he who loves finds the door open.
Rabindranath Tagore

Children should know that they are loved now, which is forever, and that someone was here to comfort them in their huge sorrows and in the hungers and fears of their days and nights. This is why I believe that to be able to remember the gift of love in one's childhood is the greatest gift any man shall have received in his life—because from the gift of love, a man can become the whole person he was meant to become in the sight of God.
Richard Cardinal Cushing

We can live if we can love. Love is the medicine for the sickness of mankind. Love is the greatest thing in the world, whether one calls it God or an instinct. To give one's life away to what one knows to be of highest worth, not only for oneself but for all mankind, is the most mature experience open to man.
Karl Menninger

If a woman told us that she loved flowers, and we saw that she forgot to water them we would not believe in her "love" for flowers. Love is the active concern for the life and growth of that which we love.
Erich Fromm

Love is probably the most overworked word in the English language. So many human tragedies have occurred because of the misuse of and lack of understanding of what it means . . . When someone tells you that he loves you, don't ask him "how much"; just "how?"
George B. McLaughlin

Not to understand that a demand may be part of God's love for man is to misunderstand love as meaning unconditional acceptance without demand, and to sentimentalize love, emptying it of any real content.
Maurice Friedman

Samuel Johnson, the great English writer, spent much of his time in the company of Oliver Goldsmith, the famous author of *The Vicar of Wakefield.*

One day, as the huge Johnson strode the streets of London, with little Goldsmith tagging along beside him trying to keep up, Johnson suddenly exclaimed, "Goldie, do you see that man across the street? I hate him." "But Samuel," protested Goldsmith, "you do not even know the man." "That's why I hate him, Goldie, that's why I hate him. If I knew him I might love him."
Source Unknown

It behooves every man to reflect: Whence is the source which evokes in me feelings of love, if not the love of God for His creation?
Baal Shem Tov

There is a land of the living and a land of the dead and the bridge is love, the only survival.
Thorton Wilder

A father once complained to the Baal Shem Tov that his son had forsaken God. "What, Rabbi, shall I do?" "Love him more and more" was the reply.
Hasidic Lore

---

20   Universal is over all

In our world of today, due to the influence of many factors, a new international consciousness is beginning to develop. Men increasingly realize that they have an allegiance to mankind as a whole as well as to their own sections of it.
Dag Hammarskjold

We are in the world and the world is in us.
Alfred North

Every man takes the limit of his own field of vision for the limit of the world.
Johann Uhland

When the two brave explorers came down from the summit of Mount Everest, Tenzing Norkay, the native of India, was beset by newspapermen, each eager for him to promote some special aim or other. One wanted him to give his adventure an Indian Nationalist slant, another a Communist interpretation, and so on. Mr. Norkay made a simple comment: "The world is wide. Nobody sees all of it, not even from the top of Mount Everest."
Ethical Outlook

All people smile in the same language.
The Christian Athlete

"I am a citizen, not of Athens or Greece, but of the world." These are the words of Socrates, the ancient Greek philosopher, and perhaps the wisest man that ever lived. Despite

his words, Socrates lived and died a good and patriotic citizen. He found no conflict between the laws of his little community and the greater laws of reason by which all men should be governed. Today, Socrate's words have greater force than ever. Either we must all think of ourselves as part of mankind; or mankind will, within our own time, sink to the level of the beasts of the jungle.
Clifton Fadiman

When the world was large and it took months to travel from one place to another, we could afford to be little men. Now that the entire world is a small neighborhood, we need big men and big minds.
Harry Emerson Fosdick

All of us in our present civilization are dependent upon one another to a degree never before known in the history of mankind, and in the long run we are going to go up or down together.
Theodore Roosevelt

We travel together, passengers on a little spaceship, dependent on its vulnerable reserves of air and soil; all committed for our safety to its security and peace; preserved from annihilation only by the care, the work, and I will say the love, we give our fragile craft. We cannot maintain it half fortunate, half miserable, half confident, half despairing, half slave to the ancient enemies of man, half free in liberation of resources undreamed of until this day. No craft, no crew can travel safely with such vast contradictions. On their resolution depends the survival of us all.
Adlai E. Stevenson

The League of Nations might have succeeded if the peoples of the world had wanted it to succeed.
Winston Churchill

From family to clan, from clan to nation, from nation to federation, enlargements of allegiance have occurred throughout the history of mankind without weakening the earlier loves. We can develop a rational loyalty to planet earth while maintaining an emotional attachment to our prized diversity.
Rene Dubos

Ethics is the maintaining of life at its highest point of development—my own life and other life—by devoting myself to it in help and love; both these things are connected. This Ethic, profound, universal, has the significance of religion. It is religion.
Albert Schweitzer

All creation, with its multitude of diversities, comprises a unity similar to that of an individual human being. It has differentiated parts, but those parts are merely distinctive organs complementing one another in the larger life of the whole.
Maimonides

3

The world around us

21 The greatness of the outdoors

Linnaeus saw a bank of flowers and paused to pray, because God in His majesty was passing very near.
Source Unknown

Nature makes the man from the child, and the hen from the egg, but God makes the man and then the child, the hen and then the egg.
Johannes Eckhart

... Always night and day
I hear lakewater lapping with low
   sounds by the shore;
While I stand on the roadway, or on.
   the pavements gray
I hear it in the deep heart's core.
William Butler Yeats

Some warm day lie down on the earth. Get your ear down close to the ground and listen. You'll hear all manner of sounds—the wind in the trees and the murmur of insects, and you will discover presently that there is in all these sounds a well-regulated tempo. You cannot get that tempo by listening to traffic in the city streets, for it is lost in the confusion of sound. But the peaceful sounds of the earth are entirely different.
Norman Vincent Peale

The sun is 92 million miles from the Earth; it is the center of the solar system, and by the power of gravity holds every planet in its orbit. Yet that very same sun can ripen a bunch of grapes as though that were all it had to do.
Galilei Galileo

Sometimes as I drift idly along Walden Pond, I cease to live and I begin to be.
Henry David Thoreau

The parable is told of a king who once demanded of his counselor a sign of the wondrous works of God. The counselor replied, "Here are four acorns. Will your majesty stoop and plant them—then stoop and look into this pool of water?"

The king looked and saw four oak trees where he had planted the acorns. "Wonderful," said the king, "this is indeed the work of God."

"How long were you standing by the pool of water?" asked the counselor.

The king looked at his garments and found they were threadbare. He saw his reflection in the water and realized that he had become a very old man. "There is no miracle here," said the king.

"Yes," replied the counselor, "it is God's work whether He did it in one second or eighty years."
Source Unknown

Two Americans visiting Switzerland were discussing Europe. One of them said, rather cynically, that there was nothing beautiful in Europe: "Cathedrals are old and dusty; the castles are without bathrooms; the art is not beautiful, for the most part it is religious art, having none of the squares and circles that you find in our progressive American art; there is nothing beautiful in Europe."

His compatriot, pointing to the Alps, said, "But don't you think Switzerland is beautiful?"

His answer was, "Take away the scenery and what have you got left?"
Fulton J. Sheen

It is the course of wisdom to set aside an ample portion of our national parks and reserves, thus insuring that future generations may know the majesty of the earth as we know it today.
John F. Kennedy

Half of our misery and weakness derives from the fact that we have broken with the soil and allowed the roots that bound us to the earth to rot. We have become detached from the earth, we have abandoned her. And a man who abandons nature has begun to abandon himself.
Pierre Van Paasen

Be still, my heart, these great trees are prayers.
Rabindranath Tagore

A Garden

A garden is a lovely place
Where seeds burst through the sod.
A garden is a partnership
Between two hands and God.

A garden is a restful place
Where gentle breezes blow . . .
A family of growing things
Where souls can also grow.

A garden is a peaceful place
Where I can go apart
To think, to meditate, to pray
And listen with my heart.
William Arthur Ward

Most people enjoy getting out in the woods and fields or out on a lake or stream (fishing and hunting are good excuses), and springtime is an

ideal season as the deciduous flora "comes to life." Nature is not just a place to escape from daily responsibilities but gives man a chance to "Be still and know . . . "; and to be revitalized, rejuvenated, and be re-created. Since in nature there can be more awareness of the Creator than in the asphalt and concrete jungle where the creations of man predominate.
George Purvis

Look then to the simplicity of nature and thence to the anxieties and complexities we have created.
Paul Boese

When we become too wrapped up in the doings of man, it is time to go out on a warm spring night; to look up into the sky, and compare the greatest of men's satellites with the great satellite that God has already put in orbit—the one we commonly call the moon. It is time to ponder the mystery of seed that grows even while a man sleeps, and a kingdom that comes "in the fullness of time" as surely as springtime follows winter, grass grows, flowers bloom, and birds build nests and sing, even when we have not shown them how to do it.
Don Ian Smith

22 Science—servant of humanity

America is an affluent society in what, with proper turns of events and uses of technology, could be an affluent world.

Never has it been as true as now to say the human species has the keys to heaven or hell on earth in its hands. Science could turn our planet into a modern Garden of Eden. It could also turn our earth into a lifeless wasteland.

But science is only a tool. The good or harm it does depends on how men use it.

Man has done wondrous things with science. His conquests and exploits are awesome. But man the individual, man the social animal, has not yet truly conquered and civilized himself.
Indianapolis Star

The devices which science has given us are neither good nor evil in themselves. Their capacity for good or evil lies in the use we make of them. Thus, not in the laboratory, but in the human heart, in the realm of the spirit, lies the challenge of the future.
David Sarnoff

The fun in science lies not in discovering facts, but in discovering new ways of thinking about them.
William Lawrence Bragg

Science, when she has accomplished all her triumphs in her order, will still have to go back when the time comes to assist in building up a new creed by which man can live.
John Morley

Science made gods of us before we had earned the right to be people.
Jean Rostand

What a deep faith in the rationality of the structure of the world, and what a longing to understand even a small glimpse of the reason revealed to the world there must have been in Kepler and Newton to enable them to unravel the mechanism of the heavens in long years of lonely work.
Albert Einstein

Science should be the greatest ally, not the worst enemy of mankind.
Albert John Luthuli

Science had better not free the minds of men too much, before it has tamed their instincts.
Jean Rostand

After all his achievements in science, Isaac Newton said that he felt like a boy playing with pebbles on the shore of truth.
Source Unknown

With every new answer unfolded, science has consistently discovered at least three new questions.
Wernher von Braun

A prominent doctor, who was asked how he happened to choose medicine as a career, said, "As a small boy my younger brother took very ill. The doctor was sent for and came as fast as horse and buggy could transport him. As the doctor entered, I hid behind the sofa on which my brother lay. Here I observed my anxious parents and the country doctor with knitted brows, hovering over my sick brother. Finally the doctor arose and said, 'You need not worry, the child will get well.' A heavenly light fell across the faces of my parents, which was wonderful to behold. I decided then, as a child, to bring light to the faces of others through service in medicine."
Jas Paul Kennedy

Medicine is more than a profession. Medicine has a soul, and its calling involves not only the application of knowledge and the exercise of skill but also facing a human situation. It is not an occupation for those to whom career is more precious than humanity or for those who value comfort and serenity above service to others. The doctor's mission is prophetic.
Abraham Joshua Heschel

A motto for science classes could be: "We learn to discover and we discover to learn."
Joseph Crescimbeni

Penicillin was indeed the product of an accidental discovery, but the discovery was made, and the knowledge developed, because certain scientists had definite goals in mind. "Chance," Pasteur wrote, "favors only the prepared mind." The mind must be prepared not only by scientific training and technological know-how, but also by the awareness of social needs.
Saturday Review

23 The wages of war

War is clearly waste—waste of the lives of the killed; waste of the physical well-being of the maimed; waste of the time of the men who are fortunate enough to come home safe and sound, despite their loss of productive years; and it is waste of munitions consumed and stockpiled unused as well as the capital goods worn out in producing them. It is a wasteful activity from an economic point of view, no matter how successful it may be politically, nor how quick the victory. I am neither a pacifist nor a peace-at-any-price man. I happen to believe that, given the world in which we live, force does change things and that the purpose of waging war is to win decisively at the least possible cost in order to impose one's will upon the vanquished. But I deplore war as waste of human and material resources.
Willard M. Fox

War is not an "art." It is a surrender to the lowest animal instincts, ignoring the reasoning power which supposedly makes us superior. That war should still be considered a way of settling anything is a disgrace to civilization. Today it means nothing but reciprocal suicide.
Sigmund Spaeth

Mankind must put an end to war, or war will put an end to mankind.
John F. Kennedy

Peter Ustinov likes to tell a story about a newspaperman who was observing the Italian Army on maneuvers. Everything went wrong. Tanks bumped into each other, wrong signals were sent, messages never got through. The newspaperman made some appropriate comment to the general. "I, too, get depressed at this," the officer sighed. "But remember, the enemy has generals, too."
Virginia Kelly

We are all familiar with the famous thing which General William T. Sherman said about war. Here is something else he said. Remember this is not the word of a preacher, but of a soldier: "I am sick and tired of war. Its glory is all moonshine. It is only those who have never fired a shot, nor heard the shrieks and cries of the wounded, who cry aloud for blood, more vengeance, more desolation."
Halford E. Luccock

The question of war is in the first place a question of the scale of values. When the might of the state and the nation is looked upon as greater than man, war has in principle already made its appearance, everything has been made ready for it spiritually and materially . . . War and everything connected with it, is not only the most extreme form and the utmost limit of violence, it is also the most extreme form and the utmost limit of anti-personalism, it is a denial of personality. In consenting to war, man ceases to be a personality and he ceases to regard other people as personalities.
Nicholas Berdyaev

War spawns many evils: swollen budgets, the dislocation of young manpower, inflation, surly attitudes of other nations, restrictions on investment abroad, a perishable prosperity, and the brooding danger that our economy may be forced into the straitjacket of wage-and-price controls and perhaps higher taxes. And the evils rising from the crucible of conflict will multiply.
Everett M. Dirksen

As long as war is regarded as wicked it will always have a fascination. When it is looked upon as vulgar, it will cease to be popular.
Oscar Wilde

Several years ago an aged warrior of the Civil War was being interviewed by a reporter from a metropolitan newspaper who informed him: "You and two others are the sole survivors of the Confederate Army, and there is only one Union soldier still alive."

"Well, now's the time to attack!" snapped the Rebel, "We've got them outnumbered at last!"
The Catholic Layman

If my soldiers were to begin to think, not one would remain in the ranks.
Frederick the Great

When figures were published on fatalities in a war, someone said they were "statistics with the tears wiped off."
Author Unknown

It costs as much to acquire and maintain a squadron of supersonic aircraft as it does to build and maintain a university.
Abraham Ribicoff

A conscientious man would be cautious how he dealt in blood.
Edmund Burke

---

24 Art endures

A man becomes truly Man only when in quest of what is most exalted in him. True arts and cultures relate Man to duration, sometimes to eternity, and make of him something other than the most favored denizen of a universe founded on absurdity. Each hero, saint or sage stands for a victory over the human situation. All art is a revolt against man's fate.
Andre Malraux

Art and religion are the soul of our civilization. Go to them, for there love exists.
Frank Lloyd Wright

As a simple, unpretentious admirer of fine art, Elbert Hubbard derived much pleasure from visiting the great art galleries. One day he was admiring a priceless painting in a New York gallery when a friend chidingly remarked, "Elbert, why do you allow yourself to become so enthused over things you can never afford to own?"

"'Harry,' replied the sage of East Aurora, "I would rather be able to appreciate things I cannot have than to have things I am not able to appreciate."
Highways of Happiness

Works of art are of an infinite loveliness and with nothing to be so little reached as with criticism. Only love can grasp and hold and fairly judge them.
Rainer Maria Rilke

When Goethe said, "Art is long, life is short," he meant that universal values are to be found in those works of men which survive the ages. That is why the study of the arts enriches the education of men in any era and at any period of their individual lives.
Theodore P. Gnagey

Science proves to the mind; art reveals to the heart.
Max Weber

All art is a wedding of technique and emotion. Without emotion all the technique in the world will not produce art.
Richard Rodgers

Too often the tendency is to regard the arts as something pleasing but peripheral. I feel the time has come when we must accord them a primary position as essential to the nation's well being. In our increasingly mechanized and computerized world, the arts afford a measure of consolation and reassurance to our individuality, a measure of beauty and human emotion that can reach and move most men. They are indispensable to the achievement of our great underlying concern for the individual, for the fullest development of the potential hidden in every human being.
David Rockefeller

The purpose of art is to help us to be able to put up with life, and sometimes it helps us to get a little more out of it.
W.H. Auden

The best of artists has that thought alone
Which is contained within the marble shell;
The sculptor's hand can only break the spell
To free the figures slumbering in the stone.
Michelangelo

Every child, every man, every culture gives form to its feelings and ideas through art. Art is the essence of that which is human; it is the embodiment of the human experience and goal. From the moment in our history when man became distinguishable as man, art was the mark that distinguished him, and ever since, man has continued to be an artful creature.
D'Arcy Hayman

There is only one thing valuable in art: the thing you cannot explain.
Georges Braque

Art must contain a human experience and through the personality of an artist, skillfully communicate

this experience in an understandable language to the greatest number of thinking people for the longest length of time.
Frank Reilly

Art is a mode of knowledge, and the world of art is a system of knowledge as valuable to man as the world of philosophy or the world of science.

Herbert Read

Art seems to me to be a state of soul, more than anything else.
Marc Chagall

Art is like a border of flowers along the course of civilization.
Lincoln Steffens

Art is the stored honey of the human soul, gathered on wings of misery and travail.
Theodore Dreiser

25 The melody lingers on

Making music is an act of love.
Eugene Istomin

Examinations of the texts of many hundreds of African songs underlines the universal quality found in all genuine folk musics: Namely, that people sing about themselves and in doing so create not only entertainment but social adjustment. The good are praised, the evil lampooned, individual sorrows are shared and a sense of community is enhanced; in other words folk music, properly and naturally employed, is therapeutic.
Hugh Tracey

Everything will perish save love and music.
Scottish Proverb

A little boy who loved music was bitterly disappointed because he could neither play nor sing. But Amati, the violin-maker, said:

"There are many ways of making music. What matters is the song in the heart." So Antonio Stradivarius was encouraged to become the world's greatest violin-maker.
Edgar Chrisemer

Out of loneliness I will fashion a song
And when I find someone who can hear my song
We will sing it together.
A. M. Sullivan

When Sir Malcolm Sargent volunteered for the forces early in World War II, the government told him that the best service that he could render was—to music. On the home front he kept up morale with his concerts. On one occasion in the North of England he was on the rostrum when the sirens sounded: "Anyone who wants to leave may do so now," he told the audience, "but the orchestra will carry on. We may

be killed but we shall play something that Hitler cannot kill." Not a single person left. Sargent raised his baton and the orchestra intoned the opening theme of Beethoven's Fifth Symphony.
Illustrated London News

Serious nations, all nations, that can still listen to the mandate of nature have prized song and music as the highest; as a vehicle for worship, prophecy, and for whatsoever within them was divine.
Thomas Carlyle

Nature is saturated with melody; heaven and earth are full of song.
Nahman of Bratzlav

There is an old Jewish legend about the origin of praise. After God created mankind, says the legend, He asked the angels what they thought of the world He had made. "Only one thing is lacking," they said. "It is the sound of praise to the Creator." So, the story continues, "God created music, the voice of birds, the whispering wind, the murmuring ocean, and planted melody in the hearts of men."
The Midrash

I'm passionately involved in life. To be alive, to be able to speak, to see, to walk—it's all a miracle. I have adopted the technique of living life from miracle to miracle. I feel what people get out of me is this outlook on life, which comes out in my music.
Artur Rubinstein

Music is a language of emotions with a power for good or ill. It can shock; it can soothe. It can offend, it can comfort. It can agitate, it can inspire. Victor Hugo has said, "Music expresses that which cannot be put into words and that which cannot remain silent."
Audrey Nossaman

A few can touch the magic string
And noisy fame is sure to win them
But alas for those who never sing
But die with all their music in them
Anonymous

Music speaks with emotion that words alone do not arouse. This emotional content may stir us to noble action, or quietly establish a sense of peace that sets us free from the disturbances of outer conditions. Being free from language barriers, its function affects most people, and its influence remains far-reaching. Although a baby does not understand the words to the lullaby that puts him to sleep, his body responds to the tender love that is expressed in the lilt of his mother's song. He relaxes, sleeps in peace, and awakes refreshed and contented. Music continues with us throughout life to give us comfort, to inspire, and to refresh us. When we listen, it brings us into rhythmic action and causes us to move with greater ease and lightness of heart.
Science of Mind

Dear Lord, let me catch the music of the world.
John Greenleaf Whittier

26 Action and passion

Life is both action and passion. A man should share the passion and action of his time at peril of being judged not to have lived.
Oliver Wendell Holmes

Once the eminent philosopher John Dewey found his son in the bathroom. The floor was flooded. The professor began thinking, trying to understand the situation. After working a few minutes the son said, "Dad, this is not a time to philosophize. It is a time to mop."
Source Unknown

Truth exists only as the individual himself produces it in action.
Soren Kierkegaard

A ship in harbor is safe, but that is not what ships are built for.
J.A. Shedd

A sane society whose riches are happy children, men and women, beautiful with peace and creative activity, is not going to be ordained for us. We must make it ourselves. Our destiny is our responsibility, and without faith we cannot meet it competently. Long enough have we been told that faith is impracticable, that we must trim our sails to whatever winds that blow. Now the truth is burning in us that indifference and compromise are chaos.
Helen Keller

Let us sort out the music for the sounds, and again respond to the trumpet and the steady drums.
Adlai E. Stevenson

Fields can lie fallow, but we cannot; we have less time.
Mignon McLaughlin

Don't look at the world with your hands in your pockets. To write about it you have to reach out and touch it.
Mark Twain

A busy preacher was telling a Quaker all the things he had to do during the coming week. There were three sermons to deliver, two weddings to perform, two special addresses to be made, and nearly two dozen sick calls! Raising his hand, the Quaker interrupted quietly and remarked dryly: "If thou doest so much talking, when hath the Lord a chance to talk to thee?"
Herman W. Gockel

Stand still and silently watch the world go by—and it will!
Construction Digest

It is easier to write ten volumes of philosophy than to put one principle into practice.
Leo Tolstoy

Tell your tale before midnight. It is later than you think.
Virgil

Iron rusts from disuse, stagnant water loses its purity and in cold weather becomes frozen; even so does inaction sap the vigors of the mind.
Leonardo DaVinci

If we are—
Too busy to read a book that promises to widen our horizons;
Too busy to keep our friendships in good repair;
Too busy to conserve our health in the interest of our highest efficiency;
Too busy to keep the warm and vital loves of our own fireside glowing;
Too busy to cultivate the sense of a personal acquaintance with God;
Too busy to spend one hour during the week in worship;
Too busy to give time to the culture of our own souls—
Then we are indeed too busy.

Source Unknown

For every achievement there is a price. For every goal there is an opponent. For every victory there is a problem. For every triumph there is sacrifice.

William Arthur Ward

People are in great danger when they know what they should do and refuse to act upon what they know.

James Baldwin

What is used, develops, and what is left unused, atrophies, or wastes away.

Hippocrates

One hears that it does not matter what one believes so long as he is sincere. The fact that segregationists are sincere is somehow thought to render the attitude less harmful. Dietrick Bonhoeffer rightly points out in his "Letters and Papers from Prison" that the folly of a sincere person can be much worse (even morally) than conscious malevolence. We have the obligation not just to be sincere but to study carefully the full consequences of our actions.

Phillips Moulton

27 On taking a chance

Once when Carol Heiss (woman figure skater) was struggling over a fifth-grade composition on the American frontier, her mother told her something she never forgot. "Everyone has his own frontier—in the mind. On one side of it, everything is known, tried. On the other side is the part of yourself that hasn't yet been explored. All life's great adventures," she emphasized, "are on that other side."

Source Unknown

A thought, a sword, and a spade should never be allowed to rust.

Irish Proverb

Every forward step achieved by man has been due to the adventurous attitude. This attitude inspires dissatisfaction with the world as it is; it arouses the desire to change and improve things. The attitude of adventure is the flame that lights the fuse to explode new ideas.

Wilfred A. Peterson

When Sir Ernest Shackleton sought men to go with him to the South Pole in 1900 he inserted these stark lines in the *London Times:* "Men wanted for hazardous journey. Small wages, bitter cold, long months of complete darkness, constant danger, safe return doubtful. Honor and recognition in case of success." There were no applicants? There were no answers? Hundreds and hundreds of them from all over England.

Source Unknown

Keep on going and the chances are that you will stumble on something, perhaps when you are least expecting it. I have never heard of anyone stumbling on something sitting down.

Charles F. Kettering

A young man, eager to be on time on his first day of work, fell clumsily to the sidewalk in front of a bench filled with village loafers. As he dusted himself off amid their raucous laughter, he said: "Go ahead, laugh. You'll never fall because you're never going anywhere."

Robert Janacek

There is a story related by Conrad Hilton, the famous hotel owner, which illustrates something of what it means to be a "pioneer of faith." When Mr. Hilton was a young man trying to make up his mind what he would do with his life, his mother once said to him, "You will have to find your own frontier. A friend of your father's, a great pioneer out here in the West, once said, 'If you want to launch big ships, you have to go where the water is deep.'"

John Thompson

I never condemn a man for making a mistake. I will condemn a man who plays it cozy, who refuses to expose himself to failure. Such a man is worse than useless. He tends to spread the paralysis of caution up and down and across an organization. Such a man has no faith in himself or in others. And faith in people, I believe, is an important requirement in a man.

Murray D. Lincoln

There was nothing original in the conception that the world was round; it was held by all educated astronomers of the time. The greatness of Columbus was rather in the courage that he displayed in venturing into the unknown sea to prove the validity of his thesis and his pertinacity in the pursuit of his project.

Theodor Herzl

Our Father, who has set a restlessness in our hearts and made us all seekers after that which we can never fully find . . . Keep us at tasks too hard for us, that we may be driven to Thee for strength.

Eleanor Roosevelt

In order to profit from your mistakes, you have to get out and make some.

Leroy B. Houghton

28 A thing of beauty

Beauty is not, as Emerson observed, its own excuse for being. It is not a thing apart, an isolated abstraction removed from the general scheme of things. It is woven into the very texture of everyday life.
Sikh Review

In Connecticut the state police tried out the efficacy of multiflora hedges as road dividers on the Wilbur Cross Parkway. At varying speeds and angles, a car is slowed from 30 mph to 5 mph crashing a single row of roses. Highway officials think a double row would be just about perfect. This safety barrier is much cheaper than concrete or steel rails, and makes a beautiful highway.
Source Unknown

We live only to discover beauty. All else is a form of waiting.
Kahlil Gibran

One of the unexpected benefits of beautification came to light in Washington, D.C. Nine Washington schools were landscaped, and the window breakage was cut in half in these particular schools, while it continued at the same old rate at the other city schools. Perhaps beauty begets a regard for itself which will pay off in more than one way.
Atlantic News-Telegram

Religion and beauty are very closely allied. Some who think they have never had a religious experience have really had one through beauty without knowing it. If you have ever felt your spirit lifted and enlarged in the presence of a great canyon or waterfall, or a majestic storm, or a flaming sunset, or the soft hush of summer twilight, or the play of northern lights, or the flashing of stars in illimitable distances—then you ought not to say carelessly that you have never had a religious experience. If you have ever sensed something holy in a baby's smile or an old man's face, in an early morning bird song or a great oratorio, in Beethoven's Hymn to Joy or in a forest of great pines whose music lets one understand the legend of the Aeolian harp, then the presumption is strong that you have grasped something of the meaning of worship.
Source Unknown

We are lovers of beauty without extravagance and lovers of wisdom without a loss of manliness.
Pericles

Find some time each day to be alone—a time for listening. You may hear a mockingbird, or the wind in the trees, or a brook running over polished stones, or some other music of our earth—or even the hushed voice of Him who created all this beauty.
Harriet Hall

The relation of art to scholarship in the modern world requires scholars who have a share in esthetic creation, and artists who have a taste for scholarship. Given cooperation among such men who have overcome the modern tendency toward increasing specialization, we may be able to lay the basis for the more complete interplay of thought between the creative artist and the technical scholar. There may emerge from cooperation and mutual understanding between the discoverer of truths and the creator of works of beauty a new phenomenon in civilization, the team of scholar-artist.

Louis Finkelstein

A little girl was tacking up a new wall calendar, containing unfamiliar figures of the new year which was about to begin.

"It's going to be a beautiful year!" she exclaimed.

Someone, who heard the girl's prediction, asked, "How do you know it is going to be a beautiful year? A year is a long time, and you never know what will happen."

"Well," she answered, "a day isn't a long time, I know, because I'm going to take a day at a time, and make it beautiful. Years are only days put together, and I'm going to see that every day in the new year gets something beautiful into it."

"Then," the friend said, "it will be a beautiful year."

Sunshine Magazine

It isn't being in love; it's loving that makes you happy. It's like the difference between beauty and charm. What is left when your beauty has gone, when the tide is out? Charm is high tide forever.

Elizabeth Bibesco

Those who contemplate the beauty of the earth find reserves of strength that will endure as long as life lasts.

Rachel Carson

Beauty is mind-deep. You are as pretty—or as ugly—as you think you are. Visualize yourself as a pleasant, friendly, cheerful, laughing, sparkling person and your imagination will make you into that kind of person.

Author Unknown

Like the showers of rain which bring needed life-giving energy to grow, art is the rain of beauty falling from heaven to earth. It is God speaking, showing His heart to the world, filling it with fresh memories of the beauteous realms above.

Charles W. Haddock

Great art can be a revelation of God. We believe that God is love, truth and beauty. The service or the worship of God must not be clothed in ugliness or cheap sentimentality. The highest end of all that is true, beautiful and good is to serve and glorify God. Let us, "Worship the Lord in the beauty of holiness" (I Chronicles 16:19).

Anonymous

There are two men, one of whom is very happy and one of whom is very miserable. The essential difference between them is that one loves the beauty of the world, and the other hates its ugliness.

Thomas Dreier

29 The natural law and the universe

The flowers of the earth do not grudge at one another, though one be more beautiful and fuller of virtue than another, but they stand kindly one by another, and enjoy one another's virtue.
Jacob Boehme

There is no unbelief;
Whoever plants a seed beneath the sod
And waits to see it push away the clod
He trusts in God.
Lizzie York Case

Ah, how wonderful is the advent of spring—the great annual miracle of the blossoming of Aaron's rod, repeated on myriads and myriads of branches.
Henry Wadsworth Longfellow

Some years ago, the *Boston Globe* wrote a little story related to the philosopher George Santayana. He chose an April day in 1912 to bring to a close his professional career as a teacher at Harvard University. While he was engaged in his last lecture at University Hall a robin landed on the windowsill. He looked at it for a moment, then sighed softly, "Gentlemen, I have a date with spring." With that he went out the door and closed his career.
W. Ballentine Henley

Summer is the month of the poor. The sun gives warmth; the gardens, food; the flowers, beauty; the lakes and seas, fun and play.
Italian Proverb

I behold the great scheme of evolution unfolding despite all the delays and waste and failures, and the higher forms appearing upon the scene. I see on an immense scale, and as clearly as in a demonstration in a laboratory, that good comes out of evil; that the impartiality of the Nature Providence is best; that we are made strong by what we overcome; that man is man because he is as free to do evil as to do good; that life is as free to develop hostile forms as to develop friendly; that power waits upon him who earns it; that disease, wars, the unloosened, devastating power elemental forces have each and all played their part in developing and hardening man and giving him the heroic fiber.
John Burroughs

I care not, Fortune, what you me deny;
You cannot rob me of free Nature's grace,
You cannot shut the windows in the sky.
James Thomson

Every spring
Surprises me
With new arrangements
Of old botany.
Beulah M. Huey

But what of those whose vision on the ophthalmologist's chart is fine, but who are blind to the world, who look, but do not see—sunrise and sunset, ocean, hill and valley, spring and autumn? A rich man once proudly escorted an artist over his

lavish estate. "You see," said the millionaire, with a lordly sweep of his arm, "I own all this land." "Yes," replied the artist, "but it is I who own the landscape."
Source Unknown

What riches are ours in the world of nature, from the majesty of a distant peak to the fragile beauty of a tiny flower, and all without cost to us, the beholders! No man is poor who has watched a sunrise or who keeps a mountain in his heart.
Esther Baldwin York

In the first place, the human mind, no matter how highly trained, is not capable of grasping the Universe. We are like a little child entering a huge library. The walls are covered to the ceiling with books in many different tongues. The child knows that someone must have written these books. It does not know who or how. It does not understand the languages in which they were written. The child notes a definite plan in the arrangement of the books—a mysterious order which it does not comprehend, but only dimly suspects. That, it seems to me, is the attitude of the human mind toward God. And because I believe this, I am not an atheist.
Albert Einstein

We cannot command nature except by obeying her.
Francis Bacon

The views of nature held by any people determine all their institutions.
Ralph Waldo Emerson

There are no seven wonders of the world in the eyes of a child. There are seven million.
Walt Streightiff

---

30 Inner space and outer space

Seek truth in all things. God reveals Himself through the created world.
Thomas Aquinas

He reneweth in His goodness, every day continually, the work of Creation.
Jewish Prayer Book

If God can be found through any drug, God is not worthy of being God.
Mehere Baba

While man is living here, walking these common streets, living in closest intercourse with other men, he is already in the Everlasting Presence, and his Heaven has begun.
Phillips Brooks

When the Baal Shem's father was about to die, he took his young son into his arms and said: "My time has come and it has not been permitted me to rear you to man-

hood. But, dear son, remember all your days that God is with you and around you and beside you whenever you call upon Him, and that because of this, you need fear nothing in all the world."
Hasidic Lore

Every child born into the world is a new thought of God, an ever-fresh and radiant possibility.
Kate Douglas Wiggin

If we consider the whole universe, the mind refuses to look upon it as the outcome of chance.
Charles Darwin

At times in the silence of the night and in rare lonely moments, I experience a sort of communion of myself with something Great that is not myself.
H.G. Wells

God is subtle, but He is not malicious.
Albert Einstein

I have sought Thy nearness.
With all my heart have I called Thee.
And going out to meet Thee I found Thee coming toward me.
Judah Halevi

Thou hast made us for Thyself, O Lord, and our heart is restless until it finds its rest in Thee.
Augustine

I know well that God is nearer to me in my art than to others. I consort with Him without fear, have always recognized and understood Him, nor am I at all anxious about the fate of my music; its fate cannot be other than happy; whoever grasps it shall be absolved from all the misery that bows down other men.
Ludwig von Beethoven

It's wonderful to climb the liquid mountains of the sky. Behind me and before me is God and I have no fears.
Helen Keller

God does not lie on the day when we cease to believe in a personal deity, but we die on the day when our lives cease to be illumined by the steady radiance, renewed daily, of a wonder, the source of which is beyond all reason.
Dag Hammarskjold

The Divine Architect of the Universe has not built a stairway that leads to nowhere.
Robert Millikan

4
The function of faith

31 A faith for living

Man is so made that he lives by faith in God, or else by faith in idols. When he loses his faith in God, he falls into idolatry.
Nicholas Berdyaev

Belief is easy in June, with summer all around you. In fact, doubt is difficult in a green and hospitable world. The test comes in December, when you have to believe that onsetting winter will pass. You have to muster the deep-down belief that hope is not foolish and faith is not futile. You have to believe in your own believing.
Hal Borland

We reject the religious heritage, first because to master it requires more effort than we are willing to make, and second because it creates issues that are too deep and too contentious to be faced with equanimity. We are afraid to face any longer the severe discipline and the deep disconcerting issues of the nature of the universe and of man's place in it and of his destiny.
Walter Lippmann

Nothing before, nothing behind;
The steps of faith
Fall on the seeming void, and find
The rock beneath.
John Greenleaf Whittier

The longer I live, the more obvious it is to me that the most sacred act of a man's life is to say and to feel "I believe."
Thomas Huxley

A belief is not merely an idea the mind possesses; it is an idea that possesses the mind.
Robert Bolton

Happy are the mass of believers who do not seek to be too clever in their relation to God, but follow the law of God with simplicity.
Joseph Albo

The "Battle of the Warsaw Ghetto" began on April 19, 1943; and lasted for nearly a month. The heroic defenders knew from the start that they could not win; but they fought to the end with gallant courage. In their death they bore testimony to a faith that pervaded the Jewish masses even when they did not have the means of physical resistance. This faith was expressed in a Yiddish song widely sung in the ghettos and death camps:

"Never say that you walk the last road;
The leaden skies foretell a bluer day.
Our longed-for hour will yet come;
Our marching footsteps will proclaim: We are here."
The Jewish Press

Nothing worth doing is completed in our lifetime; therefore, we must be saved by hope. Nothing true or beautiful or good makes complete sense in any immediate context of history; therefore, we must be saved by faith. Nothing we do, however virtuous, can be accomplished alone; therefore, we are saved by love. No virtuous act is quite as virtuous from the standpoint of our friend or foe as from our standpoint. Therefore, we must be saved by the final form of love which is forgiveness.
Reinhold Niebuhr

I don't know what will happen now. We have difficult times ahead, but it doesn't matter with me because I've been to the mountain top. Like anyone else I would like to live a long life. But I'm not conerned with that.

I just want to God's will, and He has allowed me to go up the mountain. I see the promised land. I may not get there with you, but I want you to know that we as a people will get to the promised land. I am happy that I am not worried about anything. I'm not fearing any man. Mine eyes have seen the glory of the coming of the Lord.
Martin Luther King

Nothing in life is more wonderful than faith—the one great moving force which we can neither weigh in the balance nor test in the crucible.
William Osler

Learning and faith cannot be bequeathed to others. They must come as the result of one's own efforts. They must be gained by honest intellectual labor and be tested in the laboratory of one's own mind. Inherited beliefs are likely to be no more valuable to the possessor than inherited wealth to one who has no idea of how it was gained.
Godfrey T. Anderson

32 The Bible is basic

Someone has described the Bible as "a letter from God to mankind," addressed "to whom it may concern."
William T. McElroy

Freedom will speak everywhere, and its speech will be Biblical.
Heinrich Heine

It is noteworthy that the Bible does not argue the existence of God nor seek to demonstrate it with logical proofs. This it takes for granted. The great burning issue is the problem of human suffering. To it the greatest book in the Bible, the book of "Job," was addressed; with it, the Scribes and the Prophets wrestled; over it, the Psalmists and the Sages agonized.
Robert Gordis

The Bible is intended to be a guide and not a set of rules to be observed rigidly.
Viscount Montgomery

A Chinese woman had just learned to read. "Lord," she said, "we are going home to many who cannot read. Make us living Bibles, so that those who cannot read the Book, can read it in us."
Source Unknown

The Bible is a book of faith, and a book of doctrine ... but it is also a book which teaches man his own individual responsibility, his own dignity, and his equality with his fellow-man.
Daniel Webster

Three men were talking about some of the recent translations of the Bible. One said, "I like the new version of the Bible. It's easy reading. The Revised isn't bad either."

"Maybe," the second man shrugged his shoulder. "But, believe me, nothing compares with the King James version."

"I know a better one," the third man said.

"I like my mother's translation best. She translated the Bible into life, and it was the most convincing translation I ever saw."
Sunshine Magazine

I feel that a comprehensive study of the Bible is a liberal education for anyone. Nearly all of the great men of our country have been well versed in teachings of the Bible.
Franklin Delano Roosevelt

Think for a moment how in the course of a single day spent in the homely, necessary details of living we clarify and illuminate our talk with one another by the often unconscious use of the Bible's language. An unwelcome neighbor becomes "gall and wormwood" or "a thorn in the flesh"; a hated task "a millstone about our neck"; we escape from one thing or another "by the skin of our teeth"; we earn our bread "by the sweat of our faces"; ... in moments of anger we remember that "a soft answer turneth away wrath"; intrusions upon our sleep are the "pestilence that walketh in darkness"; we warn our children to be "diligent in business" so that they may not "stand before mean men," or prophesy that if "they sow the wind they shall reap the whirlwind" . . . we heap "coals of fire" on the heads of recalcitrant children or of harassed wives or husbands; having no servants we are ourselves "hewers of wood and drawers of water"; we long for a time when men "shall beat their swords into ploughshares and their spears into pruning hooks."

Mary Ellen Chase

Just use me—I am the Bible.
I am God's wonderful library.
I am always—and above all—the Truth.
To the weary pilgrim, I am a good strong staff.
To the one who sits in gloom, I am a glorious light.
To those who stoop beneath heavy burdens, I am sweet rest.
To him who has lost his way, I am a safe guide.
To those who have been hurt by sin, I am a healing balm.
To the discouraged, I whisper glad messages of hope.
To those who are distressed by the storms of life, I am an anchor.
To those who suffer in lonely solitude, I am a cool, soft hand resting on a fevered brow.
O, child of man, to best defend me, just use me!

Anonymous

The Bible—actually a collection of books—has been translated into 1,068 languages. It is the most widely purchased and yet the most unread, the most misunderstood, and the most venerated of all sacred literature.

Source Unknown

Preparing for a long trip, the young man said to his friend, "I am just about packed. I only have to put in a guide book, a lamp, a mirror, a microscope, a telescope, a volume of fine poetry, a few biographies, a package of old letters, a book of songs, a sword, a hammer and a set of books I have been studying." "But," the friend objected, "you can't get all that into your bag." "Oh, yes," replied the young man, "it doesn't take much room." He placed his Bible in the corner of the suitcase and closed the lid.

Source Unknown

I believe a knowledge of the Bible without a college course is more valuable than a college course without the Bible.

William Lyon Phelps

The Bible is like an old Cremona; it has been played upon by the devotion of thousands of years until every word and particle is public and tunable.

Ralph Waldo Emerson

I am profitably engaged in reading the Bible; take all of this book that you can upon reason and the balance upon faith, and you will live and die a better man.

Abraham Lincoln

33 Pathways to God

Sometimes a nation abolishes God, but fortunately God is more tolerant.
>Herbert V. Prochnow

Think not thou canst sigh a sigh
And thy Maker is not by;
Think not thou canst weep a tear
And thy Maker is not near.
>William Blake

I cannot see
The long deep roots
Of the spreading maple tree.

I cannot see
The giant whale
Down in the deep blue sea.

I cannot see
The golden sun
On a gray and cloudy day.

I cannot see
The snow on the peak
Of the mountain far away.

But though I cannot
See the roots
The whale the sun or the snow,

I know they all
Are where they are—
I know—because—I know!

I know that I
Cannot see God—
Though I look everywhere;

But I am sure
That God is near
And He can hear my prayer!
>Ilo Orleans

God is the name for that which concerns man ultimately.
>Paul Tillich

In the depth of the human soul lives and grows that which is personal; before it, before the I stands the eternal God, who thereby is the near, personal God.
>Leo Baeck

The finest fruit of serious learning should be the ability to speak the word "God" without reserve or embarrassment... And it should be spoken without adolescent resentment, rather with some sense of communion, with reverence and with joy.
>Nathan M. Pusey

Often our God is too small, limited to certain programs, a certain church, a particular denomination. The story is told of a Japanese businessman in this country who had just heard a sermon by a famous preacher. Asked what he thought of the sermon, he replied, "From listening to him you get the idea that God is a white man, an American, and a Baptist. But everyone knows that God is a yellow man, a Japanese, and a Buddhist."
>David Paul Byram

To love God truly, one must first love man. And if anyone tells you that he loves God and does not love his fellowman, you will know that he is lying.
>Martin Buber

I believe in God, the Father Almighty, because wherever I have looked, through all that I see around me, I see the trace of an Intelligent Mind, and because in natural laws, and especially in the laws which govern the social relations of men, I see, not merely the proofs of intelligence, but the proofs of beneficence.

Henry George

Who made God? A little boy asked his mother this question after she had been telling him the story of the Creation. She was puzzled for a moment, then taking off her wedding ring, she handed it to her son, and asked if he could find where it began and where it ended. God has no beginning and no ending. He is from everlasting to everlasting.

D.E. Finch

"Bring me a fruit from that tree." "Here it is, venerable Sir." "Cut it open." "It is cut open, venerable Sir." "What seest thou in it?" "Very small seeds, venerable Sir." "Cut open one of them." "It is cut open, venerable Sir." "What seest thou in it?" "Nothing, venerable Sir." Then spake he, "That hidden thing which thou seest not, O gentle youth, from that hidden thing verily has this mighty tree grown."

Upanishad

If a clock proves the existence of a clockmaker and the world does not prove the existence of a Supreme Architect, then I consent to be called a fool.

Voltaire

34 Prayer has a purpose

Little Johnnie was almost through his nightly prayer . . . "Bless my daddy, bless my mom, bless Aunt Bessie, and please make Philadelphia, Pennsylvania, the capital of the U.S.A."

"Why, darling!" exclaimed his shocked mother, "Why did you say such a thing?"

"Because," answered Johnnie, as he settled down for the night, "that's what I put on my examination paper."

The Colonel Says

Prayer is not a monologue, but a dialogue.

W.B.J. Martin

High over the ocean the occupants of an apocryphal jetliner were told by their pilot that one of the engines had failed. "Well, we'd better start praying," said a passenger. And an alarmed seat-mate asked, "Do you think it's that bad?"

Christianity Today

If on a Spring night I went by
And God were standing there,
What is the prayer that I should cry
To Him? This is the prayer:
O Lord of courage grave,
O Master of this night of Spring,
Make firm in me a heart too brave
To ask Thee anything.

John Galsworthy

The purpose of true prayer is not to tell God of something we would like for Him to do. Rather, it should first of all help us to discover what He would have us to do and to help to make us willing to be obedient to His will.
William T. McElroy

A wealthy man prayed that God would take care of the poor, and see that they were fed and clothed. When he finished praying, the man's little girl said: "Daddy, please lend me your pocketbook." "Well, what do you want with my pocketbook?" the father asked. "I just want to help you answer your prayers, daddy."
Sunday Guardian

Prayer isn't magic, nor is God a divine Magician. Prayer isn't something related to a God "up there"—He is right here. For this reason, prayer is really more a matter of attitudes and actions than simply words.
Malcolm Boyd

O Lord, Thou knowest how busy I must be this day. If I forget Thee, do not Thou forget me.
Jacob Astley

Prayer must come from the heart and not from the school board.
Maurice N. Eisendrath

Rabbi Ammi said: Man's prayer is not accepted unless he puts his heart in his hands.
The Talmud

Prayer is an invitation to God to intervene in our lives, not only through our walking in His ways, but through His entering into our ways.
Abraham Joshua Heschel

God answers sharp and sudden on some prayers,
And thrusts the thing we have prayed for in our face,
A gauntlet with a gift in it.
Elizabeth Barrett Browning

He who prays for the well-being of his fellowmen before praying for his own is rewarded by God first.
The Talmud

Every time you pray, if your prayer is sincere, there will be new feeling and new meaning in it which will give you fresh courage, and you will understand that prayer is an education.
Feodor Dostoevski

One night a little girl surprised her mother when she concluded her prayer for her family and friends by adding, "and now, God, what can I do for You?"
Sunday School Times

Prayer is nothing you do; prayer is someone you are. Prayer is not about doing, but about being. Prayer is about being alone in God's presence. Prayer is being so alone that God is the only witness to your existence. The secret of prayer is God affirming your life.
William Stringfellow

35 Theologies are many but God is one

The broad-minded see the truth in different religions; the narrow-minded see only their differences.
Lao Tse

It is clear to us that human love is but an offshoot of the divine love, for without that divine love no love could be aroused within our heart.
Nahum of Czernobel

The religious community must teach us and help us share the burdens of others. This is religion in action, as Helen Hayes learned when in 1949 her daughter, Mary died of polio. She was being tortured by the unanswerable question—Why? and accepted no professional or social engagements. A Mr. Isaac Frantz insisted, however, on seeing her, since he and his wife had endured the same tragedy. One Sunday afternoon, the two couples met. The Frantzs' owned a tiny stationary store and had to struggle for the necessities of life. Helen Hayes and her husband, Charles, had never known anything but success, fame, luxury. But the four of them suddenly had one thing to share, the tragic loss of their children. They found themselves talking about their children, Helen Hayes for the first time since Mary's death. She had finally taken her memory out of hiding. Then Mrs. Frantz told of her plans to adopt an orphan from Israel and when Helen Hayes expressed her shock, she replied: "You are thinking I am letting him take my little boy's place. No one could ever do that. But in my heart there is still love and maybe wisdom, too. No, my dear, we cannot die because our children die. I should not love less because the one I loved is gone—but more should I love because my heart knows the suffering of others." And Helen Hayes concludes the story, entitled. "In my darkest hour—hope," "When they finally rose to leave, I realized why my search for God had been fruitless— I had looked in the wrong places. He was not to be found between the covers of a book, but in the human heart."
Source Unknown

A grandfather was walking through his yard when he heard his granddaughter repeating the alphabet in a tone of voice that sounded like a prayer. He asked her what she was doing. The little girl explained: "I'm praying, but I can't think of exactly the right words, so I'm just saying all the letters, and God will put them together for me, because He knows what I'm thinking."
Charles B. Vaughan

Prayer is the language of love. Different nations have different languages: love has its own language, no matter what nation we belong to.
John Maillard

When Nobel Prize Winner S.Y. Agnon was given an honorary degree by the Weizmann Institute of Science, the Institute's Professor Pekeris declared Agnon's right to be honored by a scientific group: Agnon established his own cosmo-

logical theory. That is, you ask how God could create the world in six days. Agnon says, "He was all alone; so nobody bothered Him."
Source Unknown

Two ministers of different faiths were the best of friends, but often disagreed on religious issues. One day they had been arguing a little more than usual on some theological point, when one of them said: "That's all right. We'll just agree to disagree. The thing that counts is that we're both doing the Lord's work . . . you in your way, and I in His."
Clyde Murdock

Theology separates men:
Religion unites them.
Max Lilienthal

The art of leading others well consists in forgetting one's self, aware that one is doing God's bidding.
Saint Teresa of Avila

The Lord is One. His dominion is without limit, boundless in space and endless in time.

The Lord is One. His is the sum of all that has been, the promise of all that is to be.

The Lord is One. His is the unity that encompasses life and death, heaven and earth, light and darkness.

The Lord is One. His is the oneness that unites man with nature, the smallest grain of sand with the farthest star.

The Lord is One. His unity is manifested in the struggle to attain harmony among men and balance between man and nature.

The Lord is One. To make His purposes our own is to dedicate body and soul to His service, is to attain that love of man which is at one with the love of God.
Gershon Hadas

---

36 For God's sake

The weary Chaplain, having made a five-mile forced march with a battalion of infantry trainees and with the five miles back still to look forward to, dropped gratefully into one of a group of chairs beneath a shade tree on the side of the road. He'd removed one boot when a jeep braked beside him and a young lieutenant hurried over and said,

"Sorry, sir. The general will be along any moment to inspect the troops. The chairs are reserved for the general and his staff."

"Son," grunted the Chaplain, pulling at the other stubborn boot, "I'm on God's staff. And until someone comes along superior to Him, I'll not be moving."
Source Unknown

There is the story of the Hasidic rabbi who one day sent out an urgent call to all the people in the town to assemble at once at the market place. The artisans left their benches, the shopkeepers their stalls, the women came with their children. When they were all together the rabbi addressed them. "I have a most important message for you," he said with the holy intensity for which he was famous. "Your very lives depend on it." The mass of faces before him were turned expectantly and reverently toward the master. "This is the message," he fairly shouted: "There is a God in the world!"
Hasidic Lore

God has laid upon man the duty of being free, of safeguarding freedom of spirit, no matter how difficult that may be, or how much sacrifice and suffering it may require.
Nikolas Berdyaev

A Russian child asked his mother: "Does God know we don't believe in Him?"
Edgar Y. Harburg

We flirt with God, instead of love Him, for flirtation means attention without intention.
David Aronson

If men will not be governed by God, then they must be ruled by tyrants.
William Penn

The purpose of man's creation is that he should become a manifestation of God's attributes, in other words, the image of God.
Koran

One day when a leading layman of our denomination, highly educated, and effective as a speaker, was asked by a friend, "Don't you find lots of defects in your pastor's sermons?" his reply was: "I don't go to church to criticize the preacher; I go to worship the Lord."
Allen Bowman

More desperately than guided missiles, we need guided men and women who will direct their lives toward God in order that mankind may live by the will and ethical principles revealed to us by God.
William B. Silverman

A little knowledge may lead a man away from God but a great deal brings him back.
Francis Bacon

Now you wonder if man has much to learn from the Bible and I answer "A great deal." I believe that the Bible is almost unknown today. It isn't a book about God, though that's how it's generally considered, but a book about man. The Bible offers a sublime answer, but unless we know the question to which it responds, we can hardly understand it. The Bible is an answer to the question, "What does God require of man?"
Abraham Joshua Heschel

I once made a journey around the world. I never once saw "The Atheists' Home for Orphans," or "The Agnostics Crippleage," but everywhere I went I saw religious institutions caring for the destitute and needy.
W. E. Sangster

No man deals falsely with his neighbor until first he denies God.
The Talmud

The new pastor was being discussed at the ladies circle group and one of them said she thought he was a real smart man.

"In what way?" asked one of the ladies.

"Well," replied the first woman, "for one thing, I've noticed he's been asking God for a lot of things our old pastor never even knew God had."
Herm Albright

O Lord of the Universe, I desire not Thy Heaven, nor fear Thy hell; I seek only Thee.
Levi Yitzhak of Berditchev

---

37 Between the individual and God

O incognito God, anonymous Lord,
with what name shall I call You? Where shall I
discover the syllable, the mystic word
that shall evoke You from eternity?
Is that sweet sound a heart makes, clocking life,
Your appellation? Is the noise of thunder, it?
Is it the hush of peace, the sound of strife?

I have no title for Your glorious throne,
and for Your presence not a golden word,
only that wanting You, by that alone
I do evoke You, knowing I am heard.
Abraham M. Klein

My God, the soul You have given me is pure. You created it and You formed it. You breathed it into me and You keep it within me. A time will come when You will take it from me, but You will return it to me in the life to come. So long as the soul is within me I acknowledge You, O Lord my God and God of my fathers, Master of all creation, Lord of all souls.
Jewish Prayer Book

May the blessing of light be upon you, light without and light within. May the blessed sunlight shine upon you and warm your heart till it glows like a great peat fire, so that the stranger may come and warm himself by it, and also a friend.

And may the light shine out of the two eyes of you like a candle set in two windows of a house, bidding the wanderer come out of the storm.

And may the blessing of the rain be upon you—the soft sweet rain. May it fall upon your spirit so that all the little flowers may spring up, and shed their sweetness on the air.

And may the blessing of the great rains be on you, may they beat upon your spirit and wash it fair and clean, and leave there many a shining pool where the blue of heaven shines reflected, and sometimes a star.

And may the blessings of the earth be on you—the great and round earth. May you ever have a kindly greeting for them you pass as you're going along the roads.

May the earth be soft under you when you lie upon it, tired at the end of the day. And may it rest easy over you when at the last you lie out under it. May it rest so lightly over you that your soul may be quickly through it, and on its way to God.

Ancient Irish Prayer

God makes visible to man His will in events, an obscure text, written in a mysterious language.

Victor Hugo

Many a time as I went into the pulpit I recalled Hugh Latimer's experience that Sunday morning when, headed toward the royal chapel, he heard a voice within him say; "Latimer, Latimer, be careful what you preach today because you are going to preach before the king of England;" then another voice said: "Latimer, Latimer, be careful what you preach today since you are going to preach before the King of kings."

Source Unknown

My granddaughter once said to me: "Is God real?" I said to her, "If God is real to you, He is real."

Carl Sandburg

Some missionaries were talking with an African named Lutete, owner of the hotel where they were staying. They stopped talking to watch an airplane pass overhead. Then Lutete said, "One day I took an airplane ride that made me very happy. For the first time I saw the world as God sees it. Looking down from the air, I could see houses and people, but I couldn't tell where the white people lived and where the Africans lived. I thought, it is like that with God. . . . He doesn't see whether we are black, white, red, brown or yellow, He sees us as His children."

Alliance Witness

The smoke of my pipe can be an offering of incense to God.

Baal Shem Tov

God, You listen to prayer. Hear our prayers when they are worth listening to.

God, You are one. Hear us when we are one people. Hear each of us when he is a whole person, a single one.

God, You create. Hear us when we try to create a loving relationship, or a better ground for a growing soul, or hope.

God, You know us. Help us to summon our souls, to stretch with utmost love toward You.

Ruth F. Brin

Piety is man's reverent attachment to the sources of his being and the steadying of his life by that attachment.

George Santayana

38   Deeds not creeds

Apprehensively, man
Approaches God.

Politely, he pleads
What is required?

What is meant,
What must be done?

Circumspectly, he murmurs,
Answer me.

Open thy heart, man.
The answer lies there.

Open thy ears, man.
You will hear.

Man, shame-faced,
Turns away,

Full well, he knows
The answer.

Ethel L. Levey

I once read of a man who informed his minister he'd at last gotten religion. Asked if he'd quit sinning, he said he had. Then asked if he'd paid all his debts, he indignantly accused the preacher of changing the subject from religion to business.
Piney Woods Pete

No religion is a true religion that does not make men tingle to their fingertips with a sense of infinite hazard.
William Ernest Hocking

A young communist came to see Gandhi to convert him to a more radical program. He spend an hour with Gandhi, but when he came out finally he looked sheepish. "What fools we can be," he said. His friends inquired as to what had gone wrong. "Nothing," was the reply, "but that little man is the only true revolutionary in our country. We spend ourselves in talking and shouting, and he acts."
Chester Bowles

I'd rather see a sermon than hear one any day;
I'd rather one should walk with me than merely show the way.

The eye's a better pupil and more willing than the ear;
Fine counsel is confusing, but example's always clear.

And the best of all preachers are the men who live their creeds,
For to see the good in action is what everybody needs.

I can soon learn how to do it if you'll let me see it done;
I can watch your hands in action, but your tongue too fast may run.

And the lectures you deliver may be very wise and true;
But I'd rather get my lesson by observing what you do.

For I may misunderstand you and the high advice you give,
But there's no misunderstanding how you act and how you live.
The Lookout

Go put your creed into your deed,
Nor speak with double tongue.
Ralph Waldo Emerson

Every seed sown produces a harvest of its kind. So it is in human life. We all need to sow the seeds of compassion, sympathy and love; for we

shall reap what we sow. Every characteristic of selfishness, self-love, self-esteem, every act of self-indulgence, will bring forth a like harvest.
Ellen G. White

Religion has never been so much a discipline demanding to know "What do you believe?" as much as "What are you doing about your beliefs?"
Francis Lehr

Most people are bothered by those passages of Scripture they do not understand, but I have always noticed that the passages that bother me are those I do understand.
Mark Twain

I must lose myself in action, lest I wither in despair.
Alfred Tennyson

Barren trees make more noise than fruit-bearing trees . . . They ask fruit-bearing trees: "Why don't you make any noise?" — to which the trees reply, "Our fruits are sufficient advertisement."
The Midrash

Words without action are the assassins of idealism.
Herbert Hoover

You're always trying to analyze *why* people do things. It doesn't matter. The only thing that counts is *what* they do.
Violet Weingarten

Salvation is attained not by subscription to metaphysical dogmas, but solely by love of God that fulfills itself in action. This is a cardinal truth in Judaism.
Hasdai Crescas

39 The grandeur of God

God grows weary of great kingdoms, but never of little flowers.
Rabindranath Tagore

Man has read his vanities in God, until he has supposed that singing on themes to God's praise might flatter Him as it would flatter us. Man has read his cruelties into God, and what in moments of vindictiveness and wrath we would like to do to our enemies we have supposed Eternal God would do to us. Man has read his religious partisanship into God . . . and conceived Him to be a Baptist or a Methodist, a Presbyterian, or an Anglican. Man has read his racial pride into God; nations have thought themselves His chosen people above all others because they seemed so to themselves. The centuries are sick with a God made in man's image.
Harry Emerson Fosdick

Do you need proof of God? Does one light a torch to see the sun?
Oriental Wisdom

My religion consists of a humble admiration of the illimitable superior who reveals Himself in the slight details we are able to perceive with our frail and feeble minds. That deeply emotional conviction of the presence of a superior reasoning power, which is revealed in the incomprehensible universe, forms my idea of God.
Albert Einstein

Switfly arose and spread around me
   the peace and the joy and the
   knowledge that pass all the art
   and argument of earth;
And I know that the hand of God is
   the elder hand of my own,
And I know that the spirit of God is
   the elder spirit of my own.
Walt Whitman

The Russian government had a plan to improve the yield of potatoes. After having followed the recommendations for a season, a farmer was being interviewed by a government representative. "Why, I tell you," commented the farmer, "if I piled all the potatoes in one big pile they would reach from here to God."

"Don't say that so loud," replied the government man. "I don't want to have to turn you in. You know there isn't any God."

"And there aren't any potatoes either," said the farmer.
Source Unknown

Who has seen the wind?
Neither you nor I
But when the trees bow down their
   heads
The wind is passing by.
Robert Louis Stevenson

The heavens declare the glory of
   God,
And the firmament shows His
   handiwork;
Day unto day expresses His greatness;
Night unto night makes Him
   known.
There is no speech, there are no
   words,
Their voice is not heard.
Yet their sway extends over all the
   earth,
And their message to the ends of the
   world...
Psalm 19

Human experience bears testimony that through time, God has chosen certain dedicated men and women and made them His instruments for proclaiming His will. These men and women are not passive echoes, but active partners in the process, expressing their own vision of the truth, subject to their own limitations. Nor are we ordinary folk dependent solely upon these revelations of the Divine. The miracles of birth, of love, of death, constitute Divine elements in the pattern of life that surround us everywhere in the universe. Thus it is given to all men to hear the call, "Thus saith the Lord," however imperfectly. And it is also given to all men to answer, "Here I am."
Robert Gordis

We must believe in the conquest of the spirit of the world by the spirit of God. But, the miracle must happen in us, before it can happen in the world.
Albert Schweitzer

I pray Him bring me to repentance,
but I bring myself to sorrow
and the wish for death.

I pray Him grant me forgiveness,
but I grant myself pity
and the sweetness of despair.

I lie in darkness
searching out the shape of my shadow,
and the night wind blows across my face.

I know there is God,
but who can touch a shadow,
and who can find the wind?

I lie in darkness, praying,
and the shadow covers me,
and the wind cools me.

Then, I, who cannot touch, am touched;
and I, who cannot form, am formed,
and I, who cannot find, am found.
Ruth F. Brin

Man, who does not understand why it is the dark part of the eye that sees, shall he presume to explain the ways of God?
The Talmud

All over this earth,
And all over the planets,
And in the capacity You have given man
To reach for the planets
There You are.
Indian Prayer

---

40 *Religion is a requirement*

The Abbe preached a fastday sermon before Louis XVI, which contained a great deal of politics and government, but very little gospel.

"It is a pity," the king said to him, as he left the church, "that you did not touch on religion, then you would have told us something about everything."
American Mercury

Heavy doses of religion in itself will not make a child a happy adult and a good citizen. The instructions must be accompanied by personalized and demonstrated affection. After all, the roots of religion are planted in love—love of God, love of family, of country, of friends, of mankind. If a child isn't taught to love, he will grow up not knowing how. Then, no matter how much else he knows about religion, he will not be a religious person.
Benjamin A. Spock

Religion is "the passion for righteousness conceived as a cosmic demand."
William Ernest Hocking

There is no one without a religious need, a need to have a frame of orientation and an object of devotion.
Erich Fromm

Modern man has lost the security of the primitive myth but he has not accepted the religious insights in which he alone can feel at home. He has rejected the legend, but cannot rise to the truth. A spiritual vagabond, he is frightened at the loneliness he has created for himself. His efforts to transform his own creation —his business, his trade union, his political party, his club, his city and finally his country—into new gods are feeble and pathetic. He is too mature for effective self-deception and will not rise to the maturity where delusion is unnecessary. He knows that "patriotism is not enough" but he refuses to admit that which is.
Louis Finkelstein

The heart of religion is not an opinion about God, such as philosophy might reach as the conclusion of its argument; it is a personal relation with God.
William Temple

Efficient as we are in improving our material comfort we seem less and less capable of providing for our spiritual requirements. The affluent society has efficiently replaced the Victorian way of life. Desirable as this is in many ways it has, however, done this at great cost. Gone is the stability of the Victorian age and we all now live on the edge of a volcano which threatens to erupt at any time . . . The more man advances technically the greater indeed becomes his need for religion.
G. J. Clarke

A church membership does not make one religious any more than owning a piano makes a musician.
Douglas Meador

"Norah," said the minister to his housekeeper, "I've asked Mr. and Mrs. James to dinner at 6:30, but I think I'll give them a quarter of an hour's grace."

"Well, sir," replied the housekeeper, "I'm religious myself, but I think you're overdoing it."
Source Unknown

God has made different religions to suit different aspirants, times and countries. All doctrines are only so many paths; but a path is by no means God Himself. Indeed, one can reach God if one follows any of the paths with wholehearted devotion.
Sri Ramakrishna

True religion, I believe, seeks the world's betterment. It raises our vision to a new day in which, through faith, courage and goodwill to all mankind, peace on earth is a reality.
Joseph Krimsky

5

Each age is a stage

41 Train a child

Samuel Taylor Coleridge, the great English poet of the Romantic period, was once talking with a man who told him that he did not believe in giving children any religious instruction whatsoever. His theory was that the child's mind should not be prejudiced in any direction, but when he came to years of discretion, he should be permitted to choose his religious opinions for himself. Coleridge said nothing, but after a while he asked his visitor if he would like to see his garden. The man said he would, and Coleridge took him out into the garden, where only weeds were growing. The man looked at Coleridge in surprise, and said, "Why, this not a garden! There are nothing but weeds here!"

"Well, you see," answered Coleridge, "I did not wish to infringe upon the liberty of the garden in any way. I was just giving the garden a chance to express itself and to choose its own production."

E. Owen Kellum, Jr.

The first idea that the child must acquire, in order to be actively disciplined, is that of the difference between good and evil; and the task of the educator lies in seeing that the child does not confound good with immobility, and evil with activity, as often happens in the case of the old-time discipline. And all this because our aim is to discipline for activity, for work, for good; not for immobility, not for passivity, not for obedience.

Marie Montessori

I once asked a psychiatrist what he considered the worst mistake made by parents. He said the worst mistake most people make is saying, "My kids are not going to have it as tough as I did." "How can this be a mistake?" I asked him. His answer seems worth noting. "The thing that makes you the man you are, if you are any sort of a man at all, is the fact that it was difficult, that you had to surmount certain odds, that the deck at times was stacked against you, that it was important that you climb and creep and crawl to get to the top, if that was what you wanted out of life."
Jim Bishop

Know you what it is to be a child? It is to be something very different from the man of today. It is to have a spirit yet streaming from the waters of baptism; it is to believe in love, to believe in loveliness; to believe in belief; it is to be so little that the elves can reach to whisper in your ear; it is to turn pumpkins into coaches, and mice into horses, lowness into loftiness, and nothing into everything, for each child has its fairy godmother in its own soul; it is to live in a nutshell and to count yourself the king of infinite space.
Francis Thompson

Children need a great deal of love on the one hand and a great deal of firm guidance and correction on the other. Children who are shielded against work, against hardship, against punishment for wrongdoing, or against other unpleasant realities of life, simply cannot develop the stamina necessary to face life. At the same time children who experience only harshness and abuse turn bitter and too frequently delinquent. The middle road is the one which wise parents follow.
William A. Kramer

Some parents say that religion is an intimate, personal matter, which every child has a right to choose for himself, and that they propose to leave the child neutral while he is growing up, and then let him or her freely select his own religion. Even if we try we cannot keep the child neutral religiously. Religion is not an addition to life, but the very climate pervades the whole of living. As soon as the child is born in any home, it begins creating in him a spiritual climate teaching him basic relations to life, feelings about life, which inevitably enter into the very substance of any religion which he will ever possess.
Harry Emerson Fosdick

Each child sits before he stands; he babbles before he talks; he fabricates before he tells the truth; he draws a circle before he draws a square; he is selfish before he is altruistic; he is dependent on others before he achieves dependence on self.
Arnold Gesell

A child educated only at school is an uneducated child.
George Santayana

We spend so much time planning to give our children things we didn't have that we forget to see that they have at least some of the things we did have.
Elbert Forester

The child needs strength to lean on, a shoulder to cry on, and an example to learn from.
Hubert H. Humphrey

As a child I used to visit the Buddhist temple often with my grandmother. One morning, as we came out from prayer, a street urchin, who was no more than my own age, rushed forward and hit me with a stick. Grandmother, instead of shaking an angry finger at the boy, said quietly to him: "My child, who is your father that has so poorly trained you?" The boy stared shamefacedly at her, then hung his head and slowly backed away.
Chen Mei

To bring up a child in the way he should go, you have to travel that way yourself once in a while.
Henry Wheeler Shaw

42   Youth is a part of you

Could I climb to the highest place in Athens, I would lift my voice and proclaim: "Fellow citizens, why do you turn and scrape every stone to gather wealth and take so little care of your children, to whom one day you must relinquish all?"
Socrates

Like a trapeze artist, the young person in the middle of vigorous motion must let go of his safe hold on childhood and reach out for a firm grasp on adulthood, depending for a breathless interval on a relatedness between the past and the future, and on the reliability of those he must let go of, and those who will receive him. Whatever combination of drives and defenses, of sublimations and capacities has emerged from the young individual's childhood must now make sense in view of his concrete opportunities in work and in love; what the individual has learned to see in himself must now coincide with the expectations and recognitions which others bestow on him; whatever values have become meaningful to him must now match some universal significance.
Erik H. Erikson

Youth can be the growing edge of a creative culture . . . they can plant the seeds of disorganization, or be seduced by a Hitler and reverse the slow; slow ascent of civilization . . . The status of youth in an era of change is both fortunate and precarious.
Howard Y. McClusky

Being young is a fault which improves daily.
Swedish Proverb

When we are out of sympathy with the young, then I think our work in this world is over.
George MacDonald

Young people have always measured their parents' world against their parents' ideals and found world and parents wanting. Every so often this awareness of discrepancy becomes deep-seated discontent. It was so for Rousseau who in the 18th Century wrote a prize-winning indictment of civilization itself. Among Rousseau's intellectual heirs were the German "Storm and Stress" rebels of the 1770's characterized by an intense sense of "Weltschmerz," a rejection of society's conventions on behalf of individual justice and freedom, and romantic yearning for the beauty in the natural and authentic in folk ways and arts. Two hundred years later we see that same "Weltschmerz" widely spread and experienced both as "alienation" and as "involvement."

K. Roald Bergethon

I do beseech you to direct your efforts more to preparing youth for the path and less to preparing the path for the youth.

Ben Lindsey

What the young people want and dream across the next hundred years will shape history more than any other motivation. Youth now living and yet unborn hold the seeds and secrets of the folds to be unfolded in the shapes to come. The mystery of justice between man, nation and nation, shall take on new phases. In plain work, done with honesty, in actions of courage and endurance lighted with inner humility, lighted with a fine balance of motives as between freedom and discipline, they shall clothe human dignity with new and wider meanings. Youth is strong for struggle and not afraid of toils or punishments or dangers. The course of civilization and society across the next hundred years . . . can be read in the eyes of youth.

Carl Sandburg

Friendship, affection comes about by two people sharing a significant moment, by having an experience in common. You do not attain the affection of your teenage son by giving him an expensive car.

Abraham J. Heschel

There is the danger of alienation when young people see no future for themselves. It makes the problem of work of critical importance. To use an old Talmudic expression, "When you stop working, you're dead."

Eli Ginzberg

The knowledge of life which we grownups have to pass on to the younger generation will not be expressed thus: "Reality will soon give way before your ideals," but "Grow into your ideals, so that life can never rob you of them." If all of us could become what we were at 14, what a different place the world would be!

Albert Schweitzer

A team is where a boy can prove his courage on his own. A gang is where a coward goes to hide.

Mickey Mantle

43 The middle years can be marvelous

The middle years should abound with confidence, productivity and happiness. The tempestuous years of youth are past and the advanced years, with their profound changes are still distant. The middle-aged man usually is physically and mentally capable of good work and a good life.
The National Association of Mental Health

Middle age is that time of life when you've met so many people every new person you meet reminds you of someone else.
Kelly Fordyce

Middle age is that difficult period between juvenile delinquency and senior citizenship when you have to take care of yourself.
Ron Greer

Middle age: The time of your life when your narrow waist and broad mind begin to change places.
Balance Sheet

Any man who anticipates the advance of middle age with horror, or even with distaste, has already lost hold upon the vital forces of his life, and condemns himself to a future of vain regrets and unassuageable nostalgia.
John O'London

In our youth-oriented society, childhood gets a lot of living attention, old age is viewed with terror—and middle age is simply ignored. There isn't even an accepted specific noun for a person in this last age group. "Middle-ager," the only one listed in the dictionary, is a word you seldom hear in ordinary conversation; "middlescence," a word once suggested by columnist Russell Baker, sounds equally foreign . . . What an individual does during this period (middle age) can be destructive; on the other hand, he may achieve a new maturity and enter a new period of productiveness and creativity . . . The one thing that seems to be most immediately apparent about the middle-age crisis is that it has much in common with adolescence, which is hardly surprising, considering that both are critical developmental periods.
Barbara Fried

In practically every industry, the responsible work is being done by men and women over 50, according to Dr. Leonard Himler of the Committee of Industrial Psychiatry. Careful surveys by the Committee and other agencies show that workers over 45 are generally more valuable to their employers than workers under 45. "The real problem of the middle-aged man is not declining usefulness," says Dr. Himler. "It's the defeatist and antagonistic attitudes that people have about aging."
John Kord Lagemann

We are reminded of the father who, on reaching 50, remarked to his daughter, then in college: "I have now reached middle age."

His aplomb was dashed when she

replied: "You mean you expect to live to be 100?"
Topeka Daily Capital

Middle age is when you are impressed not with the fact that the grass is greener on the other side of the fence but rather how difficult the fence looks to get over.
North Vernon Sun

Traveling on a New York Fifth Avenue coach a middle-aged woman dropped her coin in the conductor's fare box. As she did so she looked up and smiled. To her surprise, the youthful conductor said, "Thank you for your smile, Madam. You'd be surprised how many women your age look as though life had soured on them."
Source Unknown

It makes no difference that you have seen forty or fifty springs; each one is as new, every process as fresh, and the charm as fascinating as if you had never witnessed a single one.
Henry Ward Beecher

Try to overcome the thought that you are indispensable. Persistence in leading a strenuous life, after passing middle age, more often than not shortens life. So, bring yourself to relaxing your grip, to transferring some of your burdens to younger shoulders. Be your age! Take it easy!
B.C. Forbes

A middle-aged woman who was all upset about the piling up of the years said to a much older woman who didn't seem to mind old age at all, "I wish I could grow old gracefully, like you."

"My dear," the second woman replied, "You don't grow old. When you cease to grow your are old."
Howard Whitman

I believe that "Now" is the most important word in any language—because it is only "now"—what you do in the next minute or two—that you have control over the world and yourself.
O.A. Battista

---

44 The time of your life

Someone once asked Victor Hugo, French novelist and dramatist of the 19th century, what he thought of civilization. Hugo said: "It's a good idea, someone ought to start it."
Source Unknown

A man's age does not depend upon his accumulation of birthdays, but upon the elasticity of his spirit, the vigor of his mind. It isn't the length of time one lives that is important; it's the quality of spirit resulting in creative achievement that is important. Not quantity but quality—not biology, but mentality—not body, but spirit.
Morris Chalfant

There are three ingredients in the good life: learning, earning, and yearning.
Christopher Morley

We learn, slowly but undeniably, that nothing belongs to us, completely, finally. The job is ended, the children grow up and move away, even the money (when there is money) buys little that we want. For what we want cannot be bought. And it is then, if ever, that we learn to make our peace with destiny; to accept the fact that our dreams have been half-realized, or unrealized; that we did not do what we set out to do; that our goals have receded as we approached them. There may be a sadness in this prospect, but also a serenity. Illusions lose their power to disturb us; we value life by what it has given us, not by the promise of tomorrow. For only by accepting Time can we, in a measure, learn to conquer it.
Sidney J. Harris

For the past is past and will never return, the future we know not, and only the present can be called our own.
Marie Corelli

Asked by a friend, "If you had but forty-eight hours to live, how would you spend them?" the answer was, "One at a time."
Will Rogers

You are as young as your faith; as old as your doubt; as young as your self-confidence, as old as your fear; as young as your hope, as old as your despair.
Samuel Ullman

Age is a quality of mind.
If you have left your dreams behind,
If hope is cold,
If you no longer look ahead
If your ambitions' fires are dead
Then you are old.

But if from life you take the best,
And if in life you keep the jest,
If love you hold;
No matter how the years go by,
No matter how your birthdays fly,
You are not old.
Author Unknown

It's not miserable to be old; it's miserable not to be capable of *living your age*.
Eugene P. Bertin

To fear love is to fear life, and those who fear life are already three parts dead.
Bertrand Russell

If you wish a sheltered and uneventful life, you are living in the wrong generation.
Lyndon B. Johnson

Sweet is the light
And it is good for the eyes
To see the sun!
For if a man lives many years,
Let him rejoice in them all,
And remember that the days of darkness will be many,
And that everything thereafter is nothingness . . .
Remember your Creator in the days of your youth,
Before the evil days come and the years draw near,
Of which you will say, "I have no pleasure in them."
Ecclesiastes 11:7ff

Men who have no resources in themselves for securing a good and happy life find every age burdensome.
Marcus Tullius Cicero

It is good to maintain and to encourage life; it is bad to destroy life or to obstruct it.
Albert Schweitzer

If each of us can be helped by science to live a hundred years, what will it profit us if our hates and fears, our loneliness and remorse will not permit us to enjoy them? What use is an extra year or two to the man who "kills" what time he has?
David Neiswanger

Whoever maintains that this life is worthless is in error; it is worth a great deal; only one must know how to use it properly.
Baal Shem Tov

45 The golden years

It's not how old you are, but how you are old.
Marie Dressler

The retired person has been advised to do everything under the sun with his time—polish rock, paint pictures, collect money for civic organizations—everything but take some time out to read all those books he meant to read "when he retired." Reading may be creative, too. It may be polishing ideas instead of rocks; hanging pictures in the mind instead of on the walls. There are few pleasures that can compete with the joy of reading a good book and taking off with your own thoughts. Age may limit our freedom physically, but there is no limit to our minds except our own capacities.
Helen Weber

Retirement is neither the end nor the beginning. It is a change in emphasis. It is the act of withdrawing from a primary responsibility that has been predominant and that has required increasing sacrifice of body and mind as the years go by. If retirement is resisted and an active business career is prolonged, the values of life become lost in an unsuccessful effort to maintain a degree of activity, inconsistent with the realities of age and physical strength. Retirement should be considered as a normal state of life—a part of the total concept to be planned for and accepted just as our other phases of life like childhood, youth and maturity.
Gilbert W. Chapman

A man or woman of retirement age has four paramount problems to face. One is income ... A second problem is health ... A third problem is appropriate housing and living arrangements. Fourth is in-

terest and purpose in life . . . We have made substantial progress in the first three of these areas in recent years . . . The last of the four problems is often the least recognized and the most neglected. Yet, it is at the heart of many of the difficulties of retirement. It is the challenge of how to find meaningful activity in later years.
John W. Gardner

Sophocles wrote his Oedipus at 90 years of age; Pope Leo XIII inaugurated most of his enlightened policy after he was 70; Titian painted his masterpiece, the bronze doors of the sacristy of St. Mark's, at 85. Elihu Root died in 1937 at over 92 years of age; he was one of the greatest statesmen American ever produced and continued his activities until over 90. One thinks of Oliver Wendell Holmes, John Dewey, Bernard Baruch, Henry Ford, Arturo Toscanini, John Foster Dulles, Dwight D. Eisenhower, and others who did or are doing their best work since passing 60.
Llewellyn S. Barker

Old age is a gift, a very precious gift, not a calamity. Since it is a gift, I thank God for it daily.
John LaFarge

Those who love deeply never grow old; they may die of old age, but they die young.
Arthur Wing Pinero

Once a young girl said to her mother just after a white-haired elderly visitor had left their home, "'If I could be such a nice old lady as she is, so lovely and sweet, I wouldn't mind growing old."

"Well," her mother answered, "if you want to be that kind of old lady, you'd better begin right now. She didn't become a lady in a hurry."
Source Unknown

I know an 80-year-old man, but I don't think of him as 80. He reminds me of Auber, the father of French grand opera, who in his 80th year declared: "I am not 80, I am 4 times 20." Age seems to have quadrupled the satisfactions of his youth.
Ralph W. Sockman

Dr. Charles Mayo met an ancient lady who claimed it was her 108th birthday. The famed surgeon was skeptical but, as ever, cordial. "Well, congratulations," he said. "I hope I'll see you on your 109th birthday."

"You will," the old gal cackled contentedly.

"I will?" he asked.

"Sure," she said. "Very few people die between 108 and 109. Look it up."
Bob Considine

Old age is like a plane flying through a storm. Once you're aboard, there's nothing you can do. You can't stop the plane, you can't stop the storm, you can't stop time. So one might as well accept it calmly, wisely.
Golda Meir

46 To hallow this day

What would we do if we had a bank that—credited $86,400.00 to our account each morning—carried over no balance from day to day—allowed us to keep no cash in our account—every evening cancelled whatever amount we failed to use during the day? What would we do? Well, most of us would draw out every cent! We have such a bank, you know. We call it "Time." Every morning it credits us with 86,400 seconds, and every night it writes off whatever of this we have failed to invest to good purpose. It carries over no balances. Each day it opens a new account with us . . . If we fail to use the day's deposits, the loss is ours. There is no going back. There is no drawing against the "tomorrow."

*Weirton Steel
Employees Bulletin*

A pastor, talking with a group of college students in their fraternity house, turned to the chairman of the meeting and asked, "What are you living for?" The student answered, "I am going to be a pharmacist." The pastor said, "I understand that this is how you are going to earn your livelihood, but what are you living for?"

Source Unknown

The only life we can live is lived today. Yesterday is behind us . . . cannot be lived again but only remembered. Tomorrow is before us; and however sweet its expectations, the clock must tick its patient course before we can test our hope against reality. We can live no more than one day at a time. If we do not live today, we do not live at all; and each day that we live is a lifetime complete in itself. . . . "If only I could live again!" we sometimes sigh. And we can, indeed we do! We live over and over again as day follows day with its heights to be scaled and its depths to be plumbed.

Roy Pearson

One must live so he can say every night, "I have not wasted this day."

Zohar

We understand that a drop of messianic fulfillment must be mixed with the work of every hour, or else the hour remains godless, despite all piety and religion.

Martin Buber

He only earns his freedom and existence who daily conquers them anew.

Goethe

He has not learned the lesson of life who does not every day surmount a fear.

Ralph Waldo Emerson

In the same sense that a falling tree in the forest makes no sound unless someone is there to hear, there is truth in Thoreau's statement that "Only that day dawns to which we are awake."

Edna Kaehele

Cato, the old Roman, started to study Greek when he was around

94   EACH AGE IS A STAGE

80. Someone asked why he was beginning so large a task at such an advanced age. Cato replied dryly that "it was the youngest age he had left"—and went on studying.
    Marcus Porcius Cato

The reputation of a thousand years may be determined by the conduct of one hour.
    Japanese Proverb

Enjoy your life without comparing it with that of others.
    Marquis de Condorcet

The fruit we wish to pick tomorrow lies hidden in the seed of today. The goals we are to reach and the problems we are to solve tomorrow depend upon today's diligence, hope, and faith, today's conviction of the almightiness of good.
    Ralph E. Johnson

After the death of Rabbi Moshe of Kobryn, the Rabbi of Kotzk asked one of the disciples of the deceased what had been the most important things for his master. He answered, "Always just what he was engaged in at the moment."
    Hasidic Lore

Listen to the Exhortation of the Dawn!
Look to this Day!
For it is Life, the very Life of Life.
In its brief course lie all the Verities and Realities of your Existence:

The Bliss of Growth,
The Glory of Action,
The Splendor of Beauty,

For Yesterday is but a Dream,
And Tomorrow is only a Vision:
But Today well-lived makes
Every Yesterday a Dream of Happiness,
And every Tomorrow a Vision of Hope.
Look well therefore to this Day!
Such is the Salutation of the Dawn!
    Kalidasa

---

47   The life cycle

In single file the days bring their gifts. We choose and pay for them with time. In the morning we have today; its hours are currency. At night they will have been exchanged. For what? For a task well done, a house lovingly cared for, for contentments or regrets, for a memory which blesses or burns, for a little more wisdom.
    Ralph Waldo Emerson

No one ever regarded the first of January with indifference.
    Charles Lamb

Today is Yesterday shaking hands with Tomorrow.
    Alfred Stieglitz

Time is so powerful it is given us only in small doses.
    Thoughts for Today

The sin of the old is the belief that everything ends with them. The sin of the young is to believe that everything starts with them.
George E. Failing

I wish I could stand on a busy street corner, hat in hand, and beg people to throw me all their wasted hours.
Bernard Berenson

Time is but a stream I go a-fishing in. I drink of it; but while I drink I see the sandy bottom and detect how shallow it is. Its thin current slides away, but eternity remains. I would drink deeper; fish in the sky, whose bottom is pebbly with stars.
Henry David Thoreau

Time is like money—you can only spend it once.
Arnold H. Glasgow

To everything there is a season, and a time to every purpose under the heaven:

A time to be born, and a time to die; a time to plant, and a time to pluck up that which is planted . . . a time to weep, and a time to laugh; a time to mourn, and a time to dance . . . a time to seek, and a time to lose; a time to keep, and a time to cast away; a time to rend, and a time to sew; a time to keep silence, and a time to speak; a time to love, and a time to hate; a time of war, and a time of peace.
Ecclesiastes 3:1-8

A little while and I will be gone from among you, whither I cannot tell. From nowhere we come, into nowhere we go. What is life? It is a flash of a firefly in the night. It is the breath of a buffalo in the winter time. It is as the little shadow that runs across the grass and loses itself in the sunset.
Chief Crowfoot

Fear not that your life shall come to an end, but rather that it shall never have a beginning.
John Henry Newman

It was truly a human tombstone which bore the inscription:"I expected this, but not just yet."
Source Unknown

Thomas Jefferson,
What do you say
Under the gravestone
Hidden away?

"I was a giver,
I was a molder,
I was a builder
With a strong shoulder.

"I got no riches.
I died a debtor.
I died free-hearted
And that was better.

"For life was freakish
But life was fervent
And I was always
Life's willing servant.

"Life, life's too weighty?
Too long a haul, sir?
I lived past eighty
I liked it all, sir."
Rosemary and Stephen Vincent Benet

Does automation scare you? The whole process of human life from conception through gestation to birth is entirely automated. After birth despite parental ignorance of the process, the child grows from seven to 70 pounds. Biological growth is entirely automated. For at least 2 million years, men have been reproducing and multiplying on a little automated space ship called "earth," in an automated universe in which the entire process is so successfully predesigned that men did not even know that they were automated, regenerative passengers on a space ship, and were so naive as to think that they had invented their own success as they lived egocentrically on a seemingly static earth.

R. Buckminster Fuller

There is a difference between one and another hour of life, in their authority and subsequent effect. Our faith comes in brief moments, all else is habitual. Yet there is a depth in those brief moments.

Ralph Waldo Emerson

---

48 From generation to generation

We ask the leaf, "Are you complete in yourself?" We ask the branch, and the branch answers, "No, my life is in the root," We ask the root, and it answers, "No, my life is in the trunk and the branches and leaves. Keep the branches stripped of leaves, and I shall die."

Harry Emerson Fosdick

Time is the most precious gift in our possession, for it is the most irrevocable. This is what makes it so disturbing to look back upon time which we have lost. Time is lost time when we have not tried to live a full human life, time enriched by human experience, creative endeavor, enjoyment and suffering. Time lost is time not filled, time left empty.

Dietrich Bonnhofer

Our past is our heritage, our present is our responsibility, and our future is our destiny.

Anna L. Rose Hawkes

Life is a flame that ever burns out, but catches fire again whenever a child is born.

George Bernard Shaw

A basketball coach overheard in the locker room: "Remember, boys, basketball develops leadership, initiative, and individuality. Now get out there and do exactly as I told you."

Cherryvale Republican

As my fathers planted for me, so do I plant for my children.

The Midrash

I don't know who my grandfather was; I am much more concerned to know what his grandson will be.

Abraham Lincoln

The young man who has not wept is a savage, and the old man who will not laugh is a fool.

George Santayana

Freedom dies with every individual; it is not reborn with his successors; it must be achieved anew, generation by generation.
Henry M. Wriston

Population stabilization is not a brake upon human development, but rather a release that, by assuring greater opportunity to each person, frees man to attain his individual dignity and to reach his full potential.
John D. Rockefeller III

The Bible is a seed, God is the sun, but we are the soil. Every generation is expected to bring forth new understanding and new realization.
Source Unknown

If you would civilize a man, begin with his grandmother.
Victor Hugo

When Dr. Charles W. Eliot, President Emeritus of Harvard University, was ninety years of age and his wife was dying he called at the home of his neighbor, Dr. Francis G. Peabody, and requested that an infant grandson of Mr. Peabody's might be brought down to the room. The mother brought the baby to him and he took it and held it for a while. When he got up to leave, Mr. Peabody walked out of the door with him, and there, after a moment's silence, Eliot said simply, "I wanted to hold in my arms a life that was just beginning."
Source Unknown

We live in a world of half faith and half doubt. Standing at the temple doors, head in and heart out.
Sidney Lanier

In May 1924, it was announced that Princeton University had restored a very unusual clock, which had been acquired way back in 1771, known as the Rittenhouse Orery. It showed the motions of the heavenly bodies according to the system of Newton. Also on the face, the clock told time not only by the hours, but by the centuries. "Telling time by the centuries" is a good phrase for meditation.
Source Unknown

Once, long ago, there was a man who was traveling through the desert. It was hot, and he was hungry, tired and thirsty.

Then he came upon a palm tree that bore sweet fruit and cast a comforting shadow and sheltered a spring of cool water.

He feasted upon the dates and drank his fill of the water and sat down to rest in the shade.

When the time came for the man to depart, he turned thankfully to the tree and said:

"My dear date palm, how shall I bless you? If I wish you sweet fruit—it is already sweet; if I hope you cast fine shadows—they are so now; and if it is a cooling spring I wish—you have it!"

So, then may you be blest thus:
May every sapling that grows from your seed be just like you!"
The Midrash

49   Death is a part of life

For life and death are one, even as the river and the sea are one.
Kahlil Gibran

To be really proficient in the art of living, we must know and understand something about dying.
T. Cecil Myers

The surest way to bring us near the beloved dead, the best means of seeing them again, is not to go with them into death, but to live. They live in our lives, and they die with us.
Romain Rolland

We prepare for dying from the moment we are born. Dying is not an eventuality of old age, except statistically; it is an eventuality of each moment. Anyone of us may be dead before we leave here. This is neither a gruesome nor necessarily a happy thought, but it is realistic.
Earl Loomis

The good doctor is aware of the distinction between prolonging life and prolonging the act of dying.
Norman St. John Stevas

Let me not think of death as one who
   waits to lay relentless hands on
   me.
Nay, let me rather think of him as
   one who in all kindness waits,
At the journey's end, to draw me
   gently through his gates,
And leads me like a kindly host, that
   gives some long expected guest,
The comfort that he craves the
   most, hospitality and rest.
Author Unknown

If we have the courage to live—to accept each day as it is given to us—we shall find the way to carry out the chief acceptance of all: That of the end of life, death. For what use is it to accept life, if you cannot accept that to which life leads?
John LaFarge

The righteous are considered as alive even when they are dead.
The Talmud

Be honest with children about the facts of life, the facts of birth and of death. Help them accept themselves as they are—human beings limited in many ways and bound to experience a good deal of frustration and probably pain in the course of living—but capable also of a great deal of effort and a great deal of joy. Erik Erikson wrote in his book, *Childhood and Society,* "Children will not be afraid of life if their parents are not afraid of death." The obverse is equally true: Children will not be afraid of death—if their parents are not afraid of life.
Helen Steers Burgess

People today are on a cure-all kick. They believe that all diseases will soon be conquered and they will live forever. The fact that death is inevitable is being ignored...death is far more certain than conception and far more critical than birth. It is a part of life, an experience for which everyone is destined from the moment of birth. If a man has a right to prepare himself for life, he has a right to prepare himself for

death. No matter how well he may be prepared, he still needs the love and understanding of his family, the care of a kindly doctor, and the compassion of a clergyman if he is to die in peace, with human dignity.
Catholic Digest

I bid you a fond farewell and ask you not to mourn my passing, but live together harmoniously respecting the memories of your loving, loyal and devoted parents.
Hebrew Ethical Will

When the hour arrived for Rabbi Simha Bunan of Psyshcha to depart from the world, his wife stood by his bedside and wept bitterly. He said to her, "Be silent—why do you cry? My whole life was only that I might learn how to die."
Hasidic Lore

When children worry about dying, the schoolmistress tells them "there was a time when we weren't here and we didn't worry then; and there's going to be a time when we won't be here again—and there's no point in worrying about that now." If we can just teach children that death is part of the whole thing, part of life, it will help them.
Phyllis Levin

There is a reason for coming to terms with the idea of death—not to make life endurable but to face and outface the fears that otherwise plague your joy in life.
When you know that this curious, complex, febrile thing called life can be ended at any moment, by sickness or sudden disaster, and that it is bound to end at some moment by the wearing out of the body's cells and the stopping of the heart's pumping—only then can you make peace with your own turbulent fears, and plunge deeply and irrevocably into the waters of life itself.
Author Unknown

---

50 The meaning of our memories

We are what we will to remember, and our memories make the future.
John J. Navone

It is better to be nobly remembered, than nobly born.
John Ruskin

You must know that there is nothing higher or stronger, and good for life in the future, than some good memory . . . People talk to you a great deal about good education, but some good, sacred memory . . . is perhaps the best education.
Feodor Dostoevski

Memories believe before knowing remembers, believes longer than recollects, longer than knowing even wonders.
William Faulkner

You can close your eyes to reality but not to memories.
Stanislaw J. Lee

If the memory of a friend can be evoked with a smile and his name spoken with gentle happiness, that friend has built an imperishable monument in one's heart.
Henry Berkowitz

At the rising of the sun and at its
   going down
We remember them.
At the blowing of the wind and in
   the chill of winter frost
We remember them.
At the opening of the buds and in
   the rebirth of spring
We remember them.
At the blueness of the skies and in
   the warmth of summer
We remember them.
At the rustling of the leaves and in
   the beauty of autumn
We remember them.
At the beginning of the year and
   when it ends
We remember them.
As long as we live, they too will live;
For they are now a part of us,
As we remember them.
Variation of a British Prayer
Sylvan D. Kamens

So they gave their bodies to the commonwealth and received, each for his own memory, praise that will never die, and with it, the grandest of all sepulchres; not that in which their mortal bones are laid, but a home in the minds of men, where their glory remains fresh to stir to speech or action as the occasion comes by. For the whole earth is the sepulchre of famous men, and their story is not graven only on stone over their native earth, but lives on far away, without visible symbol, woven into the stuff of other men's lives.
Pericles

The beauty of memory is that it still sees beauty when beauty has faded.
Paul Boese

When time who steals our years
   away
Shall steal our pleasures too,
The memory of the past will stay
And half our joys renew.
Thomas Moore

Lucullus and Maecenas are remembered in history because they were more than mere rich people; they were patrons of the arts, of music, poetry, literature, painting and others of the essential amenities of living, in need of which all of us stand today. We remember George Washington, not as a country squire, but as an heroic personality, willing to risk his very life for his country and its freedom. We remember Lincoln, not merely because he was an excellent, though never a prosperous lawyer, but because he led our country in its hour of crisis, evincing those spiritual qualities which have endeared him to mankind. Therefore let us endeavor to use competence and competency for character, culture, and the cultivation of the soul.
Louis I. Newman

6
Learning for living

51 What is past is prologue

If you want to understand today, you have to search yesterday.
Pearl Buck

From the day man was created he began to labor.
What did he work for?
He worked for his children. They, when they grew up, worked for their children. And so it has been from the beginning of time.
But how many of us stop and consider how many generations have labored for us?
Hayehudi

An educated man is one who understands and appreciates the cultural tradition which produced him and who is willing to spend his time, his talent, and his training in order that that precious heritage might be preserved, protected, and perfected for the generations which will come after him.
Jose Ortega y Gasset

Knowing something about his ancestors . . . gives a man a satisfying sense of being part of a continuum, of a process of birth, death and rebirth that started long before he was born, and will continue long after he is dead. And as a man's age increases, this sense of being part of the endless human parade through history is an oddly comforting sense.
Stewart Alsop

Only by acceptance of the past, can you alter it.
T.S. Eliot

To me, the supreme test of an American citizen is this: that he is one who does not conceal but affirms his origin, who is proud of whatever it may be and who recognizes that in the plurality of American life is our strength and the source of the freedom that we proudly profess in the world.
Arthur J. Goldberg

All that we are is the result of what we have thought.
Buddhist Scripture

Those who ignore the past are doomed to repeat it.
George Santayana

We must look at the past not only because it shows us how finite we are, what creatures of our determinations, but because it also shows us that we are responsible agents in history. We must study the past to free ourselves for the future. Freedom is the knowledge of necessity, though not in the way that Hegel and Marx said it was. We must have knowledge of our determinations of the past, in order that we may be free to master our destiny in the future. We must know the past, but then we must not be pre-occupied with it.
Reinhold Niebuhr

Our past is not a tomb in which to hide from progress. It is rich ground in which we drop the seeds of our aspirations. Reverence for the past gives our life style and dignity. Through history we rebuild the lost contact between the surface and the depth of civilization; wherefore, a nation with no regard for its past will have little future worth remembering.
Eugene P. Bertin

Take from the altars of the past the fire—not the ashes.
Jean Jaures

He is a wise child who chooses a good grandfather.
Oliver Wendell Holmes

While we aim to create a new society, we must not forget we are doing it with an old society.
Jimmy Yen

Once, the tale goes, there was a leaf who pined for the freedom of the birds that fluttered nearby. Every day he would watch them soaring on high, singing their songs as they flew. If only he could cut himself loose from the branch that imprisoned him. If only a big wind would come and blow him into freedom, he too could soar and climb as he willed. One day, his prayer was answered and a big wind came. Louder and louder it whined, until suddenly, with a mighty gust, it blew the leaf free from its mooring. For a fleeting moment the leaf was free. He was overcome with joy and gladness. But it wasn't long before he fell flat on his back, an easy victim of the trampling of every passerby. Very soon his color was gone, his strength was sapped, and his hope lost. He died seeking the wrong kind of happiness.
Source Unknown

52 Teaching is reaching

A teacher who is attempting to teach without inspiring the pupil with a desire to learn is hammering on cold iron.
Horace Mann

It is the supreme art of the teacher to awaken joy in creative expression and knowledge.
Albert Einstein

I recently asked a knowledgeable college president, "What do you consider the single most important factor in the success of a teacher?" Without hesitation he replied, "The man's character."
Ordway Tead

Educators are only beginning to appreciate students like the 15-year-old boy who wrote his counselor, "I'm awfully sorry I still have only B grades. But this year I read all of Shakespeare, and I was so busy learning that I just didn't have time to do all my school work."
T.F. James

The aim of education is not to add to the sum of human knowledge. Its purpose is to open the mind and not fill it, as we would an ash can or even a golden bowl.
Christian Gauss

What are the qualities we look for in a liberally educated person? He is one who is deeply interested in life and enjoys it; who is sympathetic and generous in his attitude to other people, cultures, and countries; who is sensitive to the beautiful and the ugly in actions and objects; who believes in human rights and freedom; who has a degree of knowledge and knows how to get the knowledge he does not have; and who has at least a moderate skill in the art of living.
Harold L. Taylor

The famous Dr. Arnold of Rugby, the great English school, used to always salute his schoolboys by taking off his hat when he passed them in the street. When he was questioned about this peculiar habit, he smiled and replied, "You never can tell whether or not you may be passing a future prime minister of Great Britain."
Source Unknown

Education is not given for the purpose of earning a living; it's learning what to do with a living after you earn it.
Abraham Lincoln

As an apple is not in any proper sense an apple until it is ripe, so a human being is not in any proper sense a human being, until he is educated.
Horace Mann

What sculpture is to a block of marble, education is to the soul.
Joseph Addison

The college must not be considered as a place in which the student is contained for four years within a small academic world. The college is a place where the student learns how to look at his life and his society, how to practice the skills of the intellect through the arts and sciences. He thus learns to be ready to add his own gifts to the human life.

Harold L. Taylor

Horace Mann was dedicating a recreational building for boys. "If all the money and effort you have expended," he told the assembly, "result in the salvation of just one boy, they will have been justified."

"My dear Mr. Mann," a listener asked, "do you really believe that? Weren't you exaggerating?"

Said Mann: "Not if it were my boy."

Eagle

A commentary on our civilization is tragically pointed up in the following story: A tribe of cannibals was captured and the head of the tribe announced that he had attended college in the U.S.

"Do you mean," he was asked, "that you went to college and yet you still eat human beings?"

"Sure," replied the chief, "but now I use a knife and fork."

Source Unknown

"And yet many fathers there are who so love their money and so hate their children that, lest it should cost them more than they are willing to spare to hire a good schoolmaster for them, they rather choose such persons to instruct their children as are of no worth, thereby beating down the market that they may purchase ignorance cheap."

Then Plutarch goes on to tell the story of Aristippus, the philosopher, whom a rich man tried to hire to teach his son. When asked his fee, Aristippus said: "One thousand drachmas." The father angrily exclaimed: "For one thousand drachmas I can buy a slave!"

"Do so," Aristippus retorted. "Then you will have two slaves—your son and the one you buy."

Greek Literature

53 *The benevolence of books*

When I get a little money, I buy books; and if there is any left, I buy food and clothes.

Desiderius Erasmus

There are, in actual fact, men who talk like books. Happily, however, there are also books that talk like men.

Theodor Haecker

When you sell a man a book, you don't sell him just twelve ounces of paper and ink and glue—you sell him a whole new life.

Christopher Morley

Except a living man, there is nothing more wonderful than a book.

Charles Kingsby

Make thy books thy companions; let thy case of books be thy pleasure gardens and grounds. Bask in their paradise.

Judah ibn Tibbon

Books are not men and yet they are alive,
They are man's memory and his aspiration,
The link between his present and his past,
The tools he builds with.

Stephen Vincent Benet

Libraries are the market-places of human thought.

Trevor Fawcett

Consider what you have in the smallest well-chosen library. A company of the wisest and wittiest men that could be picked out of all civil countries, in a thousand years, have set in best order the results of their learning and wisdom.

Ralph Waldo Emerson

The best single test of a nation's culture remains what it has been since the days of Gutenberg—its attitude toward books.

Allan Nevins

I think one of our problems in education is not so much the school as the home. Speaking as a teacher, I would like to say that it is very hard to get the life of the mind across to a child in school if the child comes from a home in which there are no books and in which there is no reading. If the home does not furnish a context and background of devotion to ideas, then the school can do very little. At the risk of shocking some people, I would like to say that a home without books and ideas can be almost as bad for a child as a broken home, an alcoholic home, or a criminal one, because it leaves a vacuum into which rush corrupting values.

Max Lerner

A good book is the precious life-blood of a master spirit.

John Milton

Without the love of books the richest man is poor; but endowed with this treasure of treasures, the poorest man is rich. He has wealth which no power can diminish; riches which are always increasing; possessions which the more he scatters the more they accumulate; friends which never desert him and pleasures which never die.

Leon Gutterman

Everywhere I have sought rest and found it not except sitting apart in a nook with a little book.

Thomas A. Kempis

You can look at a book
And better still, read it.
A book is a friend
When you happen to need it,

And when you are through
You can still think about it—
So, "Hurray for Books!"
Don't say it, but shout it.

Elizabeth Coatsworth

"A house without books is like a room without windows. No man has

a right to bring up his children without surrounding them with books. Children learn to read by being in the presence of books. The love of knowledge comes with reading and grows upon it." Although modern educators may regard that as somewhat old-fashioned, or as an oversimplification, they do still surround children with books, and they strive to create in the young the desire to read not only for knowledge and for the tools of thinking but also for sheer enjoyment.
Horace Mann

How many a man has dated a new era in his life from the reading of a book.
Henry David Thoreau

54 The influence of inspiration

Those having torches will pass them on to others.
Plato

The example of the parents is the most important book which children can read.
Chrysostomus

When Alfred North Whitehead was asked what courses he taught, his reply was, "Whitehead I, Whitehead II and Whitehead III."
Samuel B. Gould

The memory of a great man is precious to mankind. Great men live on in others. They live as hope, as inspiration, as example, as symbols of the worth that we must attach to life.
James T. Farrell

Before I can lead another individual to examine the universe in which he lives, I must engage actively in the same examination. I must continue to study all facets of life, not just the one subject matter area that I teach. If I am to convince students that involvement in life is a rewarding experience, I must listen to more music, read more books, examine more art, study more natural history, and seek to know more people.
Robert T. Kirkwood

Jacques Lipchitz, the sculptor, spent his youth in Paris, where he was a close friend of Soutine, Modigliani and Chagall. One day another painter complained that he was dissatisfied with the light he painted on his canvases. He went off to Morocco, seeking a change in light. He found that the light in his Moroccan canvases was no different. Lipchitz told him; "An artist's light comes from within, not from without."
Source Unknown

You do not lead by hitting people over the head—that's assault, not leadership.
Dwight D. Eisenhower

In Springfield, Illinois, where the immortal Abraham Lincoln once lived, a local mother often told her chidren the majestic story of the Great Emancipator. One evening while walking with her little girl, she paused reverently before Lincoln's old home. The lights from within the house were streaming their rays through the doors and windows. The little girl's imagination quickly caught on fire and she said, "Mommy, Mr. Lincoln left his lights on."

"Yes, Mr. Lincoln did 'leave his lights on,' that all the world might see and follow the great humanitarian principles to which his life was devoted."

Bulletin, North Lake Tahoe

We are all links in the chain of life. No one is complete in himself. We are each one daily bearing something onward—something that contributes to the world and to experience. And we never know to what end our influence has been carried.

Good Impressions

There is no teaching like a good man's life.

Ellery Sedgwick

His mortal body remains here, but we take home his influence into our being and soul.

Anonymous

The child will get a conception of goodness because you are good to him and to other people; of love, because you and your husband increasingly love each other as well as him; of truth, because you are unfailingly truthful; of kindliness of speech, because your words and tones of speech are never harsh; of constancy, because you have kept your promise; of consideration for others, because he sees things in you.

A. Fox

Were a star quenched on high,
For ages would its light,
Still traveling downward from the sky,
Shine on our mortal sight.

So when a great man dies
For years beyond our ken,
The light he leaves behind him lies
Upon the paths of men.

Henry Wadsworth Longfellow

It is too late in the day for America to try to win anyone with words, and it is even more certain that we cannot win by giving. What then can we do? We can win the world only by example—by making our way of life as good as we know how. Our main problem is not the world but ourselves, and we can win the world only by overcoming ourselves.

Eric Hoffer

This I learned from the shadow of a tree,
That to and fro did sway against a wall,
Our shadow selves, our influence, may fall
Where we ourselves can never be.

Anna E. Hamilton

55 Study is a form of worship

We live in a time of such rapid change and growth of knowledge that only he who is in a fundamental sense a scholar—that is, a person who continues to learn and inquire —can hope to keep pace, let alone play the role of guide.
Nathan M. Pusey

Learning is like water—it can remain a great source of power as long as it remains fluid, but when it is permitted to freeze over it is a useless impediment to any creative activity.
Sidney J. Harris

It is said that Woodrow Wilson, when teaching at Princeton, would stride into his classroom, greet the class, and then say, "Gentlemen, are there any questions?" If no questions were asked then the class would be dismissed, since it was Professor Wilson's contention that his young scholars had not prepared for the class that day.
Jesse Burt

There is the anecdote of Hegel, whose landlady noticed that he was not attending divine service but was staying at home with his studies. This worried her, and she spoke to him about it. Hegel, however, replied briefly: "My dear woman, thinking is also a divine service."
Philip Owens

Knowledge is the most precious treasure of all things, because it can never be given away, nor stolen, nor consumed.
Sanskrit Proverb

He who asks a question is a fool for five minutes; he who does not ask a question remains a fool forever.
Chinese Proverb

A deep and permanent love of learning does not develop automatically. It does not develop just because a child works hard at school or does his homework or passes all his tests. The crux is how a child feels about his learning, and why he studies. I worry when the reason is just to get a good grade or to get on the honor roll or be promoted, or just to please his grownups. I am delighted when a child learns, and keeps on learning because he wants to know.
James L. Hymes, Jr.

Learning does not stop as long as a man lives, unless his learning power atrophies because he does not use it.
Robert Maynard Hutchins

People learn best by experiencing, doing, participating. Passive learning is not effective learning.
Milton Hall

Only those who have learned how to learn can be independent and versatile in keeping up with a changing world.
Guy T. Buswell

With the affairs of human beings, knowledge of truth alone does not suffice. On the contrary, this knowledge must continually be renewed by the ceaseless effort, if it is not to be lost. It resembles a statue of marble which stands in the desert and is continuously threatened with burial by the shifting sand. The hands of service must ever be at work in order that the marble continue lastingly to shine in the sun.

Albert Einstein

Where knowledge could have changed the issue, ignorance takes on the guilt of vice.

Alfred North Whitehead

While in every other respect I feel the infirmities of old age, in my studies it seems to me that I grow younger every day. Therefore I shall be glad if Death come upon me while I am engaged in reading or writing.

Francesco Petrarch

Rejected by the college of his choice, the banker's son angrily accosted his father. "If you really cared for me you'd have pulled some wires!"

"I know," replied the parent sadly. "The TV, the Hi-Fi, and the telephone would have done for a start."

Anonymous

A person sarcastically asked the president of the University of Chicago if Communism was still being taught at the University. "Yes," he replied, "and cancer at the Medical School."

Harold Seymour

My mind to me a kingdom is,
Such present joys therein I find
That it excels all other bliss
That earth affords or grows by kind...

Some have too much, yet still do crave;
I little have, and seek no more.
They are but poor, though much they have,
And I am rich with little store.

They poor, I rich; they beg, I give;
They lack, I leave; they pine, I live.

Edward Dyer

---

56   The only constant is change

New occasions teach new duties;
Time makes ancient good uncouth;
They must upward still and onward,
Who would keep abreast of truth.

James Russell Lowell

If we must not change too quickly, at least we must not refuse to change at all.

Learned Hand

"My dear, we live in a time of transition," said Adam to Eve, as they walked out of Paradise.

Dean Inge

The art of progress is to preserve order amid change, and to preserve change amid order. Life refuses to be embalmed alive.

Alfred North Whitehead

The man who never alters his opinion is like standing water, and breeds reptiles of the mind.
William Blake

We cannot change human nature, but we can change belief and behavior.
Norman Angell

Between two worlds life hovers like a star,
Twixt night and morn, upon the horizon's verge.
How little do we know that which we are!
How less what we may be! The eternal surge
Of time and tide rolls on, and bears afar
Our bubbles; as the old burst, new emerge.
Lash'd from the form of ages; while the graves
Of empires heave but like some passing waves.
George Gordon Byron

Here below to live is to change, and to be perfect is to have changed often.
John Henry Newman

You cannot step twice into the same river; for fresh waters are ever flowing in upon you.
Heraclitus

History teaches us of continuity and change. The eye of the conservative goes to continuity; the liberal sees mostly change. We must constantly kindle new fires, but always with some knowledge of and continuity with the past. Do we bring from the fires of the past the ash or the spark?

As Max Lerner expressed it, our task is not merely to transmit the heritage, but to transmute it.
Don Robinson

In change we seek not the replacement of the lamp of American liberty. Instead, we ask that each American bring a new light to the old lamp.
Leroy Collins

The only man who behaves sensibly is my tailor; he takes my measure anew every time he sees me, whilst all the rest go on with their old measurements and expect them to fit me.
George Bernard Shaw

Change can be resisted, but a study of history will show that a people and a society that remains rigid will invite decay and destruction. Unless a civilization has options, it will not endure.
Bernard S. Miller

Institutional resistance is simply a painful fact of life which those who are interested in constructive change . . . must face with . . . firm purpose and intelligent forbearance.
Donald Glabe

No one will live all his life in the world into which he was born, and no one will die in the world in which he worked in his maturity.
Margaret Mead

A native of a country town, proud of his background, was celebrating his 100th birthday. His small home town gathered to pay tribute.

"I suppose you've seen a lot of changes in your day?" remarked one of his fellow townsmen.

"Yes," said the centenarian, "and I've been against every one of them."

Humour

When you're through changing, you're through.

Bruce Barton

What a dull boring thing it is to wake in the morning and find that you are the same person who went to bed.

Logan Pearsall Smith

Change does not change tradition. It strengthens it. Change is a challenge and an opportunity, not a threat.

Prince Philip

57 The good society

Most people say a society is efficient if it makes good use of natural resources. But this is not true. A society is to be judged not only by what it does with its natural resources, but more so by what it does with its human resources.

Eric Hoffer

They say that long ago in Switzerland
There was a little chapel without light,
And each who worshipped carried in his hand
His own small lantern when they met at night.
If many went, the small church shone like gold,
With its brave lanterns hanging side by side;
But if there were a few, then it was cold
And dismal in the church at eventide.
Thus each of us who takes his humble place,
And hangs his lantern with the rest will see
A light upon his neighbor's shadowed face,
And find the room of life shines graciously.

Dorothy P. Albaugh

Evil societies always try to kill their consciences.

James Farmer

It is not true that some are not qualified for education. In fact, everyone is *capable* of being educated. Clearly, people have different needs and different abilities. But, it is the duty of society to build an educational system which fits the abilities and fulfills the needs of each particular individual.

Arthur J. Goldberg

Let everyone sweep in front of his own door and the world will be clean.

Goethe

When asked, "Would it be right to repay good for evil?" Confucius replied, "No, for how then would you repay good? Repay good with good, and evil with justice."
Source Unknown

That community is already in the process of dissolution where each man begins to eye his neighbor as a possible enemy, where non-conformity with the accepted creed, political as well as religious, is a mark of disaffection; where denunciation, without specification or backing, takes the place of evidence; where orthodoxy chokes freedom of dissent; where faith in that eventual supremacy of reason has become so timid that we dare not enter our convictions in the open lists, to win or lose.
Learned Hand

A nation is held together by shared values, shared beliefs, shared attitudes. That is what enables a people to maintain a cohesive society despite the frustrations and tensions of daily life. That is what enables them to rise above the inevitable conflicts and divisions that plague any society. That is what gives a nation its tone, its fiber, its integrity, its moral style, its capacity to endure.
John W. Gardner

When the young behave badly . . . it is because society has already behaved worse. We have the teenagers, like the politicians and the wars, that we deserve.
John B. Priestley

Some would have us renege on our commitments to the developing countries on the ground that "charity begins at home." To them, let me emphasize that I have recommended no charity, nor have I suggested that we stray from home . . . Our home is this planet, and our neighbors are three billion strong.
Lyndon B. Johnson

Happy is the generation where the great listen to the small, for it follows that in such a generation the small will listen to the great.
The Talmud

The society which scorns excellence in plumbing because plumbing is a humble activity, and tolerates shoddiness in philosophy because it is an exalted activity, will have neither good plumbing nor good philosophy. Neither its pipes nor its theories will hold water.
John W. Gardner

There is a sense in this wondrous age of what man can achieve in his redeeming moments of grandeur. As we look out on the human condition our consciences cannot be clean. If they are clean, then it is because we do not think enough. It is not inevitable that we march in hostile and separated hosts into the common abyss. There is another possibility of an ordered world illuminated by reason and governed by law. If we cannot yet touch it with our hands, let us at least grasp it in our vision.
Abba Eban

58 Laugh and the world laughs with you

It takes thirteen facial muscles to smile and forty-seven to frown. But a lot of people evidently don't mind the extra muscular activity, for they walk around looking nasty and glum. They don't realize that they are neglecting one of their most attractive assets.
James Bender

There is a Swiss joke about a recruit which is characteristic of the whole nation in more ways than one. A young soldier, taking part in some military exercise, was hit by a bayonet which pinned him to a tree, so that he could not free himself for five hours. At last he was found by a comrade who asked with sympathy:
"Does it hurt?"
The man replied: "Only when I laugh."
George Mikes

We all got a schnozzola—maybe not on our faces, then in our minds, maybe in our hearts, maybe in our habits. Ridiculous, one way or another, that's what we are. Well, sir, when we admit our schnozzolas, instead of defending them, and laugh, the world laughs with us and things ain't serious no more—what a great world this would be if we all learned to laugh at our schnozzolas. We wouldn't have wars, suicides, race hatred and our souls wouldn't get sick.
Jimmy Durante

The world is a looking glass, and gives back to every man the reflection of his own face. Frown at it, and it will in turn look sourly upon you; laugh at it, and with it, and it is a jolly kind companion.
William M. Thackerey

One of America's greatest Presidents and certainly the most humorous was the one who occupied the White House during the bloody conflict between the North and South. Under the pressure of daily cares and the dark clouds of civil war, President Lincoln once confided to his cabinet, "With the fearful strain that is upon me day and night, if I did not laugh I should die."
Edwin Davis

The wonderful madness called laughter is found only in man. Nothing in lower creation produces anything resembling a laugh. Valleys do not smile, and horses do not laugh, for it is a positive break with everything below him in creation; it is a break with matter, it is the beginning of the spirit. Man is the only joker in the deck of Nature.
Fulton J. Sheen

Mirth is like a flash of lightning, that breaks through a gloom of clouds, and glitters for a moment; cheerfulness keeps up a kind of daylight in the mind, and fills it with a steady and perpetual serenity.
Joseph Addison

When you've killed the sense of humor of a nation, you've killed the nation.
Red Skelton

Humor is an antibiotic against hate.
Felix Weltsch

It is indeed God's gift to man, that he should eat and drink and be happy as he toils.
Ecclesiastes 3:13

Cheer up; God is where He was.
Russian Proverb

How far above you are the Sabbath stars,
And far more tranquil than your soul
For you are sad this day
And sadness stains the Name of God...
Abraham Shlonsky

As I was standing in line at our local supermarket checkout register, I listened to the woman ahead of me. She was tearing into the checkout girl about everything pertaining to the store: prices, arrangements of goods, and just about everything you could think of.

When my turn came, the checker greeted me with a pleasant smile. Gesturing toward the departing woman, I said, "Don't you sometimes get tired of people?"

"Oh, no," she answered with a big smile. "You see, I'm people too."
Helen LaMance

The most utterly lost of all days is that in which you have not once laughed.
Sebastian Roch Chamfort

I laugh because I must not cry.
George Gordon Byron

Laughter is the first achievement of man.
Peter Abelard

59 When trouble comes

There are two kinds of persons in the world: those who think first of difficulties, and those who think first of the importance of accomplishment in spite of difficulties.
Samuel Warren

A newly appointed bishop, received by Pope John XXIII in a private audience, complained that the burden of his new office prevented him from sleeping. "Oh," said John kindly, "the very same thing happened to me in the first few weeks of my pontificate, but then one day my guardian angel appeared to me in a daydream and whispered, 'Giovanni, don't take yourself so seriously.' And ever since then I've been able to sleep."
Pope John XXIII

No one would ever have crossed the ocean if he could have gotten off the ship in the storm.
Charles F. Kettering

When trouble comes 115

Which is the greatest virtue? Patience with other's vices.
Solomon ibn Gabirol

A man was asked to tell his favorite Bible verse. Here is what he quoted: "and it came to pass." This surprised everybody, as it possibly surprises you . . . because it is not a quoted passage, in fact not even a verse. Yet he insisted that "and it came to pass" was the one most meaningful to him. In every trouble, he explained, he thinks of this Biblical line. The problem, the difficulty, did not come to stay; it came to pass. It came to leave its imprint upon his personality and his character. It came to teach its particular lesson. But it was not, of itself, a finality. It did not come to stay. It came to pass.
Wilbert E. Scheer

Looking back, it seems to me
All the griefs which had to be
Left me, when the pain was o'er,
Richer than I'd been before.
Edgar A. Guest

Heroism consists in hanging on one minute longer.
Norwegian Proverb

It is probably impossible to mature in our society without experiencing failure. The good is not in the failure but in the overcoming of failure.
Stanley E. Diamond

If all our misfortunes were laid in one common heap, whence everyone must take an equal portion, most people would be content to take their own and depart.
Socrates

I know the world is filled with troubles and many injustices. But reality is as beautiful as it is ugly. I think it is just as important to sing about beautiful mornings as it is to talk about slums. I just couldn't write anything without hope in it.
Oscar Hammerstein

Grant us the knowledge that we need
To solve the problems of the mind,
But, dear God, light Thou our candle
And keep our hearts from going blind.
Anonymous

A woman shopping in a department store noticed that the clerk behind the complaint desk smiled at everyone who talked to her and kept her voice low and pleasant, even when irate customers spoke rudely to her. The shopper was amazed at the way the woman kept her cool.

Then she noticed the clerk's dark earrings. On one, in white lettering, was inscribed, "In" and on the other, "Out."
Good Reading

A woman reminisced that as a small girl she was given chores to do along with her brothers on the farm. One such job was hoeing grass in the cornfield. Sometimes she would do a shoddy job and simply cut off the top of the grass.

Her father remarked one day: "Dear, just cutting off the tops means you will have to do it again. Get the grass out by the roots and you'll never have to do it again."

"Now that I'm mature," the woman said, "I find trouble must

be handled like the grass in the cornfield. You must get it out by the roots if you would rid yourself of it."
A. Purnell Bailey

Troubles are like babies—they grow larger by nursing.
Lady Holland

I have learned much from my teachers, more from my books, but most from my troubles!
The Midrash

Sumatanga is a custom in some parts of India. At the side of the door as one enters the home there is a shelf. On this shelf one is to put all his troubles and woes upon entering the house.
Source Unknown

Trouble develops in us the ability to meet it. It strengthens and matures those it touches. Trouble frequently finds for us our dearest friends. *We need the night to see the stars.*
Author Unknown

60 Worship is worthwhile

A ritual is shared action expressive of common strivings rooted in common values.
Erich Fromm

There was an old gentleman who used to attend a church where I was once minister. Throughout the prayer he would sit with his head held high and his eyes wide open. Once he explained the reason for this to me. "I have always felt," he said, "that when I come into the presence of my Creator He will want me to hold my head high and look Him straight in the eye and answer for what I am and what I have done."
Source Unknown

A father was praying in a house of worship beside his son. The little boy was praying softly, the father loudly. The father nudged him and said, "Talk louder." The boy replied, "I'm not talking to you."
Author Unknown

To worship is to quicken the conscience by the holiness of God, to purge the imagination by the beauty of God, to open the heart to the love of God, to devote the will to the purpose of God.
William Temple

The distance between the mouth and the heart is less than twelve inches.

This is the distance which separates many from God.

They have God in their mouths, but not in their hearts.

To have God in the mouth, but not in the heart,
Is to have God not at all.
Anonymous

O brother man! Fold to thy heart thy brother;
Where pity dwells, the peace of God is there;
To worship rightly is to love each other,
Each smile a hymn, each kindly deed a prayer.
John Greenleaf Whittier

Prayer is an invitation to God to intervene in our lives, to let His will prevail in our affairs; it is the opening of a window to Him in our will, an effort to make Him the Lord of our soul. We submit our interests to His concern, and seek to be allied with what is ultimately right.
Abraham J. Heschel

This is my prayer to You, O God,
Guard me so that I do not turn aside from my life's path,
So that my spirit does not dry up,
So that I do not lose my thirst for You,
Or the freshness that You poured into me when I was young.

May my heart be ever open to the broken,
To every orphan, to all who trip and fall,
To all those who struggle unnoticed,
To those who feel their way in the dark.

Bless my eyes so that I can see
Man's greatness manifest in this world
And the glory of my people in its redeemed land
Spreading its fragrance over all the earth.
Strengthen my senses
So that I may absorb the greenness of the world

The budding and the blossoming of the plants.
May I learn from them the secret
Of how to grow in silence.

Grace me with the ability to give forth the best kind of fruit,
The essence of my life, blossoms that come out of my very being,
Without expecting any repayment for myself.

And when my time comes,
Grant me the ability to slip into the night
Without demanding anything
From men
Or from You,
O my God.
Hillel ha-Bavli

"Pardon me," said a student, coming upon Louis Pasteur bending over his microscope, "I thought you were praying."

"I was," replied the scientist.

For Louis Pasteur, work in the field of science was a form of prayer. There have been great men who have communed with God in the fields, in the forests, in the laboratory, at a blackboard. There have been those giants of the soul who were able to see God in whatever they did; wherever they were, not distracted or reduced by their environment.
Source Unknown

He prayeth best who loveth best.
Samuel Taylor Coleridge

My words fly up, my thoughts remain below:
Words without thoughts never to heaven go.
William Shakespeare

I asked for strength, that I might achieve;
I was made weak, that I might learn humbly to obey...

I asked for health, that I might do greater things...
I was given infirmity, that I might do better things...

I asked for riches, that I might be happy;
I was given poverty that I might be wise...

I asked for power that I might have the praise of men;
I was given weakness, that I might feel the need of God...

I asked for all things that I might enjoy life;
I was given life, that I might enjoy all things...

I got nothing that I asked for—but everything that I had hoped for.
Almost despite myself, my unspoken prayers were answered.
I am among men, most richly blessed!

An Unknown
Confederate Soldier

7
The family

61 *The art of loving*

Men who love and are satisfied do not want to build new worlds.
Henry Birne

The sound of a kiss is not so loud as that of a cannon, but its echo lasts longer.
Oliver Wendell Holmes

Love would seem to be free: If we have known love of parents, it came with no cost, and was freely given. Or, if two young hearts are in love, each would say that love was free; for a while that would seem to be true; but only for a while. Continuing and growing love is not the automatic result of marriage vows; the cost of growing love comes high. It means understanding and patience and sacrifice and wisdom; whenever we take it for granted we run the risk of losing it.
Henry Pope Mobley, Jr.

If things I give to you are small
And fade like fairy gifts away—
When I give love I give it all,
Nor keep it for another day.

Each day love gives a greater share
Of love and what love feeds on most,
And bankrupt, never seems to care,
And never stops to count the cost.

So giving, love and I give all,
And let the other gifts be small.
Ann Batchelder

You've got to love what's lovable, and hate what's hatable. It takes brains to see the difference.
Robert Frost

Toward evening on a fall day a mother placed her four-year-old son and her three-month-old baby out on the porch of their modest home to catch the last ray of a fall sunset. The little boy was impressed with the fact that he was acting as a guard over his baby brother. Nestled near his side was his fluffy three-month-old collie puppy who seemed to be perfectly content to be pressed up against his master's body. The three of them formed quite a picture there in the afternoon haze. A passer-by with an educated heart saw the beauty of the scene and paused, walked across to the little boy and spoke to him softly, "What are you doing, sonny?" he asked. And the little boy answered, "I am loving them."
Beam

When my husband's cousin left for service in Vietnam, he kissed his family good-by. A few days later, his six-year-old son said, "I shouldn't have washed Daddy's kiss off. It will be a long time before he can give me another." After a pause, he added, "That's okay. It soaked into my heart anyhow."
Mrs. Richard Otley

Just as we reveal our personalities, our inner thoughts and feelings by the way we act with friends, in school, on the job, so our behavior when in love is a reflection of what we are as people. Love does something to us, and we do even more to it. We can turn it into something which adds strength and beauty to two lives, or we can make it a device for exploiting and inflicting pain on the loved one and thereby bringing on ourselves an inevitable defeat.
George Lawton

Children are not so much upset by physical insecurity as they are by emotional upheavals, or the lack of love. During World War II, when Britain was being bombed nightly, many British parents sent their children to the country where they could be safe from the bombings. But social studies made after the war showed that the children who stayed in London with their parents, where, despite the bombings, they could have the security of love and understanding, were less disturbed than those who were isolated from home in areas of comparative safety.
Billy Graham

Faults are thick where love is thin.
Danish Proverb

Only our love hath no decay;
This no tomorrow hath, nor yesterday;
Running, it never runs from us away
But truly keeps his first, last, everlasting day.
John Donne

Love is not blind—it sees more, not less. But because it sees more, it is willing to see less.
Julius Gordon

I maintain that hell is the suffering of being unable to love.
Feodor Dostoevski

62 A man and a woman

"My girl and I split up because of religious differences," a buddy told me. "She worshipped money—and I didn't have any."
B. J. Cole

At a lecture on Long Island for a group of housewives, the subject was "A Happy Sex Life." At the conclusion there were questions and answers. Finally the lecturer asked, "Are there any more questions?" From the back of the room came: "Are there any more answers?"
Robert Sylvester

A happy marriage is a long conversation that seems all too short.
Andre Maurois

Love and respect woman. Look to her not only for comfort, but for strength and inspiration and the doubling of your intellectual and moral powers. Blot out from your mind any idea of superiority; you have none. There is no inequality between man and woman; but as often is the case between two men, only different tendencies and special vocations. Woman and man are the two notes without which the human chord cannot be struck.
Joseph Mazzini

An adolescent who had repeatedly voiced antagonism toward girls paused while mowing the lawn to look lingeringly at the pert little Miss living next door.

His father, observing from the porch, said to him, "Judging by your interest in our pretty neighbor, I'd say your opinion about girls is changing."

"You're wrong, Dad," protested the youngster, "but if ever I decide to stop hating them, she'll be the one I'll stop hating first."
Jack Kytle

No one is born a woman. One is merely born a female, and becomes a woman.
Simone de Beauvoir

A lady is a woman who makes a man behave like a gentleman.
Russell Lynes

Coincidence that we should meet,
That once you dropped a glove—
Coincidence that I was there . . .
But fate that we should love.
Catherine Haydon Jacobs

In the light of the great truths about the importance of marriage to our characters, we spend our time well in considering the vows we take. One of Scotland's greatest preachers went to the heart of this when he said, "There are two rocks in this world of ours on which the soul must either anchor or be wrecked—the one is God, and the other is the opposite sex."
Ansley C. Moore

Vernon "Lefty" Gomez, famed pitcher of the New York Yankees during the 30's, was separated for a time from his actress wife, but effected a reconciliation just before the World Series started. In the lobby of the Yankees' hotel, Gomez was accosted for an interview by a female reporter.

Gomez greeted her and then introduced Mrs. Gomez. "Oh, dear," blurted the lady reporter. "Am I to construe this as a reconciliation?"

Without batting an eye, Gomez retorted, "Well, I didn't bring her along to pitch."

Donald McGraw

The act of sexual union is holy and pure. The Lord created all things in accordance with His wisdom and whatever He created cannot possibly be shameful and ugly. When a man is in union with his wife in a spirit of holiness and purity, the Divine Presence is with them.

Moses ben Nahman

In life as well as in school, possessing so-called attributes and interests of the opposite sex is an advantage. "Children should be helped to accept their own sex with a sense of fulfillment and value the complementary role of the opposite sex," suggests psychoanalyst Dr. Irene M. Josselyn. As shrewd old Ben Franklin pointed out, "It is the man and woman united that makes the complete human being." The America of tomorrow needs men who are not limited to aggressive "masculine" characteristics but capable of showing the more "feminine" traits of warmth and sensitivity to others' feelings. And we need women who are less conforming, more original and daring in their thinking.

Jack Harrison Pollack

Man cannot degrade woman without himself falling into degradation; he cannot elevate her without at the same time elevating himself.

Alexander Walker

The average girl would rather have beauty than brains, because she knows that the average man can see much better than he can think.

Anonymous

---

63 Marriages are made on earth

A very wise man has said that matches are made in heaven, but marriages are made on earth.

Anonymous

Success in marriage does not come merely through finding the right mate, but through being the right mate.

Barnett R. Brickner

In marriage, today, as never before, a man and woman must find time, however briefly, to communicate as persons, realizing that only to the degree that they reflectively treat each other as sacred persons will they become persons. They must, in common and not just in times of crisis, discuss their goals in life, judge their values, analyze their

deepest ambitions for themselves and their chidren, and all of this in total honesty and humility.
>*Dennis Burke*

A mentally healthy person accepts sex as an important part of life, but not the whole of it; and attitudes toward the other sex which are founded upon a genuine understanding of and respect for personality of the other are the only adequate basis for marriage.
>*W. D. Wall*

Successful marriage is always a triangle: a man, a woman, and God.
>*T. Cecil Myers*

Marriage is a union of two personalities, not the submerging of one and the domination of the other.
>*Yvonne A. Ellwitz*

One does not find happiness in marriage; he takes happiness into marriage.
>*G. Curtis Jones*

Don't insist that marriage is a "50-50 proposition." At times you will demand 90%, whether you are aware of it or not. At other times you will be asked to give the 90%. But marriage is not a ball game; it needs no scorekeeper. It does not matter even whether you continually provide more than 50%. The important thing is that your contribution and your mate's add up to 100%.
>*George A. Kelly*

"Goodness," remarked a young woman as she inspected her grandmother's wedding ring, "what heavy and unwieldy things those were 50 years ago!" "Yes, dear," answered grandma, "but you must remember that in my day they were made to last a lifetime."
>*Neal O'Hara*

The great secret of successful marriage is to treat all disasters as incidents and none of the incidents as disasters.
>*Harold Nicolson*

A story of married love makes all the sizzling pictures of Purple Passion served up on the newsstands taste like ten cents' worth of cold potatoes.
>*Winston Churchill*

They were at the movies and during an intense love scene she nudged her husband and said, "Why is it that you never make love to me like that?"

"Listen," he snapped, "do you know how much they have to pay that fellow for doing it?"
>*J. J. Kelly*

Let's never forget that once we loved each other with all the radiance of young love. Why should we be ashamed to show that the years could not extinguish the spark; why not tell each other once in a while that we are still in love?
>*Author Unknown*

There is an interesting story of how the father of Matthew Henry, the commentator, won his bride. He was a minister, she was an only daughter, and heiress to a considerable fortune.

Her father objected. "You see,"

he said to his daughter, "he may be a perfect gentleman, a brilliant scholar and excellent preacher but he is a stranger and we do not even know where he comes from."

"True," replied the girl, with all the acumen and insight that her great son afterward displayed, "but we know where he is going and I should like to go with him."
Wesleyan Methodist

My grandfather used to tell young girls who came to him for advice on how to find an ideal man: "Never go out looking for an ideal man—a husband is a lot easier to find."
Herb Shriner

A man is in general better pleased when he has a good dinner upon his table than when his wife speaks Greek.
Samuel Johnson

Couples who hope for a happy marriage will do well to remember that in "wedding" the "we" comes before the "I."
Robert Brault

---

64 Parenthood is pain, privilege, and pride

The Hebrew word for parents is *horim*, and it comes from the same root as *moreh*, teacher. The parent is, and remains, the first and most important teacher that the child will ever have.
Kassel Abelson

"Listening" to a youngster is an art which every parent should develop. It is more than simply hearing what he has to say. He may be unable to put his feelings into words. We may have to receive his message by observing the way he behaves. Irritation, temper, or tears may be an indicaton of weariness or illness or of an emotional disturbance which is unrelated to the incident of the moment. He does not understand this. He expects *us* to understand, *and expects* us to *help*! So we must listen, not just with our ears, but the heart and mind as well. Then communication may become complete, and bring about a real partnership.
Science of Mind

It probably takes more endurance, more patience, more intelligence, more healthy emotion, to raise a decent, happy human being than to be an atomic physicist, a politician or a psychiatrist.
Milton R. Sapirstein

What a father says to his children is not heard by the world, but it will be heard by posterity.
Jean Paul Richter

Being a good father, though it is not easy, is the most rewarding respon-

sibility a man can undertake. A man may not always know the right thing to do, but right or wrong, if he acts with love and involvement, his children will respond with affection and respect. From that give-and-take comes the greatest satisfaction of fatherhood.
Ashley Montagu

Let every father remember that one day his son will follow his example instead of his advice.
Nuggets

He who brings up the child is to be called its father, not he who gave him birth.
The Talmud

All husbands and wives borrow their children. Our children are not our own; our children belong to God. He has loaned them to us for a season. Most marriages contain these borrowed jewels. They are not ours to keep, but to rear. They are not given to us to mold into our image. They are not given to us so that we can force them to fulfill our lives and thus, in some way, cancel our failures. They are not tools to be used, but souls to be loved.
Thomas C. Short

Give your children unconditional love, a love that is not dependent on report cards, clean hands, or popularity. Give your children a sense of your wholehearted acceptance of their human frailties as well as their abilities and virtues. Give your children your permission to grow up to make their own lives independent of you. Give them a sense of truth. Bestow upon your child the blessings of your faith. These are the laws of honoring your son and your daughter.
Joshua Loth Liebman

My parents weren't always right, but they were clear. They figured that if they didn't teach us, someone *else* would. In a moment of choice between right and wrong I could hear the echoes of their oft-repeated admonitions in my inner ear—"nagging" is what we would call it today. The need for clarity and consistency is even greater today when our teen-agers are offered more temptations and opportunities for messing up their lives than we had. Sometimes these opportunities are euphemistically labeled "advantages."
Sam Levenson

When children are around they are a pain in the neck and when they are not they are a pain in the heart.
Anonymous

As I approached my neighbor's home, I noticed her young son mowing the lawn.

"Is your mother home?" I asked the boy.

"You don't suppose I'm cutting the grass because it's too long, do you?" he replied.
Mrs. L. Binder

65 The family that stays together

In the family, children learn to be people. The boy learns from his father how to be a man, and from his mother how to care for women. The girl learns from her mother how to be a woman and a mother, and from her father what men are like. No known society has found a permanent substitute for the family as a way of shaping whole human beings. Many societies have tried other systems of child care. In our time the Soviet Union and Israel are notable examples. In both of these countries, however, a slow drift is taking place toward closer relationships between parents and children, more time together, and more individualization and intimacy.
Margaret Mead

The measure of a man's success in life is not the money he's raised. It's the kind of family he's raised.
Joseph P. Kennedy

Life has taught us that love does not consist in gazing at each other, but in looking outward together in the same direction.
Antoine de St. Exupery

There are two kinds of teenage rebellion; the normal, that leads to maturity, and the abnormal, that usually results in anarchy and destruction. Normal rebellion is constructive; it helps the teenager "shed his cocoon" and start to use his own wings. Or, to use another image, it means cutting the apron strings but not the heartstrings. Normal rebellion actually opens communication between parents and teenagers . . . but abnormal rebellion is quite another matter. It closes communications between parents and their teen.
Warren W. Wiersbe

If a child is going to internalize our values, the child must know what our values are. They must be spelled out for him in words and deeds. No discipline in terms of building inner controls can be accomplished without a warm and accepting relationship with an adult.
John Costello

As we went up in the elevator, the small child, maybe two years old, was bawling at the top of his lungs, and the mother was vainly trying to shush him. When they got off at the tenth floor where the dentists' offices are, we said to the elevator operator, "I suppose you carry a lot of howling children. An elevator must be pretty frightening the first time."

"No, I don't," was the answer. "Most of the youngsters who come in here just hold onto their mothers' hands and stay still as mice. You know the reason? Trust. If a child is brought up to trust that wherever his parents take him is a safe place, you won't get any hysterics. Trouble with that little fellow is he doesn't really trust his mother."
Presbyterian Life

A person who succeeds in marriage is a real success in life although he may fail in many other things, while

any other success will hardly comfort one who makes a failure at home.
Leland F. Wood

Above all, children need adults about them whose behavior makes sense, who live a consistent set of values and after whose image they can form a personality.
Bruno Bettelheim

It is the men who make the roads, but it is the women who teach the children to walk on them.
French Proverb

Man's higher thoughts are written down in books for posterity, but woman's are written in the hearts of their children.
Arlene Henkel

One cannot be a successful father or mother by merely reading a book on the subject . . . The successful family is not an accident, but an achievement.
H. Henlee Barnette

Marriage is not a one sided affair. The man has obligations as well as the woman. First, he must have as high a regard for his wife as he has for himself. He should sacrifice his personal needs in order to provide more abundantly for his wife and children. Above all, he should treat his wife with love and sympathy, for she is part of him and depends on him. Children of a loveless marriage are likely to be of inferior quality. Faithfulness is one of the essential conditions of an ideal marriage.
Menorat HaMaor

66 Home is more than a house

I think it must somewhere be written, that the virtues of the mothers shall be visited on their children as well as the sins of the fathers.
Charles Dickens

Parents wonder why the streams are bitter when they themselves have poisoned the fountain.
John Locke

Scotland, with her well known reverence for motherhood, insists that, "An ounce of mother is worth more than a pound of clergy."
H.H. Birkins

Guests are an important part of family life. They broaden our interests and help us in making the social contacts we need. Even the caller who stays for only a few minutes may bring something of value from the outside world—a piece of news, a fresh idea, a worthwhile opinion.
Norah Smaridge

True refinement, like true and good manners in the deepest sense, begins in the home and with the members of one's own family.
Author Unknown

Peace, like charity, must begin at home.
Yitzhak Ben Zvi

My mother taught me not only the three R's, but she implanted in my mind the love and purpose of learning. My mother was the making of me. She understood me; she let me follow my bents.
Thomas A. Edison

The most influential of all educational factors is the conversation in a child's home.
William Temple

A woman at a gathering was so serene and lovely to look at that an older woman was surprised to learn she was the mother of seven young children. When two of the children entered the room, both about the same height, the older woman remarked that it must have been hard having them all so close together.

"Not at all," the mother said. "We adopted Debbie three years ago."

'Good heavens!" the other exclaimed. "You mean you adopted one? Didn't you have enough of your own?"

"Yes, of course," was the reply. "But Debbie had no one at all."
Helen Bender

Light your lamp first at home and afterward at the mosque.
Indian Proverb

Every person who has a family worthy of the name should be able to rush home with one sure conviction in his soul. "They may not agree with me, they may not be able to help me; but at least they will all listen to me!" No matter how old we are, it is a great force for sanity to know that there is one group in a preoccupied world at whose feet we can dump our pack of trouble and have it looked over with wide resourceful eyes.
Frances Lester Warner

The ancient Chinese philosopher Lao-tzu wrote that the meaning of a room is not in the four walls, but in the space between them. A home is the atmosphere of our thinking outpictured. Just as we cannot breathe easily in polluted air, we cannot live harmoniously in a discordant atmosphere.
Science of Mind

It is far better to establish a home than an opinion.
Edmond Cahn

For a child, home is not a fine house in the best part of town, with a color TV, a hi-fi, wall-to-wall carpeting, and fine furniture. It is brothers and sisters and mother and father. It is where someone loves him, is interested in him, and cares what happens to him.
Willa Fogle

There are no real difficulties in a home where the children hope to be like their parents one day.
William Lyon Phelps

A child may have a beautiful home, vacations at the shore, sacks of toys and everything that money can buy, but if his parents show in their own behavior that they care little about education, scorn the life of the

mind, and show no concern for high standards of conduct or performance in their own lives—then it is inaccurate to speak of the child as having had every advantage. It would be better to say that he has had almost every disadvantage.
John W. Gardner

The sense of community must begin in the home. The family in essence, is a miniature of the community, with all the inevitable conflicts between differing viewpoints and the need for cooperative action. The child's future attitudes as a member of his community and as a citizen of his nation will be influenced first by the degree to which he is made to feel a part of the family and the extent to which he feels responsible for sharing the duties of life in the home.
Hubert H. Humphrey

67 Habit and discipline

We are creatures of habit. Any habit, good or bad, once formed is difficult to break. John Dryden once said, "Habits gather by unseen degrees, as brooks make rivers, rivers run to seas."
Gundar A. Myran

Patience and courage is a more powerful force than rage.
French Proverb

If thou hearest that a mountain has moved, believe it; but if thou hearest that a man has changed his character, believe it not.
Mohammedan Proverb

Many years ago a Czar came upon a sentry standing at attention in a secluded spot in the palace garden. He asked the man, "Sentry, what are you guarding?"

"I don't know, Sire," the guard replied. "I was ordered to my post by the Captain of the Guard."

The Czar then questioned the Captain of the Guard who likewise could not give him a reason, only that "Regulations called for a sentry at that particular spot."

The Czar then ordered the archives to be searched for the origin of the regulation which kept that lonely spot under surveillance day and night, year after year. Finally it was learned that Catherine the Great had planted a rose bush there and ordered a sentry to keep it from being trampled. The rose bush had been dead over one hundred years, but the regulation providing for a guard still remained.
Milo L. Arnold

Simply to tell men what is virtue, and to extol its beauty, is insufficient. Something more must be done if the characters . . . are to be molded and the inveterate vices eradicated.
William Edward Harpole Lecky

Whatever the color of the thought most frequently before the mind, that color will the mind take, for the mind is dyed by its thoughts.
Marcus Aurelius

Sow a thought, you reap an act; sow an act, you reap a habit; sow a habit; you reap a character; sow a character, you reap a destiny.
Anonymous

No one becomes bad suddenly.
Latin Proverb

Character is long-standing habit.
Plutarch

A city man watched a rancher firmly grind a cigarette butt into the snow-covered ground. "You can't start a fire with snow on the ground," the city man told him. "No," was the response, "but I can start a habit."
Izaak Walton Magazine

Habit is like a soft bed—easy to get into, hard to get out of.
Kelly Fordyce

Self-discipline means doing one's work and doing it at the top of one's bent. I need hardly add that this often involves simple drudgery. There is no way to avoid it, whatever profession or calling you enter. There is drudgery in housework, in office work, in acting, painting, writing; it cannot be avoided, and the habit of self-discipline is the habit of doing what has to be done, even when dull. At any age, the ability to dodge disagreeable tasks comes naturally . . . Mental discipline is like physical discipline. It becomes easier through practice.
B. J. Chute

Prayer is often used as a substitute for a gavel. People say the meeting will be opened with a "few words of prayer," and that's all it usually amounts to—words. Prayer is the achievement of a relationship with God that grows only from inner, spiritual discipline.
Edgar N. Jackson

Accustom thyself to habitual goodness for a man's character is what habit makes it.
Maimonides

We live by the thousand small decisions of every day. These decisions make our morality. The intended function of small, daily religious observances is to keep our self-discipline and our sense of marvel constantly exercised and supple and responsive; they *remind*...
Gerda Charles

What a man believes may be ascertained not from his creed, but from the assumptions on which he habitually acts.
George Bernard Shaw

We build our lives each day with the bricks of habit we have made.
Megiddo Message

Habit is a cable; we weave a thread of it every day, and at last we cannot break it.
Horace Mann

68   Margin for error

He who lives without committing any folly is not so wise as he thinks.
Francois La Rochefoucauld

I have told of my failings and mistakes, if only because I have found that failure is a far better teacher than success.
Bernard Baruch

To admit errors sets one free as the truth always does.
Hans Kung

The sages do not consider that making no mistakes is a blessing. They believe, rather, that the great virtue of man lies in his ability to correct his mistakes and continually to make a new man of himself.
Wang Yang-Ming

A dwelling which should be condemned as unsafe is the dwelling on one's own mistakes.
William Arthur Ward

To avoid all mistakes in the conduct of great enterprises is beyond man's powers.
Fabius Maximus

The man who makes no mistakes does not usually make anything.
William Connor Magee

A man who has committed a mistake and does not correct it, is making another mistake.
Confucius

Sir Eardley Wilmot was asked by a friend in public office who felt that he had been wronged by a fellow official: "Don't you think it would be manly to resent this offense?"
"Yes," replied Sir Eardley, "it would doubtless be manly to resent it, but it would be godlike to forgive."
Cincinnati Enquirer

The immature get and forget, the mature give and forgive. The selfish take and mistake. The patient bear and forbear.
Author Unknown

A chip on the shoulder is the heaviest load a man can carry.
Anonymous

There is nothing final about a mistake, except its being taken as final.
Phyllis Bottome

To make mistakes as we are on the way to knowledge is far more honorable than to escape making them through never having set out to seek knowledge.
Richard C. Trench

During a long life I have had to eat my own words many times, and I have found it a very nourishing diet.
Winston Churchill

Looking back . . . over the long and labyrinthine path which finally led to the discovery of the quantum theory, I am vividly reminded of Goethe's saying that men will always be making mistakes as long as they are striving after something.
Max Planck

A church is a hospital for sinners, not a museum for saints.

Abigail Van Buren

Clara Barton, founder of the American Red Cross, was once reminded of an especially cruel thing that had been done to her years before. But Miss Barton seemed not to recall it.

"Don't you remember it?" her friend asked.

"No," came the reply, "I distinctly remember forgetting the incident."

Sunshine Magazine

If you were to ask what is the hardest task in the world you might thing of some muscular feat, some acrobatic challenge, some chore to be done on the battlefield or the playing field. Actually, however, there is nothing which we find more arduous than saying, "I was wrong."

Sunshine Magazine

---

69 The importance of little things

Sometimes when I consider what tremendous consequences come from little things— a chance word, a tap on the shoulder, or a penny dropped on a newsstand—I am tempted to think . . . there are no little things.

Bruce Barton

A traveler in ancient Greece who had lost his way and was seeking to find it, asked directions of a man by the roadside who turned out to be Socrates. "How can I reach Mount Olympus?" asked the traveler. To this Socrates is said to have replied gravely, "Just make every step you take in that direction."

Dialogues of Socrates

I don't know how long God will let me live, and while I do live, He may let me do very little, but the little He will let me do, I intend to do it all.

Pope John XXIII

An actor, Charles Brookfield by name, was once mistakenly reported to be dead, and so had the unusual opportunity of reading his own obituary notices. He always remembered one of them. One could not blame him. It ran like this: "Never a great actor, he was invaluable in small parts." While he may not have taken this as a compliment, nothing much more worth while could be said of anyone.

Harry Emerson Fosdick

A little more kindness and a little less creed,
A little more giving and a little less greed
A little more smile and a little less groan,
A little less kicking a man when he's down;
A little more "we" and a little less "I"

A little more laugh and a little less cry;
A few more flowers on the pathway of life,
And fewer on graves at the end of the strife.
Anonymous

Small deeds done are better than great deeds planned.
George Marshall

Little drops of water,
Little grains of sand,
Make a mighty ocean,
And the pleasant land.

Thus the little minutes,
Humble though they be,
Make the mighty ages
Of eternity.
Ebenezer Brewer

When our PTA honored Miss Bestwick, retiring teacher, someone asked where she learned to be so tolerant. In her first year, she explained, when a mole on a little boy's neck turned out to be a spot on her eyeglasses.
Burton Hillis

Saints are not formed in great crises but in the ordinary grind of daily life.
Everyday Saint

Someone asked a famous conductor of a great symphony orchestra which orchestral instrument he considered the most difficult to play. The conductor thought a moment, then said: "Second fiddle, I can get plenty of first violinists. But to find one who can play second fiddle with enthusiasm—that's a problem. And if we have no second fiddle, we have no harmony!"
Grit

Life is not lost by dying! Life is lost
Minute by minute, day by dragging day,
In all the thousand small, uncaring ways,
The smooth appeasing compromises of time.
... Life can be ...
Lost without vision but not lost by death,
Lost by not caring.
Stephen Vincent Benet

Wars are never caused by the little man, just fought by him.
Bob Robison

All are architects of Fate,
Working in these walls of Time;
Some with massive deeds and great,
Some with ornaments of rhyme.

Nothing useless is, or low;
Each thing in its place is best;
And what seems but idle show
Strengthens and supports the rest.
Henry Wadsworth Longfellow

Life is made up of little things. It is seldom that occasion offers itself for doing a great deed. True greatness consists in being great in all little things. Let us be willing to keep doing a little good rather than waiting to do a great deal of good all at once.
W.S.K. Yeaple

70 Making a life

Life is not simply something which is capable of being enjoyed, but something capable of being improved, and the greatest of pleasures is to work for its improvement.
Andrew Martin Fairbairn

Sow yourselves, sow the living part of yourselves, in the furrows of life.
Miguel de Unamuno

Human life is best lived in the magnetic field between the poles of togetherness and aloneness.
Lynn White

The man who insists upon seeing with perfect clearness before he decides, never decides. Accept life, and you must accept regret.
Henri Frederic Amiel

Some years ago, a Westerner interviewed the great Indian poet Tagore. To the statement that science was lengthening the life span, he replied: "Why? What are you living for?"
Journal of the American Association of University Women

If life were predictable it would cease to be life and would be without flavor.
Eleanor Roosevelt

The life of every man is a diary in which he means to write one story and writes another; and his humblest hour is when he compares the volume as it is with what he hoped to make it.
James M. Barrie

The Mexican matador, El Cordobes, was asked if he was afraid of death, "No," he replied. "Only life scares me."
Dallas Morning News

I, who am blind, can give one hint to those who see: Use your eyes as if tomorrow you would be stricken blind.
Helen Keller

I shall not die, but live, and declare the works of the Lord.
Psalms 118:17

Life and death are brothers that dwell together; they cling to each other and cannot be separated. They are joined by the two extremes of a frail bridge over which all created beings travel. Life is the entrance; death is the exit; life builds, death demolishes; life sows, death reaps; life plants, and death uproots. Know that yesterday shall never come back; nor should you say: "I shall do it tomorrow." Hasten to do your task every day, for death may at any time send forth its arrow-like lightning.
Bahya ibn Pakuda

Life is the sum total of everything we hold dear, everything we feel . . . from the first breath to the last. It can be likened to, and for some encompasses, a good marriage that keeps its youthful romantic aura of mutual regard, despite the arguments and adversities to which lovers are prone. In fact, our feelings may be intensified and

strengthened by occasional setbacks, if we but acknowledge the significance of our love.
Max L. Berges

Life is too short to be little.
Benjamin Disraeli

Let us endeavor so to live that, when we come to die, even the undertaker will be sorry.
Mark Twain

There are obviously two educations. One should teach us how to make a living. The other should teach us how to live.
James Truslow Adams

Let us devote our lives to worthwhile actions and feelings, to great thoughts, real affections and enduring undertakings.
Andre Maurois

You made such an outcry about life yesterday
I thought you meant more than undisturbed breathing
Christopher Fry

8
Character is the key

71   The greatest ability is responsibility

It is safer in the end to blunder occasionally in the attempt to fulfill the high responsibilities of his office than to make his work one chronic blunder by refusing to face these responsibilities.

John Kelman

One of the great sources of moral and political breakdown in our day is the reluctance of ordinary people to accept responsibility.

W. T. Purkiser

The question of responsibility was posed in a great courtroom trial a few years ago, in Israel. Judge Landau, later the presiding judge in the Eichmann case, sat in judgment. A Jewish officer was charged with leading a raid on an Arab village and ordering the slaughter of a number of innocent Arab civilians. His defense was simple: "I am a soldier," he said. "I was simply obeying military orders to preserve the security of Israel."

Judge Landau's historic pronouncement goes to the very heart of the moral issue: "You, and you alone, are responsible for the moral consequences of your actions."

The Jerusalem Post

If a man knows any evidence in favor of the defendant, he is not at liberty to keep silent regarding it, for thus he may become responsible for the man's death. If a man sees another in mortal danger by falling into a river, through an attack by robbers, or some other evil, he is duty bound not to stand idly by, but must come to his rescue. Moreover, if he sees one man pursuing another to kill or to ravish, he is in duty bound to prevent the commission of the capital crime even by taking the life of the offender.

The Midrash

There are plenty of recommendations on how to get out of trouble cheaply and fast. Most of them come down to this: Deny your responsibility.

Lyndon B. Johnson

Reverence for life . . . does not allow the scholar to live for his science alone, even if he is very useful . . . the artist to exist only for his art, even if he gives inspiration to many . . . It refuses to let the business man imagine that he fulfills all legitimate demands in the course of his business activities. It demands from all that they should sacrifice a portion of their own lives for others.

Albert Schweitzer

"What is life's heaviest burden?" asked a youth of a sad and lonely old man. "To have nothing to carry," he answered.

E. Scott O'Connor

A wrongdoer is often a man that has left something undone, not always he that has done something.

Marcus Aurelius

Old Faithful is not the largest geyser, nor does it reach the greatest height. Nevertheless it is by far the most popular geyser. Its popularity is due mainly to its regularity and dependability. You can count on Old Faithful. Nothing in life can take the place of faithfulness and dependability. It is one of the greatest virtues. Brilliance, genius, competence—all are subservient to the quality of faithfulness.

Wallace Fridy

In the play *The Andersonville Trial* the following are the words that the prosecuting attorney spoke to the commander of the Andersonville camp where 14,000 Union prisoners died as the result of his excessive cruelty. When the camp commander attempted to vindicate himself by referring to orders received from a superior officer, the prosecuting attorney said: Your superior had no absolute authority over you. He was not your superior insofar as morals were concerned. No man has authority over the soul of another. As we are men, we own our own souls; and, as we own them, we are equal as men . . . Why couldn't you disobey?

Saul Levitt

A rabbi once passed through a field where he saw an old man planting an oak tree. "Why are you planting that tree?" he asked. "You surely do not expect to live long enough to see the acorn grow into an oak?"

The old man replied: "My ancestors planted trees that I might enjoy their shade and their fruit. I am doing likewise."

The Talmud

72 Integrity is integral

A devout Negro clergyman was asked by one of his parishioners to explain the doctrine of election. His reply was: "You know what an election is, when we elect the President and the governor. In the Kingdom of God there is always an election going on. Only three votes are cast. The Lord always votes *for* you. The devil always votes *against* you. And you have the deciding vote."
Alliance Witness

A man who has reformed himself has contributed his full share toward the reformation of his neighbors.
Norman Douglas

To help put meaning into a single life is the best kind of individual responsibility.
Norman Cousins

Question: Why is it written: "In the day that God created a man on earth," and not "in the day that God created man on earth?"
Answer: You shall serve your Creator as if there were only one man in the world, only you yourself.
Martin Buber

Each self is not only a knot of purposes and predilections but has its own particular and private character. Each man and child is not a unit or a statistic only, but a person. In any plans that we may have for man, this unique individuality of every member of his race must never be disregarded. Dollars are all alike, and miles and pounds, but not men. There is no Bureau of Standards to make them uniform, and let us hope there never will be.
Edmund W. Sinnott

He who comes to defile, the path is opened for him, and he who comes to purify, assistance is rendered him.
The Talmud

Every life is a profession of faith, and exercises an inevitable and silent propaganda. As far as lies in its power, it tends to transform the universe and humanity into its own image. Every man's conduct is an unspoken sermon that is forever preaching to others.
Henri Frederic Amiel

Each of us is placed here on earth and given life for some grand purpose. Each of us has been given a talent. It was put in us to develop and through its development to bless humanity. That is the ordained purpose behind each of our lives. And that purpose can be accomplished only by the individual.
Alden Palmer

Character is like a tree, and reputation is like a shadow. The shadow is what we think of it; the tree is the real thing.
Abraham Lincoln

A famous psychiatrist conducting a university course in psychopathology was asked by a student, "Doctor, you've told us about the abnormal person and his behavior; but what about the normal person?"

"If we ever find him," replied the psychiatrist, "we'll cure him."
Source Unknown

Man alone is conscious of his individuality.
Leo Baeck

God give us men! A time like this demands
Strong minds, great hearts, true faith and ready hands;
Men whom the lust of office does not kill;
Men whom the spoils of office cannot buy;
Men who possess opinions and a will;
Men who have honor; men who will not lie;
Men who can stand before a demagogue
And damn his treacherous flatteries without winking;
Tall men, sun crowned, who live above the fog
In public duty, and in private thinking.
J. G. Holland

Man only exists for the purpose of proving to himself that he is a man and not an organ-stop! He will prove it even if it means physical suffering; even if it means turning his back on civilization.
Feodor Dostoevski

If all mankind minus one were of one opinion, and only one person were of the contrary opinion, mankind would be no more justified in silencing that one person than he, if he had the power, would be justified in silencing mankind.
John Stuart Mill

---

73 To tell the truth

Are we disposed to be of the number of those who, having eyes, see not, and having ears, hear not the things which so nearly concern their temporal salvation? For my part, whatever anguish of spirit it might cost, I am willing to know the whole truth; to know the worst and to provide for it.
Patrick Henry

To give up pretensions is as blessed a relief as to get them gratified; and where disappointment is incessant and the struggle unending this is what men will always do . . . How pleasant is the day when we give up striving to be young—or slender. Thank God! we say, those illusions are gone. Everything added to the self is a burden as well as a pride.
William James

Half the misery in the world comes of want of courage to speak and to hear the truth plainly and in a spirit of love.
Harriet Beecher Stowe

Sin has many tools, but a lie is the handle which fits them all.
Oliver Wendell Holmes

Sometimes the kindest thing you can do for a person is to tell him a truth that will prove very painful. But in so doing, you may have saved him from serious harm or even greater pain. In a world such as ours, people must learn to "take it." A painless world is not necessarily a good world.
Sylvanus and Evelyn Duvall

Any truth is many-sided, even simple truth. But the complex truth of today needs approach by many different methods and many different types of mind before we can arrive at even an approximation of the truth.
Josiah Charles Stamp

From the cowardice that shrinks from new truth,
From the laziness that is content with half-truths,
From the arrogance that thinks it knows all truth,
O, God of Truth, deliver us.
Prayer of the Scholar

Facts do not cease to exist because they are ignored.
Franklin Field

A little girl came to her mother very early one morning and asked, "Which is worse, Mamma, to tell a lie or to steal?" The mother replied that both were so sinful that she could not tell which was worse.

"Well, Mamma," replied the little one, "I've been thinking about it, and I think it's much worse to lie than steal." When asked for her reason she said, "Well, you see, Mamma, if you steal a thing you can take it back, unless you've eaten it, and if you've eaten it, you can pay for it; but a lie is forever."
Hy Pickering

Self-respect cannot be hunted. It cannot be purchased. It is never for sale. It comes to us when we are alone, in quiet moments, in quiet places, when we suddenly realize that, knowing the good, we have done it; the beautiful, we have served it; knowing the truth, we have spoken it.
A. Whitney Griswold

When I see a bird that walks like a duck and swims like a duck and quacks like a duck, I call that bird a duck.
Richard Cardinal Cushing

A truth that's told with bad intent, beats all the lies you can invent.
William Blake

Truth, like justice, beauty and contact lenses, is in the eye of the beholder.
Gene Klavan

Know truth and you will know its source—God— for He is the Creator of all reality.
Shem Tov ibn Palkira

I have discovered the art of fooling diplomats; I speak the truth and they never believe me.
Benso di Vacour

Every time a creative man presents living, profound truth, most people

cannot endure it. They are only interested in bourgeois trials and tribulations, politics, the petty happenings of every day. They are afraid of looking the sun and death in the face.
Eugene Ionesco

When her little daughter told a lie, mother told her if she kept telling lies she wouldn't go to heaven. The little girl asked if her father, aunts, and uncles ever told a lie. Mother replied, "I think everyone has told a lie one or twice."

"It must be awful lonesome in heaven with nobody there but God and George Washington," the little girl replied.
Helen Bender

Men occasionally stumble over the truth, but most of them pick themselves up and hurry off as if nothing happened.
Winston Churchill

74 To walk humbly

When a caller on John D. Rockefeller, Jr., noting his modest office surroundings, remonstrated, "How can you hope to impress people in an office like this?" Mr. Rockefeller asked simply, "Whom do I have to impress?"
Source Unknown

Humility is a strange thing; the minute you think you've got it, you've lost it.
E. D. Hulse

The great act of faith is when man decides that he is not God.
Oliver Wendell Holmes

Once when Rabbi Pinhas entered the House of Study, he saw that his disciples, who had been talking busily, stopped when he entered. He asked them: "What were you talking about?"

"Rabbi," they said, "we were saying how afraid we are that the Evil Urge will pursue us."

"Don't worry," he replied. "You have not gotten high enough for it to pursue you. For the time being, you are still pursuing it."
Hasidic Lore

A haughty lawyer once asked a sterling old farmer, "Why don't you hold up your head in the world as I do? I bow my head neither before God nor man."

"Squire," replied the farmer, "see that field of grain? Only those heads that are empty stand upright. Those that are well filled are the ones that bow low."
Capper's Weekly

I believe that the test of a truly great man is his humility. I do not mean by humility doubt of his own power. But really great men have a curious feeling that the greatness is not in

them but through them. And they see something divine in every other man, and are endlessly, foolishly, incredibly merciful.
John Ruskin

Both (north and south) read the same Bible and pray to the same God; and each invokes His aid . . . against the other. The prayers of both could not be answered fully. The Almighty has His own purposes . . . With malice toward none, with charity for all and with firmness in the right as *God gives us to see the right,* let us strive on to finish the work we are in . . .
Abraham Lincoln

A Vatican official, learning that the new Pope wished to take a daily walk in his garden, told him arrangements had been made to screen his path from the view of nearby residents.

"Why?" asked the Pope, "Don't I look respectable?"
Daily Telegraph

The greatest of faults is to be conscious of none.
Thomas Carlyle

There is no room for God in him who is full of himself.
Martin Buber

To know one's ignorance is the best part of knowledge.
Lao Tse

From early youth until his death at the age of 78, through periods of poverty and crippling arthritis, Auguste Renoir, the French painter, devoted himself fanatically to his work.

Shortly before he breathed his last, he looked up at those gathered at his bedside and murmured: "What a pity! I was just beginning to show a little promise."
Milwaukee Journal

A mountain shames a molehill until they are both humbled by the stars.
Old Adage

O burning bush: Not because you are tall, but because you are lowly, did God reveal Himself in you.
The Talmud

The one great solution for all passion, emotionalism and intolerance is the broad knowledge that none of us knows he is right.
Willit C. Jewell

Booker T. Washington was standing in the lobby of a hotel in one of our western states when a salesman came rushing in loaded down with baggage, and ordered Mr. Washington to carry his bags up to his room. "Yes, sir," was Mr. Washington's reply. He completed his errand and returned to the lobby where his friends, who had come to hear him lecture, were waiting aghast at the nerve of the salesman.

"The gentleman even gave me a tip," he said. "I took it so as not to embarrass him. It will help one of my boys toward an education."
Uplift

75 The right kindness

A man may carp and criticize—provided he does so with respect and gentleness.
Maimonides

The Lord, the Lord God is gracious and compassionate, slow to anger, abounding in kindness and faithfulness, assuring love for a thousand generations, forgiving iniquity, transgression and sin, and pardoning the penitent.
Exodus 34:6-7

No tranquilizer can be found
Through any magic art
As fine as that which must abound
Within a peaceful heart.

No drug or dope can take the place
Of peace within the mind,
Of those who have the friendly grace
To be gently, just, and kind.
Edith H. Shank

A youngster with a mirror was seen throwing rays of sunshine toward the upper story of a house. An old man nearby was curious and asked why he was doing it. "I'm throwing a little sunshine up to my friend's room. He's my pal. He broke his leg last week and today is our school debate and my friend can't be with us—so I'm sending him a little sunshine to let my friend know that we're thinking of him."
Source Unknown

There is a story of a young boy who was asked to give a definition of kindness. He replied, "If I was hungry and you gave me a piece of bread and butter, that would be kindness." I feel that if you put jam on the bread, the result would be loving kindness. What this world needs today, in these trying times, is more jam.
Faye Boggs

A man should accustom himself to be pleasant to people.
The Talmud

Kindness in words creates confidence, kindness in thinking creates profoundness, kindness in giving creates love.
Lao Tse

A boy was asked by his mother what he wanted for breakfast. He replied, "Puffed wheat, an egg on toast, and a kind word."
Ross Blake

Do not forget little kindnesses, but do not remember small faults.
Oriental Proverb

One of the nicest guys I know rarely returns a kindness. Instead he passes it along wherever it's needed most.
Burton Hills

Do it now. It is not safe to leave a generous feeling to the cooling influences of a cold world.
Thomas Guthrie

It is never too soon to do a kindness, for one does not know how soon it will be too late.
Friendly Chats

Join the great company of those who make the barren places of life fruitful with kindness. Carry a vision of heaven in your heart, and make the world correspond to that vision.
Helen Keller

Kind words are the music of the world.
Megiddo Message

Better do a kindness near at home than walk a thousand miles to burn incense.
Defender

Shall we make a new rule of life from tonight: always to try to be a little kinder than is necessary.
James M. Barrie

To give pleasure to a single heart by a single kind act is better than a thousand head-bowings in prayer.
Judah Saadi

Have a heart that never hardens, a temper that never tires, a touch that never hurts.
Charles Dickens

The Bible begins and ends with kindness: God clothing Adam and Eve, and burying Moses (Genesis 3:21, Deuteronomy 34:6).
The Talmud

Constant kindness can accomplish much. As the sun makes ice melt, kindness causes misunderstanding, mistrust and hostility to evaporate.
Albert Schweitzer

76 Conscience—the still small voice

With a good conscience our only sure reward, with history the final judge of our deeds, let us go forth to lead the land we love, asking His blessing and His help but knowing that here on earth God's work must truly be our own.
John F. Kennedy

Mass opinion has shown itself to be a dangerous master of decisions when the stakes are life and death.
Walter Lippmann

History shows too many times where the majority led a society over the abyss and where the truth was to be found in a minority report.
Gerald Kennedy

To thine own self be true,
And it must follow, as the night the day,
Thou canst not then be false to any man.
William Shakespeare

Cowardice asks, is it safe? Expediency asks, is it politic? Vanity asks, is it popular? But conscience asks, is it right?
Anonymous

Conscience—the still small voice

It is easy in the world to live after the world's opinion; it is easy in solitude to live after our own; but the great man is he who, in the midst of the crowd, keeps with perfect sweetness the independence of solitude.
Ralph Waldo Emerson

Anyone who has had a tiny pebble or coarse grains of sand in a shoe knows how uncomfortable it feels. In Roman times the chances of getting sand or pebbles in footwear were greater than today, because the Romans wore sandals. The Latin word for a small, sharp pebble was "scrupulus." The Romans compared the pricking of one's conscience with having a pebble in one's sandal. This mental uneasiness was described as "scrupulus," which became "scrupule" in French and "scruple" in English.
William Penfield

Once Michelangelo, painting frescoes in the Sistine Chapel, was lying on his back on a high scaffold, carefully outlining a figure in a corner of the ceiling. A friend asked him why he took such pains with a figure that would be many feet away from the viewer. "After all," said the friend, "who will know whether it is perfect or not?" "I will," said the artist.
Source Unknown

On theological matters everyone is welcome to his own opinion.
Josephus

Yet still there whispers the small
   voice within,
Heard through Gain's silence, and
   O'er Glory's din;

Whatever creed be taught, or land
   be trod,
Man's Conscience is the oracle of
   God.
George Gordon Byron

Unless the vessel is clean, whatsoever you pour in it becomes soiled.
Horace

A young lad knocked on the door of a woman's house and asked her if she would like to buy some of the berries he had just picked. "Yes," she said, "and I'll take your pail in the kitchen and measure out two quarts."

The boy stood outside and played with the dog. "Why don't you come in and see that I measure your berries right?" inquired the woman. "How do you know that I may not cheat you?"

"I am not afraid," replied the lad, "for you would get the worst of it."

"Get the worst of it," replied the woman, "what do you mean by that?"

"Why, Ma'am," said the boy. "I would only lose the berries; you would make yourself a thief."
A. Purnell Bailey

I hope I shall always possess firmness and virtue enough to maintain what I consider the most enviable of all titles, the character of an "honest man."
George Washington

The idea of conscience embarrasses Modern Man. Moral consciousness is something that bio-chemists, psychologists and sociologists have tried to tie down with their straight

pins of statistics and theory. But conscience is a live thing. Slice it up and it still squirms. Cut off its tail and it grows a new one.
Cyrin Maus

In these times one must write with one's life. This is the challenge to all of us.
Antoine de St. Exupery

Create in me a clean heart, O God; and renew a right spirit within me.
Psalms 51:10

A man lays the foundation of true greatness when he becomes more concerned with building his character than with expanding his reputation.
William Arthur Ward

---

77 Thankfulness—the greatest of all virtues

It was Thanksgiving Day, and we gathered as usual with our nine children around the dining-room table. Following an old family custom, we went round the table from one to another, asking each what he was most thankful for this year. The typical answers of "home," "Church," "family," were given. Finally we got down to Bobby, our five-year-old.

Loud and clear he spoke up: "I want to thank God for making daddy strong enough to carry home this big turkey!"
Catholic Digest

The man who has forgotten to be thankful has fallen asleep in the midst of life.
Robert Louis Stevenson

In the eighteen-sixties, Dr. Edson, rector of St. Anne's Church and best loved citizen of Lowell, Massachusetts, said to a friend, "Good morning, how are you today?" "I am very well thank God," came the reply.

"I am so glad to hear you thank God for it," said the old rector. "For twenty years everyone in Lowell has been thanking *me.* They always say, 'I am very well, thank *you,* Dr. Edson.'"
Source Unknown

We need Thanksgiving, and specifically, Thanksgiving Day, because we need to give thanks for all that we have received and for the blessings that too often we take for granted. The person who has known sickness, hospitalization, and surgery this past year, but who now is restored to the fullness of life, wants to give thanks for God's merciful acts through the healing arts. The man who has been promoted and has known success this past year feels the need to give thanks for the good fortune that has come his way. Those family circles that have been reunited again so that every seat at the Thanksgiving table is filled know the reason why we give thanks.
Maurice E. Roberts

A thankful heart is not only the greatest virtue, but the parent of all the other virtues.
Marcus Tullius Cicero

One moment of thinking of our blessings will require an hour of thanking.
Wilfred A. Peterson

I have thought fit, according to the ancient and laudable practice of our renowned ancestors, to appoint a day of public thanksgiving to God, for the great benefits which He has been pleased to bestow upon us, in the year past . . . That He would graciously be pleased to put an end to all tyranny and usurpation, that the people who are under the yoke of oppression may be made free; and that the nations who are contending for freedom may still be secured by His almighty aid, and enabled under His influence to complete wise systems of civil government, founded in the equal rights of men and calculated to establish their permanent security and welfare. And, finally, that the peaceful and glorious reign of our Divine Redeemer may be known and enjoyed throughout the whole family of mankind.
Samuel Adams

A man was called upon at a dinner of the Pilgrim Fathers to respond to the toast, "The Pilgrim Fathers."

After paying tribute to the Pilgrim Fathers for enduring the rigors of the New England winters and the privations and dangers of life in the little settlement of Plymouth, he paused.

"But let us give thought," he added with a grin, "to the Pilgrim Mothers. For they not only had to endure everything the Pilgrim Fathers endured, but mark this, they had to endure, also, the Pilgrim Fathers."
C. Kennedy

Two little girls, one Jewish and the other Christian, were the best of friends. After Easter the little Christian girl was asked by her grandfather what her best friend got for Easter. "Oh," she replied, "she didn't get anything for Easter. You see, I'm Easter and she's Passover. I'm Christmas and she's Hanukkah." Then with a big smile she added, "But we're both Thanksgiving."
Source Unknown

If you can't be thankful for what you receive, be thankful for what you escape.
Grit

For each new morning with its light,
Father, we thank Thee,
For rest and shelter of the night,
Father, we thank Thee,
For health and food, for love and friends,
For everything Thy goodness sends,
Father, in heaven, we thank Thee.
Ralph Waldo Emerson

There are two kinds of gratitude: the sudden kind we feel for what we take, and the larger kind we feel for what we give.
Edwin A. Robinson

78   Honest to God

Behold, you desire truth in the inward parts.
Psalms 51:8

The difficulty is not that men are ignorant of the truth; it is that they have not yet dared to live by it.
Morton J. Cohn

Accept the truth from whatever source it comes, even from your inferiors. If you keep a secret it is your prisoner; but if you disclose it, you become its prisoner. Why are the wise more often at the doors of the rich than the rich at the doors of the wise? Because the wise appreciate the advantage of wealth, while the rich do not know the value of wisdom.
Solomon ibn Gabirol

Hell is truth seen too late.
H. G. Adams

Truth is the hardest missile one can be pelted with.
George Eliot

The truth or falsehood of an idea has nothing to do with the person who advances it or even with his motives for advancing it; and we must diligently search for the truth that may be wrapped in the ideas that come our way.
Irwin Miller

Be ye lamps unto yourselves.
Be your own reliance.
Hold to the truth within yourselves
As to the only lamp.
The Buddha

In troubled water you can scarce see your face, or see it very little, till the water be quiet and stand still. So in troubled times you can see little truth; when times are quiet and settled, truth appears.
John Selden

Man with his burning soul,
Has but an hour of breath
To build a ship of Truth,
In which his soul may sail,
Sail on the sea of death;
For death takes toll
Of beauty, courage, youth,
Of all but Truth.
John Masefield

Four are asked what is strongest. One suggests wine; the second, the king; the third, women; and the fourth says "above all things Truth beareth away the victory." The verdict is: "As for the truth, it endureth, and is always strong; it liveth and conquereth forevermore."
First Esdras, 3 and 4

What does it mean, when people will say that Truth goes all over the world? It means that Truth is driven out of one place after another, and must wander on and on.
Baal Shem Tov

The only way to speak the truth is to speak it lovingly.
Henry David Thoreau

Seek truth in all things, for God reveals Himself in the created world.
Thomas Aquinas

Pay little attention to Socrates, but much more to the truth; and if I appear to you to say anything true, assent to it; but if not, oppose me with all your might.

Plato

The greatest and noblest pleasure which men have in this world is to discover new truths; and the next is to shake off old prejudices.

Frederick the Great

A newspaperman once asked Sam Rayburn, "Mr. Speaker, you see probably a hundred people a day. You tell each one 'Yes,' or 'No,' or 'Maybe.' You never seem to make notes on what you have told them, but I never heard of your forgetting anything you have promised them. What is your secret?"

Rayburn's hot brown eyes flashed: "If you tell the truth the first time," he replied, "you don't have to remember."

D. B. Hardeman

Truth is great and will prevail if left to herself ... she is the proper and sufficient antagonist to error, and has nothing to fear from the conflict unless by human interposition disarmed of her natural weapons, free argument and debate.

Thomas Jefferson

---

79 Beliefs that matter

Religion is not a way of looking at certain things. It is a certain way of looking at everything.

Robert E. Segal

We have just enough religion to make us hate, but not enough to make us love one another.

Jonathan Swift

I would not give a farthing for a man's religion if his dog and cat are not the better for it.

Rowland Hill

It is customary for us to equate religion with theology. This has led to many difficulties. Religion is more than any theology, more than any dogma or creed. Religion may be defined in many different ways, but in its essence it is the total meaning of life.

I. Lynd Esch

At a faculty-student reception, Yale's chaplain, the Reverend William Sloane Coffin, Jr., met with an intense sophomore with the light of battle in his eye. "Sir," said the boy belligerently, "religion is a crutch!"

"Sure it is," agreed Coffin. And before the flabbergasted student had time to respond he added, "But who isn't limping?"

Mrs. W. W. Johnson

Religion is behavior and not mere belief.

S. Radhakrishnan

Religion has not been tried and found wanting. It has been found difficult and never sufficiently tried.
G. K. Chesterton

There is the story about a young minister who wanted to make his sermon a memorable one. He planned to attack horse racing, but an older minister reminded him that several congregation members raised horses. Then the young man wanted to attack tobacco. This was turned down for the same reason. Likewise moonshine. Finally, he asked what was "safe" to condemn. The older preacher said, "Preach against them heathen witch doctors. There ain't one of them within 4,000 miles."
Don Maclean

True prayer is a way of life; the truest life is literally a way of prayer.
Alexis Carrel

Religion does not exist to describe the furniture of heaven and the temperature of hell.
Reinhold Niebuhr

A farmer whose corn crop had done poorly decided to "borrow" a few bushels from a neighbor. On a dark night, the farmer and his eight-year-old son headed for a distant corner of his neighbor's field, carrying several bushel baskets. When they reached the fence separating the two farms, the farmer looked furtively to the right, to the left, ahead and behind. Just as he was about to step into the heavily laden acres of corn, the tense silence was broken by his small son. "Daddy," said the little boy, "you didn't look up."
Star Reporter

All progress is made by men of faith who believe in what is right, and even more important, actually do the right in their private affairs. You cannot add to the peace and good will of the world if you fail to create an atmosphere of harmony and love right where you live and work.
Thomas Dreier

Greater is he who is commanded and fulfills the commandment, than one who is not commanded and fulfills it.
The Talmud

While in college I was talking to my college church pastor on one occasion and said to him: "Doesn't it make you nervous to know that you are preaching to a college president and faculty members who know theology backwards and forwards. Doesn't it make you feel uneasy to know that any grammatical error will be noticed?" His answer was one that should be framed and put on the door of every church in the land. He said, "It's not the big men in the church that give you trouble; it's the little men."
Jack Wright

A prominent British churchman once wrote that he read the Bible every day in order to know what people ought to do and his newspaper in order to know what they were doing.
William T. McElroy

80 Compassion means involvement

Human sympathy, I find, is a wonderful thing; it lays a healing touch upon the new-made, grievous wound, and that which seemed unbearable becomes something with which we may live and not despair.
Maybe Dick

Our greatest threat is not the atomic bomb. Our greatest threat is the callousness to the suffering of men. The most urgent task faced by American education is to destroy the myth that accumulation of wealth and the achievement of comfort are the chief vocations of men. How can adjustment to society be an inspiration to our youth, if that society persists in squandering the material resources of the world on luxuries in a world where more than a billion people go to bed hungry every night?
Abraham Joshua Heschel

Your education has been a failure—no matter how learned you are—if it has failed to open your heart.
Royal Neighbor

One must not only preach a sermon with his voice, he must preach it with his life.
Martin Luther King

If there breathe on earth a slave, if you do not feel the chain, are you not base slaves?
James Russell Lowell

More helpful than all wisdom is one draught of simple human pity.
George Eliot

The racial problem will be solved in America to the degree that every American considers himself personally confronted with it. Whether one lives in the heart of the Deep South or on the periphery of the North, the problem of injustice is his problem; it is his problem because it is America's problem.
Martin Luther King

Sooner or later one has to take sides—if he ever is to remain human.
Graham Greene

The willingness to be involved in those experiences that we encounter both with others and with ourselves, at the moment they occur often determines the degree of the direction our lives take. These two conditions—self-acceptance and the readiness to live—are in direct relationship to our capability to realize the value of life—pleasure. In the final analysis, life is but a short experience and this temporal state with its tragic overtones knows its finest moments as pleasure and enjoyment. And the greatest of these moments is love—which is temporary if not complete departure from pure reason.
Cornelius Beukenkamp

There was a child who had to walk each evening past a haunted house which he feared. His elders sought to give him courage. One gave him good luck charms to ward off the ghosts. Another influenced the city council to erect a street light on the

dreaded corner. Another said earnestly: "It is sinful to be afraid. Trust your God and be brave!" Each one gave to the child, and held himself aloof. But one with charity said: "I know what it is to be afraid. I will walk with you past the house." He did nothing to remove the fear—except to lift it from the child's shoulders and place it on his own.
Robert Hoyer

Those who turn their backs do not see tears.
Paul Boese

One of President Woodrow Wilson's favorite stories was about a group of college professors at a certain university who were in the habit of meeting to consider any acts of misconduct on the part of the students. One afternoon they were talking about some such act by a certain student, and one professor who insisted upon a severe punishment for the lad said, "After all, God has given us eyes."

"Yes," replied one of his colleagues with a kinder nature, "and eyelids!"
Good Reading

The worst sin toward our fellow creatures is not to hate them, but to be indifferent to them: that's the essence of inhumanity.
Henry David Thoreau

It does take courage to care, to fling open your heart and react with sympathy or compassion or indignation or enthusiasm when it is easier —and sometimes safer—not to get involved. But people who take the risk, who deliberately discard the armor of indifference, make a tremendous discovery: *the more things you care about, and the more intensely you care, the more alive you become.*
Anonymous

One of the finest and truest definitions of sympathy is, "Sympathy is your pain in my heart."
Halford E. Luccock

He jests at scars that never felt a wound.
William Shakespeare

Give thy servant an understanding heart...
I Kings 3:9

9
The values in our lives

81 Dealing in ideals

Even on a mass scale, ideals are the very stuff of survival.
John H. Glenn

Ideals are like stars; you will not succeed in touching them with your hands. But like the seafaring man on the desert of waters, you choose them as your guides and, following them, you will reach your destiny.
Carl Schurz

Human progress inevitably depends on enough men defining the values they want to live by and then backing up those standards by wise and appropriate means.
Norman Cousins

It is our attitude toward free thought and free enterprise that will determine our fate. Restriction of free thought and free speech is the most dangerous of all subversions. It is one un-American act that could most easily defeat us.
William O. Douglas

A little before you go to sleep read something that is exquisite and worth remembering, and contemplate upon it till you fall asleep; and when you awake in the morning, call yourself to account for it.
Desiderius Erasmus

A great civilization can go down in ruins if its people are confused in values and fail to develop moral character. So long as there is effort to share the finest fruits of the culture with all the people and so

long as there is effort to develop the rich potentials in all the people, there is hope. This is the basic assumption of democratic society. This is why the schools are the most important institutions in a democratic society. It is their task to bring forth and refine the ore which is the most precious raw material, the children. They are the power plants in which is generated the moral power of the people.
Algernon D. Black

People who have no values have no value.
Burton Hills

The whole of human civilization must begin anew with each new generation. Every value of communal living must be transmitted through its inculcation into the lives of the young. If the young person comes to feel no devotion to the values and norms of his people, he will honor them only when he sees some immediate advantage in doing so. He will become a social deviant, or at best only an expedient adherent to social values. Widespread failure to achieve devoted adherence to values and norms threatens social order and in time leads to the collapse of institutions.
Dale White

Civilized men, everywhere have common ideals. One of the most important tasks of the teacher, as I understand it, is to bring to clear consciousness the common ideals for which men should live. These common ideals have a force that unites. They may prove more lasting than current conflicts; they may prove the agent for resolving or outgrowing some of these conflicts.
U Thant

Great ideas and fine principles do not live from generation to generation just because they are good, nor because they have been carefully legislated. Ideals and principles continue from generation to generation only when they are built into the hearts of children as they grow up.
George Benson

To crush a contrary opinion forcibly and allow it no expression because we dislike it is essentially of the same genus as cracking the skull of an opponent because we disapprove of him. It does not even possess the virtue of success. The man with the cracked skull might collapse and die, but the suppressed opinion or idea has no such sudden end and it survives and prospers the more it is sought to be crushed with force.
Jawaharlal Nehru

Ideals are the most powerful forces known to man. No nation's greatness long survives the lowering of the greatness of its ideals. And, as with nations, so with individuals. Low ideals and high station cannot long retain company. We all must have ideals unless we are content to drift along aimlessly, motionless, ineffectually. Ideals vitalize. Ideals energize.
B. C. Forbes

82 Understanding is essential

We do not admire what we cannot understand.
Marianne Moore

There is an incident in Dostoevski's "The Brothers Karamazov" where Alexi, disturbed at his father's behavior, tells his father that God will judge his deeds. "Yes," replies the father, "But He will also understand me."
Feodor Dostoevski

We shall never wholly understand another living creature, if only because we can't exchange biographies.
Brand Blanshard

Anyone who does not want to become a complete stranger in the world must "give the young people their due and become personally acquainted with a few of them, that he may know what the rest are doing."
Goethe

Seek not to be understood, but to understand.
Stan Finch

A little bush and a lofty pine were growing side by side. The little bush looked up at the lofty pine and said: "See how big I am." The lofty pine looked up into the sky and said: "See how small I am."
Christian W. Kocher

During a recent strike of social workers against their agency, one executive in a rare perceptive moment is quoted as saying: "There is no shortage of brains in this crowd —all we lack is understanding."
Personnel

Understanding is the wealth of wealth.
Arab Proverb

When Alexander Woollcott visited his blind friend, the famous Helen Keller, he never took roses or other flowers. He knew that color meant nothing to the blind woman. Instead, he took great bunches of geranium leaves. They gave out a spicy, fresh fragrance that appealed to her. She could touch them and smell them. Wise people always fit their gifts to the recipients.
Sunshine Magazine

O God, help us not to despise what we do not understand.
William Penn

An old ship carpenter in New England once said, concerning a difficult piece of construction: "I know that can be done." When asked how he knew, he replied: "Don't ask me so many questions: I can't understand all I know."
Robert E. Luccock

A true university is a center of independent thought.
Robert Maynard Hutchins

Some people believe they are thinking when they are only rearranging their prejudices.
Henry James

On seeing the sages of other nations, one should say: "Blessed be God Who hath imparted His wisdom to His creatures."
The Talmud

It was said of a man who regarded himself as very clever, that "He knew just enough to build walls around himself, but not enough to make doors and windows."
Halford E. Luccock

Hasn't it ever struck you as strange that men, who will bravely disregard all danger and sacrifice their lives for their fellow men on the battlefield, will make such little effort to communicate with or live with their fellow men in peace and understanding in their own cities? "To be understood is a pleasure; to reach an agreement is expedient and pleasant; to be understood and reach agreement is deeply gratifying." To be able to communicate with others has many other good results—it guards us against intolerable loneliness, engenders vitality, and gives us hope and courage for the tasks that lie ahead.
Francis J. Braceland

---

83 That which is eternal

In a sermon delivered by Dr. A. H. Boyd of England, he spoke of the rich fool and his three mistakes. He mistook his body for his soul; he mistook man for God; and he mistook time for eternity.
Halford E. Luccock

What is excellent,
As God lives, is permanent:
Hearts are dust, hearts' loves remain;
Heart's love will meet again.
Ralph Waldo Emerson

We do not know what to do with this short life, yet we want another which will be eternal.
Anatole France

This minute, too, is part of eternity.
Duncan Stuart

Religion is the vision of something which stands beyond, behind and within the passing flux of immediate things; something which is real, and yet waiting to be realized; something which is a remote possibility, and yet the greatest of present facts; something that gives meaning to all that passes, and yet eludes apprehension; something whose possession is final good, and yet is beyond all reach; something which is the ultimate ideal, and the hopeless quest.
Alfred North Whitehead

If we work upon marble, it will perish; if we work upon brass, time will efface it; if we rear temples, they will crumble into dust; but if we work upon immortal minds, if we imbue them with principles, with the just fear of God and love of our fellowmen, we engrave on those tables something which will brighten to all eternity.

Daniel Webster

Death rips off all deceptions and self-deceptions. Seen in perspective of that decisive moment, what is any man's life but a record of folly, futility and frustration? For death not only brings all our enterprises to an abrupt end; it reduces them all to nonsense . . . If there is no fulfillment more than human life or history can give, what is life but "a tale told by an idiot, full of sound and fury, signifying nothing?" Everything becomes "questionable" in the face of death. Essential to man can be that which retains its value only in the face of death, while that which does not stand this ultimate test reveals itself in its utter delusiveness.

Will Herberg

It is only by deliberately paying our attention and our primary allegiance to eternity that we can prevent time from turning out lives into a pointless and diabolical foolery.

Aldous Huxley

The tragedy of the times is that we are so obsessed with the temporal that we are ignorant of the eternal. We travel so fast that we never see the scenery.

Vance Havner

Prayer is a crucible in which time is cast in the likeness of the eternal. Man hands over his time to God in the secrecy of single words. When anointed by prayer, his thoughts and deeds do not sink into nothingness, but merge into endless knowledge of an all-embracing God. We yield our thoughts to Him who endowed us with a chain of days for the duration of life.

Abraham Joshua Heschel

I don't care what they say with their mouths—everybody knows that something is eternal. And it ain't houses, and it ain't women, and it ain't earth, and it ain't even stars—everybody knows in their bones that something is eternal, and that something has to do with human beings. All the greatest people who ever lived have been telling us for 5,000 years and yet you'd be surprised how people are always losing hold of it. There's something way down deep that's eternal about every human being.

Thornton Wilder

King Monobaz unlocked his ancestral treasures at a time of famine, and distributed them among the poor. His ministers rebuked him, saying, "Thy fathers amassed, thou dost squander." "Nay," said the benevolent king, "they preserved earthly, but I heavenly, treasures; theirs could be stolen, mine are beyond mortal reach; theirs were barren, mine will bear fruit time without end; they preserved money, I preserved lives. The treasures which my fathers laid by are for this world, mine are for eternity."

The Talmud

84 The measure of a man

The measure of a man is not the number of servants he has but the number of people he serves.
> Construction Digest

Measure me not by the heights to which I have climbed but the depths from which I have come.
> Frederick Douglass

Alexander Hamilton was an illegitimate child, Milton and Homer were blind. Beethoven probably never heard his heroic last symphonies as deafness closed in upon him. Franklin Roosevelt was a four-term President in a wheelchair. Helen Keller's unmatched courage magically overcame the triple handicap of blindness, deafness, and in consequence, inability to speak. The electrical wizard Steinmetz and the great French writer Voltaire overcame twisted bodies to go on to benefit all mankind ... It would be difficult to find a better proof of the Biblical admonition "Judge not according to the appearance."
> Saturday Review

When the other fellow takes a long time, he's slow. But when I take a long time, I'm thorough.
When the other fellow doesn't do it, he's lazy. But when I don't do it, I'm too busy.
When the other fellow does something without being told, he's overstepped his bounds. But when I do it, that's initiative!
When the other fellow takes a stand, he's bullheaded. But when I do it, I'm being firm.
When the other fellow overlooks a rule of etiquette, he's rude. But when I skip a few rules, I'm original.
When the other fellow pleases the boss, he's polishing brass. But when I please the boss, that's cooperation.
When the other fellow gets ahead, he's getting the breaks. But when I manage to get ahead, it's hard work.
> Anonymous

Your brother's sins write in the sand
Where water may erase them.
But carve his virtues in your heart
And let not time efface them!
> James Gallagher

Each man is known by three names, by the name given him by his parents, by the name he is called by others and by the name which is written in the book of his history.
> The Midrash

You can't tell what a man is like or what he is thinking when you are looking at him. You must get around behind him and see what he has been looking at.
> Will Rogers

Inevitably, a man is measured by his largest concerns and by what he regards as the ultimate questions... But if a man places a high value on life, whatever its accent or station; if he respects a mysterious but real connection between himself and the people who have gone before him and those not yet born, then there

are proportions in his measure beyond estimate. In such a man, the gift of awareness has come fully alive. His perceptions are keenest when he looks inward and sees others in himself. He will fix his mind on the things that are more important to him than whether he lives or dies. The ultimate question for him has to do not with his personal immortality but with the immortality of values and meaningful life beyond his own time.
Norman Cousins

When we take man as he is, we make him worse; but when we take man as if he were already what he should be, we promote him to what he can be.
Goethe

In every man there is something that is not of dust or earth or flesh or time, but of God.
George Fox

One cannot always be a hero, but one can always be a man.
Benjamin Franklin

The life of every man is a diary in which he means to write one story, and writes another; and his humblest hour is when he compares the volume as it is with what he vowed to make it. But moments of self-appraisal like these help place one's course of life in better perspective.
James M. Barrie

The mark of the immature man is he wants to die nobly for a cause. The mark of the mature man is he wants to live humbly for one.
William Stekel

No man can give you anything to add an inch to your stature ... If a man is a small potato, he remains so whether he is boiled, mashed or French-fried.
Abba Hillel Silver

---

85 Goals to strive for

He who will not be ruled by the rudder must be ruled by the rocks.
Megiddo Message

Professor Toy of Harvard—pioneer in giving the world modern thoughts on the Bible, was told it would be hopeless: "Why you cannot change people's views about the Bible! You couldn't do it in a lifetime; it would take 500 years."

The next day Professor Toy faced his class and began the lecture in the following manner: "I have been told that it may take 500 years to change the current view about the Bible. I am beginning this morning!"
Source Unknown

Don't be afraid to dream, and when you do, dream big, and one day translate it into deeds to match the dream.
Henrietta Szold

You must have long-range goals to keep you from being frustrated by short-range failures.
Charles C. Noble

Principles are not soft cushions to rest upon.
Willy Brandt

The ultimate goal of educators must be to help man understand how to live in harmony with his environment. This goal will not be met tomorrow, but it must be met by the day after tomorrow—if there is to be one.
Robert Arnold

Paul S. Rees tells of a minister speaking to a group of college students in their fraternity house. He turned to the chairman of the meeting and asked: "What are you living for?" The student answered: "I am going to be a pharmacist." The minister replied: "I understand that this is how you are going to earn your livelihood, but what are you living for?" After thinking about the question for a moment, the young man replied with both honesty and bewilderment: "Sir, I am sorry, but I haven't thought that through." The minister then asked the rest of the group the same question. Only two out of the thirty young men had seriously faced the central issue of existence: the reason for living.
Carroll E. Word

Let a man know what he wants to become. Let him hold on to this ideal, and make it the blueprint that guides his work. This vision, and the will to survive it, will mold the ultimate quality of our lives. It enables every man to grow toward the image of his own dream.
Ben Zion Bokser

Those psychiatrists who are not superficial have come to the conclusion that the vast neurotic misery of the world could be termed a neurosis of emptiness. Men cut themselves off from the root of their being, from God, and then life turns empty, inane, meaningless, without purpose. So when God goes, goal goes. When goal goes, meaning goes. When meaning goes, value goes, and life turns dead on our hands.
Carl Jung

Once we know the thing that we desire to be, the things that we must do will follow of themselves.
Archibald MacLeish

The awful truth is that our wisdom about ends does not match our ingenuity about means, and this situation, if it continues, may be sufficient to destroy us.
Elton Trueblood

The trouble with our age is all signposts and no destination.
Louis Kronenberger

The snow covered the ground, and the three lads were playing. A man came and said to them: "Would you like to try a race and the winner receive a prize?"

The boys agreed, and the man told them that his race would be different. "I will go to the other side of the field," he said, "and when I give you the signal, you will start to run. The one whose footsteps are the straightest in the snow will be the winner."

The race began, and the first boy kept looking at his feet to see if his steps were straight. The second lad kept looking at his companions to see what they were doing. But the third boy just ran on with his eyes steadfastly fixed on the man on the other side of the field.

The third lad was the winner, for his footsteps were straight in the snow. He had kept his eyes firmly on the goal.

Grit

The controlling factor in any man's future is not where he stands, but in what direction he is headed.

The goal toward which we move is that which our secret thoughts have set for us— "as a man thinketh in his heart, so is he."

First a man creates a vision, and then his vision creates him; for every man grows to be like the thing that he loves.

We are today where yesterday's thoughts have brought us, and we shall be tomorrow where today's thoughts carry us.

Elmer G. Leterman

Our educational process must provide for discovery and even rediscovery. It must permit the learner to be actively involved. He must be allowed the privilege of getting his hands dirty and his feet wet.

Richard Myshak

86 Life is worth living

Believe that life is worth living and your belief will help create the fact.
William James

The good life is a process not a state of being.
Carl F. Rogers

Time is perpetual presence, perpetual novelty. Every moment is a new arrival, a new bestowal. Just to be is a blessing, just to live is holy. The moment is the marvel; it is in evading the marvel of the moment that boredom begins which ends in despair.
Abraham Joshua Heschel

There is more to life than increasing its speed.
Mohandas Gandhi

Believe, when you are most unhappy, that there is something for you to do in the world. So long as you can sweeten another's pain, life is not in vain.
Helen Keller

I remember my science teacher in junior high school explaining that the life of organisms, and of man as well, was in the final analysis nothing but a process of oxidation, of combustion. I suddenly sprang to my feet and passionately threw at him the question: "If that's so, what kind of meaning does life have?" I had grasped the truth that man exists on a different plane from, say, a candle that stands on the table and burns down until it sputters out. Every life, in every situation, retains a meaning. The so-called life not worth living does not exist.

Viktor E. Frankl

Whether 60 or 16, there is in every human being's heart that lure of wonder, the sweet amazement at the stars, and at starlike things and thoughts; the undaunted challenge of events, the unfailing, childlike appetite for what next, and the joy of living.

Cheer

However good life may appear and our hopes for that life, it is also true that all of us have moments when we are overwhelmed by life. We soon discover that gratitude is not enough. Life is a most exacting and responsible gift. It must be lived somehow from day to day on the high road or the low road. It must be shared with our fathers before us and our children who come after us.

Lawrence Svane

One must learn to love life. I am well content to tell you that I cannot admire you at leisure, and hold you in high esteem as I would wish, until I perceive in you the most beautiful of all forms of courage, the courage to be happy.

Joseph Joubert

A seeker after truth once said to Pascal, "If I had your creed, I could live your life;" only to be greeted with the swift rejoinder, "If you lived my life, you would have my creed."

Robert Menzies

Each life converges to some center
Expressed or still;
Exists in every human nature
A goal . . .

Emily Dickinson

Life is not physical things. Life itself keeps life going—if you use your car a lot, the car wears out and your legs get weak, but if you walk a lot, your legs get strong. The non-living wears itself out by work; but the living builds itself up. That's one of the great differences between life and non-life.

Albert Szent-Gyorgyi

There is no cure for birth or death save to enjoy the interval.

George Santayana

When death comes to me it will find me busy, unless I am asleep. If I thought I was going to die tomorrow, I should nevertheless plant a tree today.

Stephen Girard

The first requisite for happiness in later years is a philosophy of life— an outlook comprehensive enough to include every aspect of life in its fullness.

H. Spencer Lewis

87 A standard is something to stand by

By living up to our highest ethical standard, we ourselves are, to a great degree, protected from the unethical practices of others.
Albert Reissner

Bad men hate sin through fear of punishment; good men hate sin through their love of virtue.
Megiddo Message

If idolaters order a community, "Surrender one among you that we may slay him, and if not we shall slay you all"—let them all submit to death, but they must not surrender one among them to be murdered.
Maimonides

It is easier to fight for one's principles than to live up to them.
Alfred Adler

In Germany they first came for the Communists, and I didn't speak because I wasn't a Communist. Then they came for the Jews, and I didn't speak up because I wasn't a Jew. Then they came for the trade unionists and I didn't speak up because I wasn't a trade unionist. Then they came for the Catholics and I didn't speak up because I was a Protestant. Then they came for me—and by that time no one was left to speak up.
Martin Niemoller

The word used for "worship" is one that means to crouch, to kiss, to do homage, to prostrate oneself, to reverence . . . One is reminded of the little fellow who kept standing up on the pew disturbing people during a church service. Finally his mother set him down very firmly and told him to remain seated. After a time of silence, the little fellow leaned over to his mother and said, "Mother, I am standing up inside." Too many of us talk about dedication who are standing up inside. Our spirits are not prostrate.
Ernest G. Malyon

Any man will command respect if he takes a stand and backs it up with his life.
Bobby Richardson

Our high standard of living could be causing our low standard of morals.
Clayton "Spokesman"

If our standards are low and people get so absorbed in the material side of life, then it is the beginning of the end . . . It wasn't the barbarians that destroyed Rome, it was the decline in the character of the Roman people. And we may, too. I hope not. But it's the character and standards of our people—that's what is important.
Robert E. Wood

"Can you fight?" Dr. Charles W. Eliot, president of Harvard University, once asked a young professor who had gone to him with a disconcerting problem.

"Why, yes," the man replied; "that is, I think I can."

"Can you fight when you are in the minority?"

"I have done so occasionally."

"Can you fight when everybody is against you—when not one man is ready to lend you support?"

"I am ready to try it if necessary."

"Then you need have no fear; but if you have convictions, it will sometimes be necessary to do no less."

Rollo Walter Brown

When lately I stood with a friend before the Cathedral of Amiens, he asked me how it happens that we can no longer build such piles. I replied: men in those days had convictions; we moderns have opinions.

Heinrich Heine

My own feeling as a dean is that we ought ... to make the students more aware of where we stand on moral questions, not by imposing rules but by speaking out ourselves; not by laying down the law but by clearly stating our opinions. As mature adults we ought to make it plainer that we do not consider one kind of behavior just as good as another. I believe today's students want to hear us say where we stand—if only so that they can disagree or object. We ought to give them something firm to object to, and not put them in the frustrating position of having to kick against a cloud.

J. Merrill Knapp

If a man does not know what port he is steering for, no wind is favorable to him.

Lucius Annaeus Seneca

Give us clear vision that we may know where to stand and what to stand for—because unless we stand for something, we shall fall for anything.

Megiddo Message

88 Good for something

The pleasure of doing good is the only one that will not wear out.

Oriental Proverb

If a fellow does a good deed because he thinks he is going to be thanked, he will soon grow weary of doing good deeds. For one of the most unlovely aspects of human nature is a tendency to accept favors without proper appreciation. The benefactors of mankind have seldom been rewarded by a grateful people. More often, they have been neglected and quickly forgotten. Sometimes good men have grown bitter because of such experiences and it is certainly easy to fall into the pit of self-pity when you have given without appreciation.

Gerald Kennedy

In a democracy such as ours and in the complex society in which we live, every citizen, in keeping with his time and talent, is called upon to do something for the wider social good.

Joseph L. Lennon

We refuse to recognize the greatness in ourselves. We pervert every good gift and call it evil. God gives us sex and we call it lust. He gives us aggression and we call it hate. He gives us curiosity and we call it arrogance. Seeing the good as evil makes us use it as evil—and ultimately deprives us of its use.
Noel Mailloux

That which is striking and beautiful is not always good; but that which is good is always beautiful.
Ninon De L'enclos

I live for those who love me,
Whose hearts are kind and true;
For the heaven that smiles above me
And awaits my spirit too;
For all human ties that bind me,
For the task by God assigned me
For the hopes not left behind me
And the good that I can do.
George Linnaeus Banks

He that does good to another does good also to himself, not only in the consequence, but in the very act. For the consciousness of well-doing is in itself ample reward.
Lucius Annaeus Seneca

Put an end once and for all to this discussion of what a good man should be, and be one.
Marcus Aurelius

My own definition of good and evil would be: Good is all that serves life and enhances life, and evil is all that strangles life and tries to corrupt it or to kill it.
Erich Fromm

It is better wholeheartedly to do one man good than to sacrifice oneself for humanity.
Dag Hammarskjold

The word "good" is ambiguous. For example, if a man were to shoot his grandmother at a range of five hundred yards I should call him a good shot, but not necessarily a good man.
G. K. Chesterton

To try too hard to make people good is one way to make them worse; the only way to make them good is to be good.
George MacDonald

Crime is news; good behavior, the absence of crime, is not news. So the papers report the crime, the evil, the abnormal; and they suppress the good behavior, the law-abiding, the normal conduct of the vast majority. . . . This strange definition of news, this eschewing of the good and building up of evil and wrong (which we demand in our papers) takes its toll across the world and in every area of our civilization. One of the world's leaders was talking recently with a journalist friend about the news space given failures in some efforts to help developing nations and the sparse attention given the successes achieved by thousands every day.
Source Unknown

I prefer being pious to being clever, but I prefer being good to being clever or pious.
Pinchas of Koretz

89 The importance of giving while living

You give but little when you give of your possessions. It is when you give of yourself that you truly give.
Kahlil Gibran

Not as ladder from earth to Heaven
Not as a witness to any creed
But simple service simply given
To our own kind in need.
Rudyard Kipling

It is not the shilling I give you that counts, but the warmth that it carries with it from my hand.
Miguel de Unamuno

To my grandfather, giving was as simple as taking a walk. Once he came home without his overcoat. "Where's your coat?" my grandmother asked. "Coat? What coat?" — "The coat you wore when you left the house."—"Oh, that. I gave it away."—"To whom?"—"To a man who didn't have a coat."
Anonymous

Gladly we serve
Because we gladly love.
To love or not
As is our will
By this we live and die.
Dutch Poet

The measure of a life, after all, is not its duration, but its devotion.
George Marshall

Give of yourself, give as much as you can! And you can always, always give something, even it if is only kindness! If everyone were to do this and not be as mean with a kindly word then there would be much more justice and love in the world. Give and you shall receive, much more than you would have ever thought possible. Give, give again and again, don't lose courage, keep it up and go on giving! No one has ever become poor from giving!
Anne Frank

God has given us two hands—one to receive with and the other to give with.
Billy Graham

All that we can hold in our dead hands is what we have given away.
Sanskrit Proverb

It never was loving that emptied the heart, nor giving that emptied the purse.
Proverb

You have heard people say, "If I were rich I should like to do something for people." Perhaps you've said it yourself. Well, you are richer right now than you know. You have it in your power to give things that are worth more than all the money you would like to have. Ink is inexpensive and time used in writing a worthwhile letter can be put to no better use.
Source Unknown

Rings and jewels are not gifts, but apologies for gifts. The only gift is a portion of thyself. Therefore the poet brings his poem; the shepherd, his lamb; the farmer, corn; the miner, a gem; the sailor, coral and

shells; the painter, his picture; the girl, a handkerchief of her own sewing.
Ralph Waldo Emerson

When a friend of Alexander the Great had asked of him ten talents, he gave him fifty. When told that ten was sufficient, he said, "True, ten are sufficient for you to take, but not for me to give."
Source Unknown

We should give as we would receive, cheerfully, quickly, and without hesitation; for there is no grace in a benefit that sticks to the fingers.
Lucius Annaeus Seneca

He who gives when he is asked has waited too long.
William Blake

Give all thou canst; high Heaven rejects the lore Of nicely-calculated less or more.
William Wordsworth

Behold, I do not give lectures, or a little charity. When I give, I give myself.
Walt Whitman

What you give for the cause of charity in health is gold; what you give in sickness is silver; what you give after death is lead.
Proverb

The world is full of two kinds of people: The givers and the takers.
 The takers eat well—but the givers sleep well.
Modern Maturity

---

90 Growing and glowing

The road to success is always under construction.
Grit

A small boy on his first day in kindergarten walked all around the room looking at everything; the low table and chairs, the little cupboards, the small coathangers, and the lavatory within his easy reach. Everything was just the right size for 5-year-olds. Then he walked up to the teacher to declare: "I don't like it here. There's nothing to grow up to."
Wesleyan Methodist

As the sun creates your shadow, God creates your soul—but in each case it is you who determine the shape of it.
The Country Parson

Become what you are.
Pindar

Many years ago a man was afflicted with a bad back. Every time he lay on it, he felt pain. He was troubled, too, by an obstruction in his nose which would close when he lay on his back. Yet he spent many months on his back and produced on the

ceiling of the Sistine Chapel in Rome some of the world's greatest paintings. His name, of course, was Michelangelo. Another man, although his birthplace was a British castle, was born with a palate so defective he lisped. Yet his oratory moved mankind during some of the great crises of history. His name was Winston Churchill.
Norman Vincent Peale

There is power within every man which he himself does not know exists. No one ever uses his total abilities or capacities. That is why so many who reach go far beyond the goal set and must reset the goal time and time again. The greatest problem of society at all times is to keep men reaching.
Ralph E. Lyne

Growth is life . . . Not knowledge, but the capacity to acquire knowledge is power.
Henrietta Szold

Sooner or later you young folks will discover that the more you grow up, the less you blow up.
Burton Hillis

There's not a man that lives who hath not known his godlike hours.
William Wordsworth

Come now, be content.
I will come back again to you, I swear I will,
And you will know me still.
I shall be only a little taller
Than when I went.
Edna St. Vincent Millay

He who is silent is forgotten; he who does not advance falls back; he who stops is distanced; he who ceases to grow greater becomes smaller; he who leaves off gives up.
Henri Frederic Amiel

There is a story of Napoleon stretching to reach a book on a high shelf. An adjutant said: "Let me get it for you. I'm bigger than you." Napoleon replied, "You are taller than I am, not bigger."
Source Unknown

When you reach for the stars you may not quite get one, but you won't come up with a handful of mud either.
Leo Burnett

Nothing affects attitudes toward the future more powerfully than what might be termed self-images of growth. The society, organization or individual that sees itself as young and growing will look eagerly to the future. In our early days as a nation, self-images of growth were particularly vivid and affected our whole national temper. In the development of the West one can readily trace the effect of such self-images in generating optimism and receptivity to change.
Alexis de Tocqueville

Somebody once asked Archie Moore, the ageless prize-fighter, how he overcame the juvenile delinquency that plagued him as a child.
"Simple," said Archie. "I grew up."
Source Unknown

10
The better part of wisdom

91 The use of judgment

Meditation is not merely a halt to frantic activity, but is actually one of the most positive stimulators of stability and spiritual integrity available to us. It can be a timely end to past blunders and foolishness, and the gateway to wiser, more enlightened moves.

Miles Eisele

If the rule of reason brings you to the position that happens to be the liberal position, it is the one you have to take—but not just because it is liberal.

John F. Kennedy

The following qualities are criteria of emotional maturity: The ability to deal constructively with reality; the capacity to adapt to change; relative freedom from symptoms produced by tensions and anxieties; the capacity to find more satisfaction in giving than receiving; the capacity to relate to others in a consistent manner with mutual satisfaction and helpfulness; the capacity to sublimate; the capacity to love.

William C. Menninger

A Quaker's advice to his son on his wedding day: "When thee went a-courting I told thee to keep thy eyes open; now that thou art married, I tell thee to keep them half shut."

Chester Duncan

There had never been any argument about it: Julius was the wisest and shrewdest man in town. One day a youth of the community questioned him on the subject.

"Julius," he said, "to what would you attribute the fact that you know so much?"

"Good judgment," replied Julius readily. "I'd say it was my good judgment."

"And where did you get your good judgment?"

"That I got from experience."

"Where did you get your experience?"

"From my bad judgment."
Abner Biberman

Do not judge a man until you have walked in his moccasins seven days.
Indian Prayer

What the colleges—teaching humanities by examples which may be special, but which must be typical and pregnant—should at least try to give us is a general sense of what, under various disguises, superiority has always signified and may still signify. The feeling for a good human job anywhere, the admiration of the really admirable, the disesteem of what is cheap and trashy and impermanent—this is what we call the critical sense, the sense for ideal values. It is the better part of what men know as wisdom.
William James

During our entire lives we undergo the judgment of others. But the one judgment that really counts is the one we make of ourselves. It is far from a once-in-a-lifetime judgment. We make it every day. The conclusions we reach about ourselves are usually conceded inside us. Thus, our potential is like an iceberg. Part of it can clearly be seen and measured, but most of it is below the surface. Only you know what is underneath.
Howard R. Dressner

We cannot evade the necessity and the responsibility for using the mind to make judgments. It is not a matter of choice. "Life is fired at us point-blank" as Ortega said, and there is really, literally, no place to hide. I was discussing these matters with a young man recently and he said, "I don't mind making judgments that involve myself alone but I object to making judgments that affect the lives of other people." I sympathized with his position but had to tell him that his reluctance would make it impossible for him to be a second grade teacher, a corporation president, a husband, a politician, a parent, a traffic policeman, a weather man, a chef, a doctor, or a horse race handicapper—in fact it would force him to live a hermit's life.
Author Unknown

Wisdom is knowledge that has been cured in the brine of tears.
Richard Armour

Though a man may become learned by another's learning, he can never be wise but by his own wisdom.
Montaigne

A wise old Scotsman, who was a judge, was once asked to settle a dispute between two brothers about the fair division of a large estate left them by their father. The Scotsman's decision is classic:

"Let one brother divide the estate, and let the other brother have first choice."
Humor Variety

Man learns little from victory, but much from defeat.
Anonymous

A man who had been the pilot of a boat on the Mississippi River for thirty-five years was asked, "I suppose you know where all the rocks and sand banks are?" The pilot replied, "No, but I know where the deep water is."
Ilion T. Jones

The well disciplined adult is never absolutely free to make decisions. But he has learned to make most of his decisions wisely.
Frank Howard Richardson

92 Knowledge is basic

Knowledge is the beginning of tolerance and tolerance the beginning of understanding.
John Wesley Coulter

Not ignorance, but the ignorance of ignorance is the death of knowledge.
Alfred North Whitehead

More important than the three R's are the three "knows." The three "knows" are: "know your world, know your craft and know yourself."
Max Lerner

Our major need today is not for more knowledge as to how to fly through the stratosphere, but more understanding of how to walk upright on the face of the earth.
Julius Mark

Knowledge is a torch of smoky pine that lights the pathway but one step ahead, across a void of mystery and dread.
George Santayana

The great scientific discoveries of the past hundred years have been as child's play compared with the titanic forces that will be released when man applies himself to the understanding and mastery of his own nature.
Melvin J. Evans

Nobody can give you wiser advice than yourself.
Marcus Tullius Cicero

There are people who seem to believe that youth can do no wrong —perhaps because they hope thereby to recapture their own youth. Foolish parents coddle their darling young rebels in a vain hope to keep them from flying the nest. In my experience, there is nothing intrinsically wise about age. There is nothing intrinsically virtuous about the young. What is *more* important than youth or age is intelligence—intelligence tested by experience.
Sidney Hook

Tertullians' aphorism, *credo quia absurdum*, "I believe because it is absurd," is far better replaced by the utterance of Anselm, *credo ut intelligam*, "I believe in order that I may understand." Belief must nurture understanding, as surely as understanding must ultimately flower into belief.
Anonymous

Dialogue opens up that which is not accessible by any other route.
Martin Buber

Most of today's women I meet have nothing to complain about, nothing to fight about in their own lives. Now, they must accept more responsibility in the area of world problems. There is nothing women can't do if they want. We need the minds especially of the brilliant women. Nature does not dole brains out by sex. The world's problems are too stupendous for only one-half of the population to shoulder them.
Pearl S. Buck

He who knows is clever, but he who knows himself is enlightened.
Lao Tse

There was once a man who wanted to embrace the globe, but his arms were too short.
Malay Proverb

Try to offer your services only where they will be welcome. Do not be like the overly enthusiastic Boy Scout who, when asked why he was late for Scout meeting, explained, "I was helping an old lady across the street." "Fine," the scout master said commendingly, "but why did it take you so long?" "She didn't want to go," answered the scout.
Edna Kaehele

There is no king who has not had a slave among his ancestors, and no slave who has not had a king among his.
Helen Keller

There are two contrasting views about education: Hellenistic—for the purpose of knowledge, and Hebraic—for the purpose of living. It is certainly not right that knowledge is just for knowledge's sake. There is a great danger that knowledge is the sole aim of education. Knowledge can be of great use to raise the standard of living, but it can also be used to annihilate mankind.
Timothy Y. H. Chow

Until man comes to know himself, all other knowledge that he gains is incomplete.
Edmund W. Sinnott

A student once asked:
"Is there anything I can do to learn the art of conversation?"
"Yes, there is one thing. If you will listen, I will tell you."
For several moments, there was silence. Then the student said: "I'm listening, professor."
"You see! You are learning already."
Professor Charles T. Copeland

93 The very best

There are loyal hearts, there are spirits brave,
There are souls that are pure and true;
Then give to the world the best you have,
And the best will come back to you.

Give love, and love to your life will flow,
A strength in your utmost need;
Have faith, and a score of hearts will show
Their faith in your word and deed.

Give truth, and your gift will be paid in kind,
And honor will honor meet;
And a smile that is sweet will surely find
A smile that is just as sweet.

Give sorrow and pity to those who mourn;
You will gather in flowers again
The scattered seeds of your thought outborne,
Though the sowing seemed but vain.

For life is the mirror of king and slave—
'Tis just what we are and do;
Then give to the world the best you have
And the best will come back to you.
                    Madeline Bridges

Life does not require us to make good; it asks only that we give our best at each new level of experience.
                    Harold W. Ruopp

After a spill at a hunting meet, the nouveau riche matron was rushed to a hospital. The doctor told her, "I think I'm going to give you a local anesthetic."

"Nothing doing," the injured woman wailed. "We can afford the best. Give me some imported!"
                    Anonymous

The future belongs to those who see and trust the best things in the worst times.
                    Harold Blake Walker

We cannot have excellence if everyone is expected to think as everyone else does, and never to challenge anyone or anything. Especially is this true if we place such strictures upon our youth, since if they accept every idea with docility during their formative years, they will be sheeplike as adults. Show me the university, or, indeed, the community where no unpopular idea can find opportunity for utterance, where the status quo can never be challenged, and I will show you a place of sterility and inaction, of self-satisfaction bordering on the reactionary. Show me the organization where everyone must conform in order to advance or even survive, and I will show you a place where excellence in its true meaning has been sublimated to a condition of mediocrity.
                    Samuel B. Gould

The other day I flew over the Okefenokee Swamp. We were down low and I could see an ugly green film over the water. It looked dirty and unclean—a breeding place for health-destroying creatures. At one time the water in that swamp was sweet and pure, coming from clear springs high in the mountains. But in that low place it had stopped, and having stopped it had stagnated.

So in life. If you stop when you hit low places, your life begins to stagnate.

Charles L. Allen

What the members of any culture will contribute to life in the year 2000 will depend not on their physical characteristics as a group, but on what they have learned and are learning about every subject in the total human curriculum that infants and children and grown men and women must learn if they are to be fully human: How to trust, how to learn, how to relate to other living things and the inanimate world, how to dream beyond the present, how to cherish the best of the past while constructing a future that transcends the present.

Margaret Mead

Good taste develops slowly but surely, through listening to and living with the best continually.

Esther Knefelkamp

The great man is the one who shows others some new dimension of life or takes them further along the dimensions they already know. The scientist who enlarges our notions of the physical world; the artist who discloses to us some new dimension of beauty; the reformer who introduces into society some new dimension of justice or humanity; the saint who reveals to us more of life's spiritual dimensions. If you needed a test of greatness, surely this would serve.

W. Donald Hudson

Being educated means to prefer the best not only to the worst but to the second best.

William Lyon Phelps

If you pay in peanuts you must expect to get a monkey.

Leslie Coulthard

High individual performance will depend to some extent on the capacity of the society or institutions to evoke it. And woe to the society that loses its gift for such evocation! When an institution, organization, or nation loses its capacity to evoke high individual performance, its great days are over.

John W. Gardner

Culture is to know the best that has been said and thought in the world.

Matthew Arnold

There is practically no job in the world that a good education can't help you to do better. And more important, a good education helps you to live better. I'm not just talking about better jobs and better salaries. I'm talking about living with yourself. A liberal education broadens your perspective, enriches your personality and gives you a truer sense of values. It opens up new worlds of interest and enjoyment. It can even teach you to relax!

Abigail Van Buren

94 Together and alone

If I am not for me, who will be?
But if I am concerned only with myself, what am I?
And if not now, when?
Hillel

All children have an innate need of a place for solitary reflection. Every one of us can remember such a spot—an attic, a corner, a grape-arbor, a hay-mow, a fencerow, or a willow tree whose drooping branches walled in a room without windows. These were our private retreats where oldsters did not penetrate, and where there was quiet enough for dreams to sprout and grow. Each escape spot was a haven where we could retire to lick our imagined or real wounds after a lost bout in the adult world. In those early years we did not realize that even grown-ups often can't find a sense of reason in their world; that they, also, need a place to sit down and sort out their problems and confusions.
Helen Virden

Nothing can be accomplished without solitude. I have made a kind of solitude for myself which nobody is aware of. Today it's very difficult to be alone because we have watches. Have you ever seen a saint wearing a watch?
Pablo Picasso

The focus of prayer is not the self. A man may spend hours meditating about himself, or be stirred by the deepest sympathy for his fellow man, and no prayer will come to pass. Prayer comes to pass in a complete turning of the heart toward God, toward His goodness and power. It is the momentary disregard of our personal concerns, the absence of the self-centered thoughts which constitute the art of prayer. Feeling becomes prayer in the moment in which we forget ourselves and become aware of God.
Abraham Joshua Heschel

To be rooted is perhaps the most important and least recognized need of the human soul. It is one of the hardest to define. A human being has roots by virtue of his real, active and natural participation in the life of a community, which preserves in living shape certain particular treasures of the past and certain particular expectations for the future. This participation is a natural one, in the sense that it is automatically brought about by place, conditions of birth, profession and social surroundings. Every human being needs to have multiple roots. It is necessary for him to draw well-nigh the whole of his moral, intellectual and spiritual life by way of the environment of which he forms a natural part.
Simone Weil

Everyone, male and female, regardless of age, has one desire second only to the desire to survive. It is to be wanted.
Percy M. Hansen

A committee is a group that keeps minutes and loses hours.
Milton Berle

The most wonderful of all things in life, I believe, is the discovery of another human being with whom one's relationship has a glowing depth, beauty, and joy as the years increase. This inner progressiveness of love between two human beings is a most marvelous thing; it cannot be found by looking for it or by passionately wishing it. It is a sort of Divine accident.

Hugh Walpole

Most of our suspicions of others are aroused by what we know of ourselves.

Anonymous

Loneliness is a universal experience and it comes to all of us. We all need something in the bank for these times. Specialists in aging tell us that an interest other than one's self that can be pursued throughout life, wherever one is, is one of the greatest protections against unhappiness in old age.

Anthony Del Vecchio

In her first appearance as Queen of The Netherlands, Wilhelmina Helena Pauline Maria stood on the balcony of her palace in Amsterdam and stared with a small child's wonder at her cheering subjects. "Mama," she asked, "do all these people belong to me?" "No, my child," replied the Queen-Regent, "it is you who belong to all these people."

Time Magazine

---

95 The eyes of the wise

Wisdom grows when knowledge is lived.

Sidney B. Simon

The wise man reads both books and life itself.

Lin Yutang

Knowledge without wisdom breeds arrogance; intellect without character breeds danger.

Samuel B. Gould

Wisdom consists of the capacity to confront disturbing ideas, even intolerable ideas, with equanimity.

Leo Rosten

The universe is full of ideas, but we need wisdom to make the right selection.

C. R. Cantrell

"Lover of wisdom" is the basic meaning of the term "philosopher." Its earliest usage was wide enough to include those lines of inquiry which in their developed state today are covered by the term "science;" but there has always been implied by it something beyond scientific truth. For philosophy is the sustained attempt to discover the fundamental character of the universe.

John Pitts

The price of wisdom is eternal thought.
Frank Birch

Patient: "Doctor, I'd like something to make me smarter."
Doctor: "Take these pills and come back to see me next week."
Patient [*next week*]: "Doc, I don't think I'm any smarter."
Doctor: "Take these pills and come back to see me next week."
Patient [*next week*]: "Doc, I don't think I've gotten any smarter yet. Are you sure these pills aren't candy?"
Doctor: "Now you're getting smarter."
Deryl Martin

Wisdom is the salvation attained by the righteous man.
Levi ben Gershon

Real wisdom is more than knowledge. Knowing is the accumulation of facts: wisdom is the interpretation of facts. Knowledge is culled from textbooks; wisdom comes out of life.
Wallace Fridy

"Integrity and wisdom—these are the keys to business success," the old man was telling his son. "By integrity," he went on, "I mean that when you promise the delivery of goods on a certain day, you must do so even if it bankrupts you."
"Well," said the son, "what is wisdom?"
"Don't make such promises."
Jobber Topics

We learn wisdom from failure much more than from success. We often discover what will do, by finding out what will not do; and probably he who never made a mistake never made a discovery.
Samuel Smiles

The more science we have, the more we are in need of wisdom to prevent its misuse. The imminent tragedy of the contemporary world is written in the fact that positivistic modern culture has magnified science and almost completely emancipated itself from wisdom.
Mortimer J. Adler

The imprudent man reflects on what he has said; the wise man, on what he is going to say.
Anonymous

Knowledge comes by taking things apart—analysis. But wisdom comes by putting things together.
Source Unknown

Wisdom begins with sacrifice of immediate pleasures for long-range purposes.
Louis Finkelstein

Wisdom denotes the pursuing of the best ends by the best means.
Francis Hutcheson

Science is wisdom; conscience is a greater wisdom; if there should come a time when these two should be divorced from each other, then hell would be let loose on earth.
Francois Rabelais

96 Caution: mind at work

Praise must be treated like perfume. It must be sniffed lightly for a little of it goes a long way.
Adlai E. Stevenson

Folks think they grow old by living; but they grow old rather by not living.
Ivan Panin

The old carpenter said it this way: "Best rule I know for talkin' is the same as the one for carpenterin': Measure twice and then saw once."
Catholic Quote

There was a man one time who was lost and asked a man by the side of the road how far it was to the city he sought. The man replied: "If you keep on going the way you are going, it is about 25,000 miles. But, if you turn back and go this way, it is only about three miles."
Gerald Kennedy

A stubborn man doesn't hold opinions. They hold him.
Grit

A little girl was trying to move a table which was in her way. Her mother called, "Mary, you can't move that table, it is as big as you are." And the little girl replied, "Yes, I can move it, for I am as big as it is."
Frederick W. Helfer

It has been said that an argument thrives on opposition and dies without it. We would all gain tremendous advantages if we could hold our arguments down to a simple discussion with modulated voices.
Paul P. Parker

God gives every bird its food, but does not throw it into the nest.
J. G. Holland

Zest is the first gift of the Immortals to man.
Anonymous

Human culture is like a fabulous tree in which each branch is formed differently, each fruit has its own special sweetness, but the branches are all shoots of the same trunk.
Kay Birket-Smith

Many years ago a student challenged President Francis Wayland of Brown University who had spoken of the great wisdom of the Proverbs. Scoffed the student: "I don't think there is anything very remarkable in the Proverbs. They are rather commonplace remarks from common people."
"Very well," said Dr. Wayland, "make one." The student beat an embarrassed retreat.
Robert E. Luccock

It is the most delightful of houses. It has fourteen doors, all opening outwards.
William James

Every man is created twice: Once when he is born; second when he repents and takes on new courage to live in ways more acceptable to God.
Hasidic Lore

The reward for a thing well done is to have done it.
Ralph Waldo Emerson

Shedding a prejudice is an agonizing experience. An illogical hatred nourished for hundreds of years for whatever reason—religious, economic or political—finally becomes a mass mental disease. The white people of this country are predominantly favorable to the Negro's demands for equality, yet many cannot shed their prejudice. When they say, "The Negro is not ready yet," what they mean is, "I am not ready yet."
Sam Levenson

Strength is an asset only when it is blended with wisdom.
Don Jennings

---

97 The practical approach

When asked to name the single book he would most like to have if marooned on a desert island, one wag eschewed the classics and suggested "A Guide to Edible Fungi."
Journal of American Insurance

There is no way to get experience except through experience.
Leo Burnett

I have often said to young parents "Don't take struggle out of your children's lives." The instinct of fathers and mothers is to do just that—to make "life easier for my boy than it was for me." It is interesting to note that youth is sounder in this matter than age. Youth revels in competitive sports, whether to do something better than his fellows, or to beat some previous record.
Samuel B. Pettengill

For weeks the couple had gone from showroom to showroom as the husband scrutinized new autos. Even after inspecting all carefully, he couldn't make up his mind.

"My, how you've changed," his wife chided him. "You married me three weeks after you saw me."

"Listen," he replied impatiently. "buying a car is serious business!"
Capper's Weekly

Horace Greeley once received a letter from a woman stating that her church was in distressing financial straits. The congregation had tried oyster suppers, grab-bags, box socials, everything. "Would Mr. Greeley be so kind as to suggest some new advice to keep the struggling church from disbanding?"

The editor replied: "Try religion."
Source Unknown

The way to say it simply is to simply say it.
Howard W. Newton

A woman stalled her car at a traffic light. She tried desperately to start the engine, while behind her an impatient man rudely honked his horn. Finally, the woman got out and walked back to the honker.

"I'm sorry," she said to the man, "but I can't start my car. If you'll start it for me, I'll stay here and honk your horn for you."

Source Unknown

All beginnings are difficult.

The Talmud

Money and time are the heaviest burdens of life, and the unhappiest of all mortals are those who have more of either than they know how to use.

Samuel Johnson

A farmer's corn was destroyed by the cranes that fed in his field. Annoyed, the farmer set a net to ensnare the birds. When he visited the snare he discovered a beautiful stork caught with the cranes. "Spare me," pleaded the stork. "I am innocent, indeed I am. I never touched any of your belongings."

"You may be telling the truth," answered the farmer, "but you are in the company of the cranes, and I judge you accordingly."

Folk Fable

There is only one way to defy Time; and that is to have young ideas, which may always be trusted to find youthful and vivid expression.

George Bernard Shaw

They who do not read can have nothing to think, and little to say.

Ben Jonson

Words are astonishingly like people. They have character, they almost have personalities . . . They shift, as people do, their conduct with their company.

Ivor A. Richards

---

98 The heart of the matter

Calisthenics can build up the body. Courses of study can train the mind. But the real champion is the person whose heart can be educated.

Fred Russell

A sage of old asked five of his disciples: "Which is the way to be cherished as good?" One answered: "Freedom from envy." Another answered: "A good friend." Another: "A good neighbor." Another: "Foresight." The last replied: "A good heart." "That last answer," said the teacher, "has my preference. It includes all the others."

The Talmud

A very young man was learning to perform on the flying trapeze. A veteran performer turned to him and said, "Throw your heart over the bars and your body will follow."

Source Unknown

The secret of the good life is the condition of a person's heart. For one to make people think he is a kindly, compassionate person when, actually, he hates people except for what they can mean to him personally, is to live a lie. A wise man long ago proclaimed a great truth when he said, "Out of the heart come the issues of life."
Erwin L. McDonald

The heart has its reasons which reason cannot know.
Blaise Pascal

Every man has a heart, but every man has not the same sort of heart. Some are empty-hearted, some are half-hearted, some are double-hearted and some are whole-hearted.
George E. Failing

The heart goes where no footstep may,
Into the promised land.
Source Unknown

If a man is to strive with all his heart, the significance of his striving must be unmistakable. The significance of the ashes of the village must be as telling as the significance of the village itself.
Antoine de Saint-Exupery

'Til the relief arrives and the guard changes
Be as a tower, that firmly set,
Shakes not its top for any blast that blows.
Dante

It is better in prayer to have a heart without words than words without a heart.
Mohandas Gandhi

Ah, how skillful grows the hand
That obeyeth Love's command!
It is the heart, and not the brain,
That to the highest doth attain,
And he who followeth Love's behest
Far excelleth all the rest!
Henry Wadsworth Longfellow

You cannot kindle a fire in any other heart until it is burning within your own.
Anonymous

Discouragements and obstacles can be used to strengthen character as dams make it possible for rivers to generate electricity: they impede the flow but they increase the power. Defeats are inescapable; failures are as certain as the sparks fly upward. By the side of every mountain is a valley, and by the side of every oasis is a desert.
Marion de Velder

Success comes only by carving through a mountain with your fingernails.
Author Unknown

People who have nothing in their insides—in their souls—they are poor. But a man or a woman who has a conviction that something is beautiful, something is profound... it helps him to overcome his grief in very sad hours.
Wanda Landowska

99 Whistle while you work

God gives us the ingredients for our daily bread, but He expects us to do the baking.
Anonymous

Thank God every morning when you get up that you have something to do that day which must be done, whether you like it or not. Being forced to work, and forced to do your best, will breed in you temperance and self-control, diligence and strength of will, cheerfulness and content, and a hundred virtues which the idle never know.
Charles Kingsley

Hard work is a virtue, but we should never work so hard and be so dedicated to our career that we endanger the greatest gift of all which is life itself.
Robert Peterson

Progress in any area . . . is nine-tenths drudgery. Great music is the final result of inspiration followed by patient rewriting and trying again. Great art is the consequence of vision plus persistent and unremitting toil. Charles Darwin was twenty years wrestling with the ideas in "The Origin of Species," testing, trying, validating his great hypothesis. He did not expect too much too soon, nor did he give too little too late.
Harold Blake Walker

Blessed is he who has found his work; let him ask no other blessedness.
Thomas Carlyle

Work has greater effect than any other technique of living in the direction of binding the individual more closely to reality; in his work, at least, he is securely attached to a part of reality, the human community.
Sigmund Freud

Work can be a great stabilizer for the human psyche. That is the reason occupation, or better, constructive activity, looms large in the therapeutic program of psychiatric hospitals. We know that idleness promotes demoralization. In the great world outside, of course, work provides man with a livelihood but, and this is important—work has more than bartering value. Work has important social implications. It is in some way the expression of the human person. It provides, or should provide, the satisfaction of fellowship and status in a group.
Francis J. Braceland

I love work, said the loafer, I could sit and watch it all day.
Author Unknown

To live in idleness, even if you have the means, is not only injurious to yourself, but a species of fraud upon the community.
William A. Alcott

All great achievements have humble beginnings. You begin to compose th Fifth Symphony by practicing your scales. You begin to invent the mass-manufacture of automobiles by learning to repair watches and

clocks on a Michigan farm. You begin to fashion the theory of relativity by learning the multiplication tables. "Whatsoever thy find thy hands to do, do it!"
Charles Templeton

Perhaps the most damaging form of personal rejection is to tell a man there is nothing in the world for him to do. For worklessness equals meaninglessness; and meaninglessness eats at the foundation of all law, all morality, all joy in human relationships.
Timothy L. Smith

No race can prosper till it learns that there is as much dignity in tilling a field as in writing a poem.
Booker T. Washington

Welfare should aim, not at adding people to its rolls, but at making them self-supporting. Give a man a fish and he eats today, but is back for more tomorrow. Teach him how to fish, and he eats for a lifetime.
Richard G. Capen, Jr.

A preacher came along and wrote on a blackboard: "I pray for all."
A lawyer came along and wrote under that: "I plead for all."
A doctor wrote: "I prescribe for all."
A workman came by, read these carefully, and then wrote: "I pay for all."
Loraine Savino

A professional is one who does his best work when he feels the least like working.
Frank Lloyd Wright

Flay a carcass in the streets and earn a living, and say not, I am a great man and the work is beneath my dignity.
The Talmud

100 A joy forever

Happiness? It is an illusion to think that more comfort means more happiness. Happiness comes of the capacity to feel deeply, to enjoy simply, to think freely, to risk life, to be needed.
Storm Jameson

Every life has its dark and its cheerful hours. Joy comes from choosing which to remember.
Construction Digest

Laughter is a healer not only of the body, but of the mind. It creates harmony, not only within yourself, but in those with whom you come in contact. Tests have proved that laughter reduces muscle tension and relaxes the tissues. In laughing, many muscles and organs of the body are stimulated, and more adrenal fluid is introduced into the blood stream.
John E. Gibson

What seems to grow fairer to me as life goes by is the love and grace and tenderness of it; not its wit and cleverness and grandeur of knowledge, grand as knowledge is, but just the laughter of little children and the friendship of friends and the cozy talk by the fireside and the sight of flowers and the sound of music.
John Richard Green

My heart leaps up when I behold
A rainbow in the sky:
So was it when my life began;
So is it now I am a man;
So be it when I shall grow old,
Or let me die.
William Wordsworth

He who binds to himself a joy
Doth the winged life destroy,
But he who kisses a joy as it flies
Lives in eternity's sunrise.
William Blake

The fruition of a sacred deed is in the joy the soul reveals. The Psalmist (100:2) proclaims: "Serve Him with joy." His service and joy are one and the same. To meet a mitzvah is to discover His presence as it is meant for me, and in His presence is "fullness of joy." What is piety? A song every day, a song every day.
Abraham Joshua Heschel

While joy and beauty and happiness and laughter are of God, as are love and faith and hope and the other emotions, and while creativity and growth inevitably flow from them in varying degrees, it is still possible that there is fulfillment at the moment they are achieved. A baby's laugh, the caress of lovers, the colors of a sunset, the pure tones of a lyric singer, and many more experiences are all phases of joy that are complete in the moment, granted that such joy spreads on and on like waves upon the surface of a pool after a pebble has been dropped into its quiet water. This I would call the "joy of joyfulness."
Source Unknown

The gift of gaiety may itself be the greatest good fortune, and the most serious step toward maturity.
Irwin Edman

An English newspaper asked this question: "Who are the happiest people on earth?" These were the four prize-winning answers:

A craftsman or artist whistling over a job well done.

A little child building sand castles.

A mother, after a busy day, bathing her baby.

A doctor who has finished a difficult and dangerous operation, and saved a human life.

No millionaires among these, one notices. No kings or emperors. Riches and rank, no matter how the world strives for them, do not make happy lives.
Treasures

Joy is an elation of spirit—of a spirit which trusts in the goodness and truth of its own possessions.
Lucius Annaeus Seneca

11

Government is for the people

101 Politics is people

Every man has a right to be heard; but no man has the right to strangle democracy with a single set of vocal cords.
Adlai E. Stevenson

Nothing is unchangeable but the inherent and inalienable rights of man.
Thomas Jefferson

Every man counts! Once the great conductor, Sir Michael Costa, was leading a rehearsal, with a vast array of musicians and hundreds of voices. As the mighty chorus rang out with the thunder of the organ and the roll of the drums, and the horns ringing and the cymbals clashing, the piccolo player stopped playing. As he sat in the corner of the orchestra, he said to himself, "In all this din it matters not what I do." Suddenly, the great conductor stopped, flung up his hands and all was still, and then he creid aloud, "where is the piccolo?" All was spoiled because it failed to take its part.
Source Unknown

Everybody wants good government —for the other guy. Everybody wants to help the poor—with the other guy's money.
Fiorello LaGuardia

A city is an assembly of people founded and based on a philosophy. Genuine cities are the milestones on the roads of advancing mankind.
E. Gutkin

Governments can err. Presidents do make mistakes, but the immortal Dante tells us that Divine Justice weighs the sins of the cold blooded and the sins of the warm hearted on a different scale. Better the occasional faults of a government, living in the spirit of charity, than the consistent omissions of a government frozen in the ice of its own indifference.
Franklin Delano Roosevelt

Bad officials are elected by good citizens who do not vote.
Source Unknown

A good leader inspires other men with confidence in him; a great leader inspires them with confidence in themselves.
Anonymous

What makes a nation great? Not its mighty armies, or its mammoth buildings, or its wealth and material prosperity, or its great king or president, or dictator. It is the character, the righteousness, of its citizens. Are they ignorant and lazy and immoral? Then the country will perish. Are they intelligent, kind and godly in their lives? Then the nation will be great.
J. Kenton Parker

Government is not something passive, not our kind of government. It has built into it the spirit of outreach, the concern for every individual. Look at the verbs in the Constitution's Preamble—*establish, insure, provide, promote, secure*. All these connote action, and all suggest that we must constantly be striving to improve the opportunities of our people.
Terry Sanford

Sacrifice signifies neither amputation nor repentance. It is, in essence, an act. It is the gift of oneself to the being of which one forms a part. Only he can understand what a farm is, what a country is, who shall have sacrificed part of himself to his farm or his country, sought to save it, struggled to make it beautiful.

We had, bit by bit, introduced a code for the collectivity which neglected the existence of man. That code explains early why the individual should sacrifice himself for the community. It does not explain clearly and without ambiguity why the community should sacrifice itself for a single member. Why is it equitable that a thousand die to deliver a single man from unjust imprisonment? . . . And yet it is this principle alone which differentiates us from the anthill and which is the source of the grandeur of mankind.
Antoine de Sainte-Euxpery

In the long history of the world, only a few generations have been granted the role of defending freedom in its hour of maximum danger. I do not shrink from this responsibility—I welcome it. I do not believe that any of us would exchange places with any other people or any other generation.
John F. Kennedy

102 This land is mine

Fix your eyes upon the greatness of your country as you have it before you day by day, fall in love with her, and when you feel her great, remember her greatness was won by men with courage, with knowledge of their duty, and with a sense of honor in action, who, even if they failed in some venture, would not think of depriving their country of their powers but laid them at her feet as their fairest offering!
Pericles

All citizens must have an understanding and appreciation of our environment, the problems that beset our quality of life and the tools necessary to wisely use, develop and protect our environment.
Robert Herbst

A day of environmental disaster is closing in on America unless we as educators and other concerned citizens immediately recognize and establish guidelines and criteria to remedy a pending holocaust.
Howard B. Casmey

The business of the American teacher is to liberate American citizens to think apart and to act together.
Stephen S. Wise

An Oriental visitor was leaving the United States at the end of his year's visit. To a question of his outstanding impression of America, he replied, "I am impressed by the size of your garbage cans."
Floyd Shacklock

The history of a nation, like the life of a man, is not a series of stills, but a moving picture, and we must see it as a whole.
Harold Macmillan

If at times we seemed to prefer justice to our country, this is because we simply wanted to love our country in justice, as we wanted to love her in truth and in hope.
Albert Camus

Nations do have souls. They have collective personalities. People who think well of themselves collectively exhibit elan and enthusiasm and morale. When nations cease believing in themselves, when they regard their institutions with cynicism and their traditions with flippancy they will not long remain great nations.
Jenkin Lloyd Jones

I haven't yet plumbed the depths of what's around me. Why shouldn't I stay in one place and dig a little deeper?
Andrew Wyeth

What is honored in a country will be cultivated there.
Plato

More and more I believe that our greatest influence in the world would be an example of justice and morality in our own country.
John Sherman Cooper

John Kennedy believed so strongly that one's aim should not just be the most comfortable life possible but

that we should all do something to right the wrongs we see . . . We owe that to our country and our country will suffer if we don't serve her. He believed that one man can make a difference, and that every man should try.
Kennedy Memorial Broadcast

The name of "American" which belongs to you, in your national capacity, must always exalt the just pride of patriotism more than any appellation derived from local discriminations. You have in common cause fought and triumphed together; the independence and liberty you possess are the works of joint counsels and joint efforts, of common dangers, sufferings, and successes.
George Washington

Nations are built by people capable of great energy and self-discipline.
Jenkin Lloyd Jones

How we treat our land, how we build upon it, and how we act toward our air and water will in the long run tell what kind of people we really are.
Laurance S. Rockefeller

103 Every day is law day

Our defense is in the preservation of the spirit which prizes liberty as the heritage of all men, in all lands everywhere. Destroy this spirit and you have planted the seeds of despotism at your own doors. Familiarize yourself with the chains of bondage, and you are preparing your own limbs to wear them. Accustomed to trample on the rights of others, you have lost the genius of your own independence and become the fit subjects of the first cunning tyrant who rises among you.
Abraham Lincoln

Do you imagine that a state can subsist and not be overthrown, in which the decisions of law have no power, but are set aside and trampled upon by individuals?
Socrates

No man is above the law and no man is below it; nor do we ask any man's permission when we require him to obey it.
Theodore Roosevelt

Law is the foundation of life. Too many people try to achieve the goal without first of all basing it on law. Whether it is an organization or a personal life, nothing can be built that will not fade unless it has the undergirding of these great principles. This is primary and elementary, and the moral framework within which we have to live can be neither defied nor ignored.
Gerald Kennedy

A community without law is but a shell.
John F. Kennedy

Law and order is not a goal, it is a matrix within which we can address ourselves to social problems.
Theodore M. Hesburgh

It is imperative that we recognize that if the law is really to come to grips with problems of racial discrimination and poverty, it must make itself felt not at the end of the policeman's nightstick, it must manifest itself in just and equitable provision for the righting of wrongs.
Arthur J. Goldberg

The greatest progress will perhaps be made if all of you can give larger thought to your duties than to your rights.

Democracy demands more obedience to the moral law than any other form of government.
Louis D. Brandeis

If one man can be allowed to determine for himself what is law, every man can. That means first chaos, then tyranny.
Felix Frankfurter

Law is an instrument of justice. Justice is rendering to every man what is due him. What is due to a man depends upon his nature, and by virtue of his nature man is a rational, free, spiritual being, whose happiness is an end in itself, and whose dignity therefore must always be respected. Law is a means to an end, and the end is the common good of man and society. If we do not respect the true nature of man and society, we will not respect the law which serves that end. Disrespect for ends is a deeper crisis than disrespect for means. If the ends are correct, the genius of a people will find the right means. If the ends are wrong, the situation is hopeless, In other words, law is designed to respect something, and if we do not respect that which the law is designed to respect, we will not respect the law itself.
Harold R. McKinnon

Wise men, though all laws were abolished, would lead the same life.
Aristophanes

---

104 The enlightened citizen

Since politics is the main means by which a democratic society determines its character and goals, it is incumbent upon everyone, including and especially the religious leader, to involve himself in the political affairs of his country and to speak and act on all public issues.
Israel Margolies

The punishment suffered by the wise who refuse to take part in the government is to live under the government of bad men.
Plato

To sit in silence when we should protest makes cowards out of men. The human race has climbed on

protest. Had no voice been raised against injustice, ignorance and lust, the inquisition yet would serve the law and guillotines decide our least disputes. The few who dare must speak, and speak again, to right the wrongs of many.
San Angelo Rotary Brand

We regard the man who holds aloof from public duties not as "quiet" but as useless.
Pericles

We cannot have enlightened government in the absence of an enlightened electorate.
John C. Stennis

I think it is good taste, and also good judgment, when a may prays for the sin of the people, that he should count himself in.
Joshua Billings

It is probably a pity that every citizen of each state cannot visit all the others, to see the differences, to learn what we have in common, and to come back with a richer, fuller understanding of America—in all its beauty, in all its dignity, in all its strength, in support of moral principle.
Dwight D. Eisenhower

Citizenship to growing children comes to mean pretty much what the community shows it means. The best way to teach young people the meaning of our democratic freedom is to demonstrate, by our own example, that we have mastered "the three R's of citzenship"— rights, respect and responsibilities.
Earl James McGrath

In every dark hour of our national life a leadership of frankness and vigor has met with that understanding and support of the people themselves which is essential to victory.
Franklin Delano Roosevelt

A patriotic American is a man who is not niggardly and selfish in the things that he enjoys that make for human liberty and the rights of man. He wants to share them with the whole world, and he is never so proud of the great flag under which he lives as when it comes to mean to other people as well as to himself a symbol of hope and liberty.
Woodrow Wilson

All that is necessary for the triumph of evil is that good men do nothing.
Edmund Burke

A state can be no better than the citizens of which it is composed. Our labor is not to mold states but to make citizens.
John Morby

Let no one be fooled: The crisis in our cities is not caused by agitators or irresponsible malcontents. It is caused by suburbanites—good people who wish no man ill. It is caused by a social system that has created an American form of apartheid that is every bit as vicious, albeit uncodified, as that in South Africa. It is caused by us good white folk who refuse to accept anyone who looks and acts differently from the way we do—or who lives in a life-style foreign to ours. It is caused by our fear of the unknown. In other words, the crisis of our cities is

caused by our failure to have faith in the God who meets us at the limit of our own understanding.
Allan R. Brockway

Any nation that thinks more of its ease and comfort than its freedom will soon lose its freedom; and the ironical thing about it is that it will lose its ease and comfort too.
Somerset Maugham

If you are better off than your neighbor, you can pay some taxes to help him.
Abraham Ribicoff

A society of sheep must in time beget a government of wolves.
De Jouvenal

A college president made this arresting statement to a class of graduating seniors: "It gets easier and easier for man to dominate his universe . . . and harder and harder for him to dominate himself."
Halford E. Luccock

Through unity of action we can be a veritable colossus in support of peace. No one can defeat us unless we first defeat ourselves. Every one of us must be guided by this truth.
Dwight D. Eisenhower

Our word "idiot" comes from the Greek name for the man who took no share in public matters.
Edith Hamilton

105 *America, God shed His grace on thee*

This country was not built by men who relied on somebody else to take care of them. It was built by men who relied on themselves, who dared to shape their own lives, who had enough courage to blaze new trails—enough confidence in themselves to take the necessary risks. This self-reliance is our American legacy. It is the secret of that something which stamped Americans as Americans. Some call it individual initiative, others backbone. But whatever it is called, it is a precious ingredient in our national character, one which we must not lose.
J. Ollie Edmunds

The founding fathers of the United States did not by accident write down the words "insure domestic tranquillity" into the preamble of our Constitution.
William G. Bray

If destruction be our lot we must ourselves be its author and finisher. As a nation of free men we must live through all time, or die by suicide.
Abraham Lincoln

Too frequently do we give credence to the notion that endeavors, because they are idealistic, are to be shunned or abused. Let me remind you that the founding fathers of this

country were unashamed idealists and visionaries not afraid to dream or to admit that they dreamed.
Arthur J. Goldberg

Things in America are never as ugly as you fear, nor as lovely as you hope.
Luigi Barzini

I am certain that in the minds and hearts of our people still—still—lie welling springs—inexhaustible and indestructible—of faith in the things we cherish, of courage and determination to defend them, of sacrificial devotion, of unbreakable unity of purpose. I am certain that, however great the hardships and the trials which loom ahead, our America will endure and the cause of human freedom will triumph.
Cordell Hull

If this nation is to succeed and flourish as it ought to, the day will come when the American people will be as willing to tax themselves for good schools as they are today for good nuclear missiles. For they will realize that they are quite able to afford both.
Walter Lippmann

This country will not be a really good place for any of us to live in if it is not a really good place for all of us to live in.
Theodore Roosevelt

There is something in the contemplation of the mode in which America has been settled that, in a noble breast, should forever extinguish the prejudices of national dislikes.

Settled by the people of all nations, all nations may claim her for their own. You cannot spill a drop of American blood without spilling the blood of the whole world. Be he Englishman, German, Dane, or Scot; the European who scoffs at an American, calls his own brother "Raca," and stands in danger of the judgment. We are not a narrow tribe of men . . . No: our blood is as the flood of the Amazon, made up of a thousand noble currents all pouring into one. We are not a nation, so much as a world.
Herman Melville

American is a people of peoples, a nation of nations.
Walt Whitman

A nation is not made great by its acres, but by the men who cultivate them; not by its great forests, but by the men who use them. America was a great land when Columbus discovered it. Americans have made it a great nation.
Lyman Abbott

Our founding fathers did not hand any generation of Americans a neatly packaged, ready-made America. Instead they handed us a set of tools—principles and institutions—for us to use in shaping the kind of nation we want. The people must win and rewin America in every generation.
George Romney

106 The democratic way of life

As soon as public service ceases to be the chief business of the citizens, and they would rather serve with their money than with their persons, the state is not far from its fall.
Jean Jacques Rousseau

The world will never be made safe for democracy; it is a dangerous trade.
G. K. Chesterton

Primarily, democracy is the conviction that there are extraordinary possibilities in ordinary people, and that if we throw wide the doors of opportunity so that all boys and girls can bring out the best that is in them, we will get amazing results from unlikely sources. Shakespeare was the son of a bankrupt butcher and a woman who could not write her name. Beethoven was the son of a consumptive mother, herself daughter of a cook, and a drunken father. Shubert was the son of a peasant father and a mother who had been in domestic service. Faraday, one of the greatest scientific experimenters of all time, was born over a stable, his father an invalid blacksmith and his mother a common drudge. Such facts as these underlie democracy. That is why, with all its discouraging blunders, we must everlastingly believe in it.
Harry Emerson Fosdick

Man's capacity for justice makes democracy possible; but man's inclination to injustice makes democracy necessary.
Reinhold Niebuhr

In a democracy—and the essence of democracy is an unbroken channel of communication between those who represent and those who are represented—the first duty of statesmen is not to sit in committee or even debate in Parliament, important though these functions are, but to speak to the people clearly and enable them to realize the issues on which their collective well-being depends and on which they have ultimately to resolve by their votes. This is something that far transcends party and party rivalry.
Arthur Bryant

The serious threat to our democracy is not the existence of foreign totalitarian states. It is the existence within our own personal attitudes and within our own institutions of conditions which have given a victory to external authority, discipline, uniformity and dependence upon The Leader in foreign countries. The battlefield is also accordingly here—within ourselves and our institutions.
John Dewey

The democratic American idea is not that every man shall be on a level with every other, but that everyone shall have liberty, without hindrance, to be what God made him.
Henry Ward Beecher

The majority is not always right. There are many tragic monuments . . . to the errors of a temporary majority.
Richard B. Russell

Freedom is not free. Shaping and preserving society necessarily involves personal commitment, costly risk, and constant effort; the cultivation of our civil liberty should be no more passive than is the cultivation of a farm.
Edmond Cahn

Democracy is the right of every individual to develop his mind and soul in ways of his own choice, free of fear or coercion, provided only that he does not interfere with the like right of others.
George Marshall

What we have most to fear is not the triumph of communism but the default of democracy.
Norman Cousins

Since primitive times, virtually all religious or social systems have attempted to maintain themselves by forbidding free criticism and analysis either of existing institutions or of the doctrine that sustains them; of democracy alone is it the cardinal principle that free criticism and analysis by all and sundry is the highest virtue.
Carl L. Becker

As I would not be a slave, so I would not be a master. This expresses my idea of Democracy. Whatever differs from this, to the extent of the difference, is no Democracy.
Abraham Lincoln

In democracy each has to be judge of issues of life and death for his fellows . . . Our Bill of Rights has become a long one. But there is no Bill of Obligations. We proclaim vociferously the rights of free speech; nowhere the obligation to listen, listen to those with whom we disagree. But any man who proclaims that he can never be wrong has closed the door on the chance of being right.
Normal Angell

107 *Power is as power does*

To act coolly, intelligently and prudently in perilous circumstances is the test of a man and also a nation.
Adlai E. Stevenson

Power is not of itself good or bad but becomes what its holder makes it. Held by a Churchill it might be good; by a Hitler, bad.
Herbert M. Baus

Power and skill are never good unless he who uses them is good.
Greek Saying

Because we belonged to a large household we had no trouble promising employment to Maria, who was a native of Chile, and wanted to come to America. One difficulty after another held her back, but finally after two years of waiting she came. She soon endeared herself to everyone, and proved a tremendous asset to the household. There seemed to be hardly anything she couldn't do, and didn't do.

One day when she was still going strong at a rather late hour I said to her, "Maria, where do you get all that energy?"

She smiled, saying first, "I don't know," but quickly added, "God works and I help."

Catholic Digest

The last temptation is the greatest treason:
To do the right deed for the wrong reason.

T. S. Eliot

Temptations are sure to ring your doorbell, but it is your fault if you invite them in for dinner.

Megiddo Message

A small boy sat on a fence eyeing the luscious-looking apples hanging from the branches of a nearby tree. Suddenly the farmer appeared, demanding, "Sonny, are you trying to steal those apples?"

"No, sir," the lad replied. "I'm trying not to!"

Highways of Happiness

God's power is always allied with His righteousness and compassion.

The Talmud

We often say how impressive power is. But I do not find it impressive at all. The guns and bombs, the rockets and the warships, all are symbols of human failure. They are necessarily symbols. They protect what we cherish. But they are witness to human folly.

Lyndon B. Johnson

I cannot say that I am in the slightest degree impressed by your bigness, or your material resources as such. Size is not grandeur, and territory does not make a nation. The great issue, about which hangs a true sublimity and the terror of an overhanging fate, is what are you going to do with all these things.

Thomas Huxley

By authority we mean legitimate power or the established right within any social order to determine policies, to pronounce judgments on selected issues, or more broadly to act as a leader or guide to other men . . . Power itself has no legitimacy, no mandate, no office.

R. M. MacIver

And ever shall this law hold good, nothing that is vast enters into the life of mortals without a curse.

Sophocles

Determined to mend his ways, Mr. Jordan did not stop at his favorite tavern on the way home. Taking a firm grip on his will power, he passed on by. After walking a few yards, he came to an abrupt stop and said to himself: "Jordan, old boy, I'm very proud of you. Come on back to the tavern and I'll buy you a treat."

The Bluejacket

108 Discontent can be divine

Discontent is the first step in the progress of a man or a nation.
Oscar Wilde

I do not know how to teach philosophy without becoming a disturber of established religion.
Baruch de Spinoza

While I am not in favor of maladjustment, I view this cultivation of neutrality, this breeding of mental neuters, this hostility to eccentricity and controversy with grave misgiving. One looks back with dismay at the possibility of a Shakespeare perfectly adjusted to bourgeois life in Stratford, a Wesley contentedly administering a country parish, a George Washington going to London to receive a barony from George III, or Abraham Lincoln prospering in Springfield with nary a concern for the preservation of the crumbling Union.
Adlai E. Stevenson

Who never broke with tears, his bread,
Who never watched through anguished hours
With weeping eyes, upon his bed,
He knows ye not, O heavenly Powers.
Goethe

I respect faith but doubt is what gets you an education.
Benjamin Franklin

Someone has made a remark worth remembering about Jane Austen, the novelist whose pictures of domestic social life in eighteenth-century England (such as *Pride and Prejudice* and *Emma*) so many have enjoyed. He said, "Jane Austen was so contented with domestic order that she neglected to look out the window and see the French Revolution."
Author Unknown

Because the world can never have perfect justice,
We will never stop fighting for justice.
Because what is built in a lifetime can be dust in a moment,
We will never stop building.
Why did You make us imperfect—
Seeking the stars and raging like children,
Eaten by hungers, and smashing our own best hopes?

Perfection never changes.
In perfection there is no hope.
So, because Your gift is Hope, and not Perfection
We will never stop struggling
For Perfection.
Joanne Greenberg

To sit by in silence, when they should protest, makes cowards of men.
Abraham Lincoln

I've heard it said that the day of demonstrations is over. I cannot agree with that. As long as these problems are with us, it will be necessary to demonstrate in order to call attention to them. A demonstration will not solve the problem of

poverty, the problem of housing, the problem in the school. But, at least, the demonstration creates a kind of constructive crisis that causes a community to see its problem and to begin moving toward acting on it.
Martin Luther King

For the first time in history the chief danger to our survival comes from ourselves instead of the forces of nature. We have not yet learned that we cannot bully nature but that we must cooperate and negotiate with it. Our pressure on nature is provoking nature's revenge, and we are sitting down to a banquet of consequences.
Laurence M. Gould

Your bowl is empty, little brother,
your hands are blue from the cold,
your face is a map of terror and pain,
old as mankind is old.

Men launch their miracles, little brother,
they send their rockets up.
but should it not be their first concern
to fill your empty cup?

Men try to reach the moon, little brother,
to lasso outer space,
but would they not come closer to God
if they wiped the pain from your face?
Anonymous

---

109 The just cause

How can we venture to judge others when we know so well how ill equipped they are for judging us?
Comtesse Diane

No greater change of environment for the U.S. Supreme Court could have been imagined when that august body moved from its dingy, smelly basement room in the Capitol Building to its present location, an awesome, sumptuous eleven-million-dollar temple of justice. At least one of the Justices was a bit unhappy over the change—Justice Brandeis.

"I would much prefer to have the Court use the little room," the troubled jurist confided to a friend.

"You would?" the other rejoined. "Why?"

"Because," replied Justice Brandeis, "our little room kept us humble."
Adrian Alexander

Everyone is a prisoner of his own experiences. No one can eliminate prejudices—just recognize them.
Edward R. Murrow

Pay attention to what a man is, not to what he has been.
Chinese Proverb

Fools speak of agitators. There is but one—injustice.
Anonymous

Give a laborer his wage before his perspiration be dry.
Mohammed

Mishpat. One word, Emma, one word of your faith . . . It means a good deal . . . *Mishpat* means that the covenant with God emerges out of social justice. You ought to remember that because you're a Jew . . . I ought to remember it because I'm a Christian.
Morton Wishengrad

My class of twelve-year-old girls was discussing the Golden Rule. I noticed that one child was unusually quiet, and soon I found out what was on her mind.

"I just thought of something we might call the 'Diamond Rule,' " she suddenly announced to the class. We all listened quiety. "The 'Diamond Rule,' " she went on, "could be, 'Think about others as you would have them think about you.' "
Betty Lee Campbell

There can be no such thing as racial justice as long as we insist on categorizing individuals as members of a particular collective—as a Jew, as Negro, as Wasp, and so on ad infinitum—rather than judging a person according to his worth as an individual.
Jerome Tuccille

Love and justice are the same; for justice is love distributed, nothing else.
Joseph Fletcher

A wise man of Athens was asked when injustice would be abolished. "When those who are not wronged feel as indignant as those who are," he said.
Arthur Mee

There is an evil which most of us condone and are even guilty of: indifference to evil. We remain neutral, impartial, and not easily moved by the wrongs done unto other people. Indifference to evil is more insidious than evil itself; it is more universal, more contagious, more dangerous.
Abraham Joshua Heschel

Justice is truth in action.
Benjamin Disraeli

Faith in the existence of God is of small value in true religion if it is not supplemented by the belief that God is just . . .
Israel Salanter

We are a nation of nation builders . . . lifegivers not life takers—that is our heritage and we must not merely be concerned with protecting the rights of man, but must also be dedicated to asserting man's rights.
Hubert H. Humphrey

The whole history of the world is summed up in the fact that, when nations are strong, they are not always just, and when they wish to be just, they are often no longer strong. Let us have this blessed union of power and justice.
Winston Churchill

110 Points of view

It isn't your position that makes you happy or unhappy—it's your disposition.

Megiddo Message

The teacher asked a question but no one answered. Finally a bright-eyed little girl in the front row said to the teacher, "Mrs. Thomas, there's a boy in the class who knows the answer to that question, but he won't speak up."

The teacher asked, "Who is it?" The little girl pointed across the room to the only non-white student in the class and said, "That boy there in the blue sweater."

Because this child had not been taught to be prejudiced she was more aware of the color of the sweater than the color of his skin. We learn our prejudices. We are not born with them.

Tal D. Bonham

Niels Bohr's view of life is beautifully illustrated by a little story he liked very much. Three Chinese philosophers came together to taste vinegar, the Chinese symbol for the spirit of life. The first philosopher, Confucius, drank of it. "It is sour," he said. The second, a philosopher of Schopenhauer's bent, pronounced the vinegar bitter. Then Lao Tse tasted it and exclaimed, "It is fresh."

Aage Petersen

What is the test of good manners? It is the being able to put up pleasantly with bad ones.

Solomon ibn Gabirol

Often short of help at Lambarene, the doctor (Albert Schweitzer) himself was helping one day as some heavy beams were moved. Seeing a young visitor watching from the shade, he invited him to help. "I am an intellectual," the young man replied, "and don't drag wood about." "You're lucky," said Dr. Schweitzer. "I too wanted to become an intellectual but I didn't succeed."

Suzanne Thomas

Two little girls were playing together in a strange garden. Soon one ran to her mother full of disappointment.

"This garden is a terrible place, mother. I have been all around, and every rose bush has sharp, long thorns on it that stick me and hurt me."

Then the second child came in breathless with excitement.

"O, mother, this garden is a beautiful place! I have been all over and every thornbush has the most beautiful roses growing on it."

And the two mothers wondered at the difference in their children.

Source Unknown

Do not do unto others as you would have them do unto you—their tastes might not be the same.

George Bernard Shaw

While supply-teaching in a grammar school, I found a book and recognized the boy's name written in it. When I gave it to him, he said, "No, this belongs to my brother—he's a class ahead of me because he's six months older than I am." Before I recovered from this remark, he added, "One of us is adopted, but I forget which one."

The words lifted my spirits as I visualized the home where being adopted made so little difference.
Margaret Carey

It is good to rub and polish our brains against those of others.
Montaigne

A five-year-old boy, riding with his mother, saw the steel work of a half-finished building and asked her: "Mother, is the building going up or down?" To a child the clutter of construction looks like the debris of destruction.
Source Unknown

A young man had determined from boyhood to serve in the ministry. He was handsome, had a brilliant mind, and was a leader in college activities. One of the vice-presidents of a large company with offices in his home town had watched his progress during his college years. He offered the young man a good salary to work for the company when he was graduated. The young man declined. The vice-president raised the salary offer several times. Still the young man steadfastly insisted that he had other work to do.

Finally, the president of the company went to him, "Isn't the salary big enough?" he asked.

"Yes," the young man replied thoughtfully, "the salary is big enough, but the job isn't."
Annie Laurie Von Tungeln

Clarence Darrow, noted criminal lawyer, and dissenter since youth, was to participate in a debate with another attorney.

"Are you familiar with the subject?" Darrow was asked.

"No," he confessed.

"Then how can you engage in a debate?"

"Easily," said Darrow. "I'll take the negative side. I can argue against anything."
Milwaukee Journal

I believe that one of the major tasks of education in our changing times is to create in our young the willingness to tolerate differences of opinion and the desire to try to understand different points of view.
U Thant

12

The meaning of each person

111   You can make a difference

In every man there is something precious which is in no one else. And so we should honor each for what is within him for what only he has, and none of his comrades.

Hasidic Lore

There is no "normal" person—there is just you, wherever you are, whatever you are. When asked his definition of a normal person Dr. Ernest Jones, world-famous psychoanalyst, said, "I have never seen one."

Lucy Freeman

The circumstances of your life, good or bad, are important, but not decisive. You are decisive. When you fail, it is not your parents' fault. They may have failed you at some crucial time, but your responsibility is not to fail life, regardless of what life may have done to you.

Theodore Parker Ferris

I'm not going to pray for you. There are certain things a man has to do for himself. He has to blow his own nose, make his own love and say his own prayers.

Fulton J. Sheen

"The Holy One, blessed be He, strikes every person from the die of the first man, but not one resembles another!" the rabbis observed, as they contemplated God's wonders as manifested in the creation of man.

The Talmud

Once, in China, Einstein needed to get someplace. But when he discovered, to get there, he'd have to ride a rickshaw that was drawn by a human being working like a horse, he refused, saying, "I'll not be a party to the making of a man a draft animal."

Western Recorder

Peter, a first grader, was so full of enthusiasm and energy that he never walked. He could only run. Coming full speed around the corner of the school one day he bumped into an elderly gentleman who asked in surprise: "Well, son, where did you come from?" Peter stopped short, and, measuring a short space between his hands, said with conviction: "This much God made. The rest I made myself."

Anna Spiesman Starr

No one person alone can change the whole world for the better; but each is needed. For each is a bit different —just as one leaf is different from the others on a tree, yet all are needed for its complete foliage.

Paul K. Povlsen

A single person is equal in value to the entire universe.

The Talmud

Among the tales of comic hairline elections is that of the man who will never again tell his wife not to vote. He was running for his third term in the Georgia House of Representatives. Feeling sure that he would have no opposition, he assured his wife that it was unnecessary to go to the polls. But little did he bargain for a spur-of-the-moment write-in vote in his district. His opponent fared so well the final results showed a surprising 254-254 tie.

If you and others stay away from the polls, your absence could change the results in hundreds of important elections. In fact, it could change history.

Nation's Business

I am only one, but I am one. I cannot do everything, but I can do something. What I can do, I ought to do. And what I ought to do, by God's grace, I will do.

Anonymous

Everything depends upon the sort of person a man is.

The Talmud

Creative ideas do not spring from groups. They spring from individuals.

A. Whitney Griswold

We are neither weak nor few.
As long as one man does what one can do—
As long as one man in the sun alone
Walks between the silence and the stone
And honors manhood in his flesh, his bone
We are not yet too weak, nor yet too few.

Learned Hand

Each and every man on the foundations of his own joys and sufferings builds for us all.

Albert Camus

Everyone shall bear his own righteousness or unrighteousness.

Apocrypha: IV Ezra

Often men are not limited so much by lack of capacity as by their unwillingness to use their capacity.
Ralph E. Lyne

It has always been my contention that an individual who can be relied upon to be himself and be honest unto himself can be relied upon in every other way. He places value—not a price—on himself and his principles. And that, in the final analysis, is the measure of anyone's sense of values—and of the true worth of man.
J. Paul Getty

---

112 The duties of the heart

Day by day, feast your eyes upon the greatness of Athens, until you become filled with the love of her; and when you are impressed by the spectacle of her glory, reflect that this empire has been acquired by men who knew their duty and had the courage to do it.
Thucydides

As William James once called for "a moral substitute for war," one may say we need a moral substitute for poverty.
   There are moral substitutes for poverty, which are simply acts of service to others.
Source Unknown

Reading maketh a full man, conference a ready man, and writing an exact man. Read not to contradict, nor to believe, but to weigh and to consider.
Francis Bacon

Learn to say "No!" It will be of more use to you than to be able to read Latin.
Charles H. Spurgeon

We do not change the world except we change men; we do not change men except we change their hearts.
Quaker Proverb

So nigh is grandeur to our dust,
So near is God to man,
When Duty whispers low, Thou must,
Then youth replies, I can!
Ralph Waldo Emerson

Plenty of people write to me in hope of getting some spectacular work to do and at the same time they fail to see the worthwhileness of the immediate duty God has given them.
Albert Schweitzer

One trouble with the world is that so many people who stand up vigorously for their rights fall down miserably on their duties.
Tit-Bits

Mazzini, when people were insisting on the Rights of Man, came forward with a list of the Duties of Man to balance the account. This is where we have been at fault. We have

made more of rights than of duties. A distaste for the very idea of responsibility is widespread. It is part and parcel of the weakness of democracy and of our moral confusion and futility. We complain loudly enough that things are not what they should be, but we are not morally sensitive about them to the extent that we feel an obligation to do something personally and specifically about putting them right.
Source Unknown

Some people strengthen the society just by being the kind of people they are.
John W. Gardner

The great tragedy of life is not that men perish but that they cease to love.
Somerset Maugham

In the deserts of the heart
Let the healing fountain start,
In the prison of his days
Teach the free man how to praise.
W. H. Auden

The best things are nearest: breath in your nostrils, light in your eyes, flowers at your feet, duties at your hand, the path of Right just before you. Then do not grasp at the stars, but do life's plain, common work as it comes, certain that daily duties and daily bread are the sweetest things of life.
Robert Louis Stevenson

Lord, make me an instrument of Thy peace. Where there is hatred, let me sow love; where there is injury, pardon; where there is doubt, faith; where there is despair, hope; where there is darkness, light; where there is sadness; joy.
St. Francis of Assisi

There is a story of a man who found frost upon his windows and tried to scrape it off. "What are you trying to do?" a neighbor asked. "I am trying to get rid of the frost," the man replied, "for I can't see out. But as fast as I get it off one pane it comes on another." The friend shook his head and said, "Let your windows alone and light a fire inside. You will then see that the frost will disappear of itself."
Source Unknown

Question: Why is it written: "In the day that God created a man on earth," and not "in the day that God created man on earth?"
Answer: You shall serve your Creator as if there were only one man in the world, only you yourself.
Martin Buber

Dignity does not consist in possessing honors, but in deserving them.
Aristotle

Naturalness is found in simplicity, and divinity in naturalness.
Pope John XXIII

Do the duty that lies nearest thee; thy next duty will then become clearer.
Goethe

113 The fullness of human experience

Oh, just to live,
To breathe, to feel, to think!
Life, Glorious Gift of God,
Most precious treasure no one else can give.
To see, to touch, to smell,
To walk, to talk,
To sing, to cry,
To shout with joy,
I am alive! I am alive!
Rose Brockman Klein

Time would be lost in which we had not lived as men, had experiences, learned, created, enjoyed, and suffered. Lost time is unfilled, empty time.
Dietrich Bonhoeffer

Crafty men condemn studies, simple men admire them and wise men use them.
Francis Bacon

We now know too much about matter to be materialists.
Arthur James Balfour

Is it really true . . . that the body and the mind are two distinct entities? Or are they merely two different manifestations of the integrated structures which make a living organism? There is at present no conclusive evidence to decide between these two alternatives so fundamentally different one from the other. However, I must acknowledge that I find the second hypothesis more congenial than the first and indeed that what we express by the word "mind" is, in my opinion, a manner of response by the living organism to the total environment —a response which is more or less elaborate depending upon the complexity of the organism, and perhaps even more upon its history.
Rene Dubos

The world is made up of people, but the people of the world forget this. It is hard to believe that, like ourselves, other people are born of women, reared by parents, teased by brothers . . . consoled by wives, flattered by grandchildren, and buried by parsons and priests with the blessings of the church and the tears of those left behind . . . It is easier to speak of fate, and destiny without realizing that people are trying to work out their own fate right now and in the immediate past and future.
Karl Menninger

You'll be old and you never lived, and you kind of feel silly to lie down and die and to never have lived, to have been a job chaser and never have lived.
Gertrude Stein

A Chinese philosopher was once asked what the most satisfying experience had been in his long life. After thoughful deliberation he replied, "I chanced to meet one day a small boy who was crying. A short conversation with the lad revealed he was lost. To the best of my ability I tried to tell him the way. Whereupon he went down the road singing."
Rodney W. Everhart

True learning is not a matter of the formal organization of knowledge of books. It is a series of personal experiences.
Harold L. Taylor

There is a Chinese story about a man who lost his ax. He suspected that his neighbor's son had stolen it. Thereafter he watched the lad very carefully. Every time the boy passed his home he looked guilty. When the lad met his neighbor he had shifty eyes, and would wring his hands as if he were to blurt out, "Sir, I took your ax!" No boy seemed to have more of the symptoms of guilt. But one day the neighbor found the ax he had considered stolen in an old ditch he was cleaning out. The next time the boy came by, the neighbor could discover none of the seeming guilt. There was no shift in the eye, no words that gave the previous hint of suspicion.
A. Purnell Bailey

Only men and women can develop the ideas that serve as the foundations for scientific and technologic process; only men and women—even in an age of giant computers—can manage organizations; only men and women can operate and repair the new machines which produce the goods which we desire; only men and women can provide services to the young and old, to the sick and well, to those seeking education or recreation. Only men and women, not financial grants or ballistic missiles, determine the strength of a country.
Eli Ginzberg

Reading makes a full man—meditation a profound man—discourse a clear man.
Benjamin Franklin

Difficulties are things that show what men are.
Epictetus

I should like to be remembered as a full man: a man who has run the gamut of human experience and emerged, like Jacob from his wrestling, limping and scarred, but having heard at last the name of the angel.
Morris West

---

114   Feelings are real

Pinch yourself and know how others feel.
Japanese Proverb

Things might happen today that so increase my tension that I feel as though I might explode. This tension is released in a game of cards, a concert, or just a good night's rest. If these outlets don't restore the vital balance I will feel worse and try harder to recover my equilibrium. I may even ask for help.
Karl Menninger

Never try to reason the prejudice out of a man. It was not reasoned into him and cannot be reasoned out.
Sidney Smith

One of the biggest troubles with success these days is that its recipe is about the same as that for a nervous breakdown.
Powerfax

About a century and a half ago, when the first American steamboat, Robert Fulton's "Clermont," was scheduled to make its trial run on the Hudson River, a crowd gathered to watch. One of the spectators was an old farmer, who predicted: "They'll never start her!" But the steamboat did start. Its speed increased. Faster and faster it went. The crowd went wild with enthusiasm.

But the old farmer turned away, shaking his head, hardly able to believe what he saw. "They'll never stop her!" he declared.
Sunshine Magazine

I was angry with my friend:
I told my wrath, my wrath did end.

I was angry with my foe:
I hid my wrath, my wrath did grow.
William Blake

To understand any living thing, you must creep within and feel the beating of its heart.
W. Macnelle Dison

One of my mother's friends was Lady Anglesey, an American woman, and she told me that she had once said to my mother: "You're so beautiful and there are so many people in love with you, why are you faithful to that ugly little man you've married?" And my mother answered: "He never hurts my feelings."
Somerset Maugham

Anger without insult is most helpful. It allows us to get our point across and enables us and our children to survive the storm with dignity . . . Our children learn from us that anger is not a catastrophic emotion, that it can be experienced and expressed harmlessly.
Haim Ginott

The two young sales girls boarding the homeward bus slumped wearily into the last remaining seats.

One of them remarked to her companion. "What a day! Sometimes I think I hate people."

"Oh, I like people all right," said the second, "but sometimes I forget that I do."
A. F. Wilson

If you don't lose your mind over certain things, you have no mind to lose.
Johann Nestroy

Mr. Jones didn't mind his wife's sniffles while they were watching a movie on their TV set, but when they went to see a double feature at the neighborhood movie theatre, that was a different story.

One feature outlined the movie heroine's pitiful struggle to find true love, and Mr. Jones became more and more annoyed with his wife's sniffles. Finally, he demanded: "For Pete's sake! Why is it you cry over the imaginary woes of people you never met?"

"For the same reason," his wife snapped back, "that you yell and scream when a man you don't know hits a home run!"
V. D. Palat

Growing up is primarily the process of outgrowing the tyranny of one's emotions. In general, this must succeed before education can succeed. It must at least begin to be successful before formal education can have a chance.
Don Robinson

The characters of men are developed more by emotional experiences than they are by mental.
Earl H. Hanson

Since the destruction of the Temple all gates of prayer have been closed, except to the cry of hurt feelings.
The Talmud

A thing only belongs to us when it is felt . . . as beautiful, necessary, and vivid.
Stefan Zweig

In the real dark night of the soul it is always three o'clock in the morning day after day.
F. Scott Fitzgerald

What is told a child he may forget, but what he feels he always remembers.
Lillian Taylor

---

115 To be aware of one's self

Men seek retreats for themselves, houses in the country, seashore and mountains; and thou too art wont to desire such things very much. But it is within thy power whenever thou shalt choose to retire into thyself.

Remember to retire into this little territory of thine own; and, above all, do not distract or strain thyself, but be free and look at things as a man, as a human being, as a citizen, as a mortal. Look within. Within is the fountain of good.
Marcus Aurelius

A man who does not respect his own life and that of others robs himself of his dignity as a human being.
Dalip Singh

If we do not have peace within ourselves, it is in vain to seek it from outward sources.
La Rochefoucauld

A man has many skins in himself, covering the depths of his own heart. Man knows so many things. He does not know himself. Why thirty or forty skins or hides, just like an ox's or a bear's, so thick and hard, cover the soul. Go into your own ground and learn to know yourself there.
Meister Eckhart

When Abraham Lincoln was a candidate for President or the United States, someone asked him about

his aspiration to that high office. He answered that he did not fear his opponents. "But," he said, "there is a man named Lincoln of whom I am very much afraid. If I am defeated, it will be by that man."
Dillard S. Miller

There are three things extremely hard: steel, a diamond and to know one's self.
Megiddo Message

The mind is its own place, and in itself can make a heaven of hell, a hell of heaven.
John Milton

The awareness of himself as a separate entity, the awareness of his own short life span, of the fact that without his will he is born and against his will he dies, that he will die before those whom he loves, or they before him, the awareness of his aloneness and separateness, of his helplessness before the forces of nature and of society, all this makes his separate, disunited existence an unbearable prison. He would become insane could he not liberate himself from this prison and reach out, unite himself in some form or other with men, with the world outside.
Erich Fromm

There are many beautiful stories of Emily and Charlotte Bronte, the novelists. One of these stories is that of a conversation between the clergyman father and Emily when she was about eight years old. The father was explaining the scenery out on the moors and particularly wished to impress his little girl with the renewal of the earth with new growth. He asked Emily, "What is here which was not here a hundred years ago?" Emily answered promptly, "Me."
Source Unknown

You tell on yourself by the friends you seek,
By the very manner in which you speak;
By the way you employ your leisure time,
By the use you make of dollar and dime;
You tell what you are by the things you wear,
By the spirit in which your burdens bear,
By the kind of things at which you laugh,
By the record you play on the phonograph;
You tell what you are by the way you walk,
By the things of which you delight to talk;
By the manner in which you bear defeat,
By so simple a thing as how you eat;
By the books you choose from the well-filled shelf,
In these ways and more you tell on yourself;
So there's really no particle or sense
In an effort to keep up false pretense.
Source Unknown

Not in the clamor of the crowded street,
Not in the shouts and plaudits of the throng,
But in ourselves are triumph and defeat.
Henry Wadsworth Longfellow

We see things not as they are, but as we are.

Immanuel Kant

At a memorial service for the late Justice Brandeis, another great jurist tried to convey the substance of Brandeis' message. "You build your towers of Babel to the clouds, you may try to circumvent nature by devices beyond the understanding of all but a handful; you may provide endless distraction to escape the tedium of your lives: it shall avail you nothing. The more you struggle, the more you will be enmeshed. Not until you have the courage to meet yourself face to face, will you have taken the first steps along the path of wisdom."

Seymour J. Cohen

The real fool, such as the gods mock or mar, is he who does not know himself.

Oscar Wilde

116 Your neighbor as yourself

There is no ethical development more important than the sharpening and enrichment of neighborly obligation.

James Rowland Angell

Treat all men with respect and amiability. Bring happiness to one another by kindly social relations. Let there be no dissension of any kind, but let love and brotherliness reign. Forgive one another and live in amity for the sake of God.

Elijah of Vilna

Prejudice is not taught so much as it is assimilated, absorbed from the attitudes of the people around us.

Lannelle Stiles

Our youth can afford idealism because they are the first generation of the affluent society. Yet they cannot afford materialism—dialectical or capitalistic—because they are the first generation that might truly see the end of the world. Our young men and women are educated enough to know that only an ideal of human brotherhood can save their world and them.

L.J. West

Men pass, side by side, as hurried and distracted travelers without exchanging a word, nor a fraternal handshake nor a smile . . . A first revolution will be made if men learn simply to speak to each other and not only to co-exist side by side.

Leon-Joseph Cardinal Suenens

We want to travel to the moon, but we don't visit the lonely soul next door.

Orland Ruby

It is easier to love humanity as a whole than to love one's neighbor.

Eric Hoffer

We may not speak the same tongue as our foreign neighbors, but we smile in the same tongue.
Sunshine Magazine

Two men were seated in a lobby of a hotel. One was a gentleman from New York and the other an Apache Indian. The New Yorker stared at the Indian for a few moments and then could no longer restrain his curiosity. "Are you really a full-blooded Indian?" he asked.

"Well, no," replied the Apache thoughtfully, "I am short one pint of blood which I gave to save a white man's life." A real person is one who is short pints of blood which he gave for the well-being of others.
Source Unknown

When God sends the dawn, He sends it for all.
Miguel de Cervantes Saavedra

A genuine conversation means stepping out of the I and knocking on the door of the You.
Albert Camus

We are constantly thinking that there are occasions on which we are justified in treating people without affection. There are never such occasions.
Leo Tolstoy

I tell my grandchildren that people come in as many flavors and colors as ice cream and we would be silly not to enjoy the differences.
Paul C. Johnson

One's love for God is equal to the love one has for the man he loves least.
John J. Hugo

Maturity begins to grow when you can sense your concern for others outweighing your concern for yourself.
John MacNaughton

I hate labels and I wear no labels. When a man has to put something around his neck that says I am, he isn't.
Pearl Bailey

He who would preserve his own freedom must preserve the freedom of others. He cannot save that piece which he desires while denying someone else the portion that is his.
Bryce W. Anderson

The road to world peace is the street where we ourselves live. The first steps to world peace are steps to the stranger in need or the sorrowful next door, be his race or religion what it may . . . To those who, through ignorance or malice, would infect us with the spiritual disease of bigotry or the contagious germs of racial hatreds, and thus serve the enemies of God and of country, I say:
    Whoever degrades another degrades me,
    And whatever is said or done against another,
    Returns in the end to hurt me.
Richard Cardinal Cushing

117 Personal and private

We strive continually to adorn and preserve our imaginary self, neglecting the true one.
Blaise Pascal

Our inner world is reality, perhaps even more real than the apparent world.
Marc Chagall

There are some problems in life that cannot be delegated. One's religion cannot. One's integrity cannot. One's conscience cannot. And one's freedom cannot. These are personal matters, and the effect their implementation has on our national life is a matter of our individual responsibility.
Howard Appling

The patient stripped to his waist for the chiropractor, who immediately went to work on him. After vigorously manipulating a few joints, the chiropractor sighed.
"By golly," he said, "it's going to rain."
The patient looked up. "What makes you say that?" he asked.
"Well," shrugged the other, "I can feel it in your bones!"
Visitor

We are not in danger of becoming slaves any more, but of becoming robots.
Adlai E. Stevenson

Some years ago a mother was carrying her baby over the hills of South Wales. But she never reached her destination alive. A blizzard overtook her and a search party later found her frozen beneath the snow.
The searchers were surprised that she did not have outer garments on but soon discovered why. She had wrapped them around her baby. When they unwrapped the child they found baby David Lloyd George alive and well.
David Lloyd George grew up to become the prime minister of Great Britain during World War I and one of England's great statesmen. The vital contribution which he made to humanity was possible because his mother had given her life to save him.
B. Charles Hostetter

Adam is not the cause, save for his own soul, but each of us has been the Adam of his own soul.
Apocrypha, Baruch 54:19

In a certain sense, every single human soul has more meaning and value than the whole of history and its empires, its wars and revolutions, its blossoming and fading civilizations.
Nicholas Berdyaev

Many people seem to get along quite happily without exploring their inner life or even paying much attention to it. Isn't the inner life an affair for artists, mystics, psychoanalysts—of those breeds of queer fish—to dabble in? Self-discovery is the most important of all human discoveries.
C. Day-Lewis

So, then, to every man his chance—
To every man, regardless of his birth,
His shining, golden opportunity—
To every man the right to live,
To work, to be himself.
Thomas Wolfe

The sacredness of a person represents an unchanging and eternal fact with which we must come to terms. Persons are final values in this world, and if we deny it, ill fares the land.
Gerald Kennedy

Who sees the whole man? The doctor sees the organ or tissue of his specialty. The dentist sees mostly a mouth. The lawyer sees a litigant. The realtor sees a prospect and may never know the tragedy that makes the seller sell. The mechanic under the car sees the client feet-to-feet at best. The undertaker does not see the whole man. He sees what is left of the whole man. The newsman sees only some extraordinary aspect that makes a man into news. The salesman looks only for the prospects and so does the professional pastor. We almost never see the whole man: how far his past, how high his future, how deep his hurts, how great his powers, how short his time, how presumptuous his claims, how real his death, how arrogant his projections. Who sees the whole man?
Carlyle Marney

Every man is an island and often you row around and around before you find a place to land.
Harry Emerson Fosdick

Religion is what a man does with his solitariness.
Alfred North Whitehead

The soul selects her own society,
Then shuts the door;
On her divine majority
Obtrude no more.
Emily Dickinson

---

118 Our real needs

What man's mind can create, man's character can control.
Thomas A. Edison

It is related of Socrates, the Greek philosopher of ancient times, that he visited the public marketplace of his native Athens. Upon returning, he was asked what he had learned from his trip. His reply was, "I never knew there were so many things in the world which I don't want."
Source Unknown

Reading maketh a full man, conference a ready man, and writing an exact man. Read not to contradict, nor to believe, but to weigh and to consider.
Francis Bacon

The proper contribution of the schoolboard member is not expertise, but wisdom; not detailed knowledge, but high values and sound judgment.
John Fischer

There are two ways of treating gossip about other people, and they're both good ways. One is not to listen to it, and the other is not to repeat it.
George Horace Lorimer

If I could get to the highest place in Athens, I would lift my voice and say, "What mean ye, fellow citizens, that ye turn every stone to scrape wealth together, and take so little care of your children, to whom ye must one day relinquish all!"
Socrates

The traditional liberal approach is to look at human needs and try to figure out how to meet them. Now we must ask which are the legitimate human needs.
Harvey Cox

Man will ever stand in need of man.
Theocritus

Lord, in whom I delight,
Being who needs me as I need Thee,
God who asks only that I walk in His ways,
Let me be brought to Thy attention.
Guard my foolish tongue, whose guile is a by-product of the terrifying pace of my generation's journey through space to
Thee, essence of life.
Ethel L. Levey

You must never deprive your body of the necessities of life, nor procure too much for the soul at the expense of the body; in weakening the body, you weaken both. Offer the body the food that will sustain it, and offer your soul doctrines of wisdom and morality.
Bahya ibn Pakuda

Needs are looked upon today as if they contained the totality of existence. Needs are our gods, and we toil and spare no effort to gratify them. Suppression of a desire is considered a sacrilege that must inevitably avenge itself in the form of some mental disorder. We worship not one but a whole pantheon of needs and have come to look upon moral and spiritual norms as nothing but personal desires in disguise.
Abraham Joshua Heschel

An old professor often talked to students about thoughts that came to him in his garden. He spoke so vividly that they came to visualize the place as a broad expanse, agleam with shrubbery and flowers. One evening they visited him and found him seated in a tiny space, shut in by walls.

One exclaimed, "Your garden! It's very narrow."

"Yes," smiled the professor as he looked upward into a sky bright with stars, "but see how high it is!"
L. Kytle

Charlton Heston was cast in the role of Moses in Cecil B. DeMille's motion picture, "The Ten Commandments." But even on location he found it difficult to get into the Old Testament mood. For instance, the original Moses climbed Mount

Sinai on foot. Whereas, for the movie shots, Heston was taken up the mountain three times a day by helicopter! So it is that our times are strangely different from Bible times. How is it that the words of the Bible after 2,000 years can have authority for us in an atomic and helicopter age! The answer lies in the fact that the needs of the human heart are much the same today as in those days.

Author Unknown

That which is to be most desired in America is oneness and not sameness. Sameness is the worst thing that could happen to the people of this country. To make all people the same would lower their quality, but oneness would raise it.

Stephen S. Wise

If a man repents of his evil deeds and then returns to the same deeds, he has not truly repented.

The Midrash

The courage to think, and the ability to love . . . these gifts, plus a modicum of strength, are all I care to ask for in this life. And I do not believe that there is any other.

William Warren Bartley III

119 Achievement that matters

An American painter, John Singer Sargent, once painted a panel of roses which won the praise and admiration of other artists. Although offered a high price on many occasions, he refused to sell it. Whenever he was deeply discouraged, Sargent would look at his panel of roses and remind himself, "I painted that." Somehow confidence and skill came back to him.

We have all of us done something of which we are justly proud. We should remember it always. Perhaps that memory will restore our faith in our ability to meet the challenge once again.

Nuggets

Make the most of yourself, for that is all there is of you.

Ralph Waldo Emerson

I once said to Kreisler, "Why do you spend your genius on trifles, instead of using it in the service of great or less familiar music, which is worthy of it?"

Kreisler said to me: "There is, in my opinion, as much artistic merit and satisfaction in doing a little thing perfectly as in doing a big thing; in writing a perfect sonnet as in building a Milan Cathedral."

Stephen Williams

We never know how high we are
Till we are called to rise;
And then, if we are true to plan,
Our statures touch the skies.

Emily Dickinson

One cannot always be a hero, but one can always be a man.

Goethe

It is no small a thing
To have enjoyed the sun,
To have lived in the spring,
To have loved, to have thought, to have done;
To have advanced true friends, and beat down baffling foes.

So live, that when thy summons comes...
Thou go not, like the quarry-slave at night,
Scourged to his dungeon, but, sustained and soothed
By an unfaltering trust, approach thy grave,
Like one who wraps the drapery of his couch
About him, and lies down to pleasant dreams.
William Cullen Bryant

It is high time the ideal of success should be replaced with the ideal of service.
Albert Einstein

Courage is bearing one's own personal tragedies without dramatizing them to others.
William Feather

It is when we forget ourselves that we do things that are most likely to be remembered.
Grit

In one of his books Bertrand Russell tells of what the painter Haydon, who wasn't a very good painter but who wanted to be, once recorded in his diary: "Spent a miserable morning comparing myself with Raphael." Instead of appreciating what he already possessed, including a great ability to paint, Haydon derived little satisfaction from his work because someone else was better.
Bertrand Russell

He who wants to improve conditions must propagate a new mentality, not a new institution.
Ludwig von Mises

To do the proper thing properly— that is a mediocre virtue. To convert the improper thing into a proper one —that is the virtue of the righteous, of the world redeemers.
Nahum Klatzkin

I don't know who—or what—put the question,
I don't know when it was put.
I don't even remember answering.
But at some moment I did answer
To someone or something YES
And from that hour I was certain
That existence is meaningful
And that, therefore,
My life, in self-surrender, had a GOAL.
Dag Hammarskjold

You've got to do your own growing, no matter how tall your grandfather was.
Anonymous

What is defeat? Nothing but education, nothing but the first step to something better.
Wendell Phillips

120 Choose life

The universe resounds with the joyful cry: "I am, I am!"
Anonymous

William Barclay tells of a church in England which during World War II was planning a Thanksgiving service. They had a big shock of corn in the altar of the church in preparation for the service, and that night an air-raid came and left the church in a heap of ruins and rubble. Winter came and then spring. And someone noticed in the springtime that on the rubble where the church had once stood little green shoots of corn were growing; they flourished through the summer; and in the autumn, among the ruins, there was a patch of corn. Bombs and the rubble and the destruction could not stop the force of life.
C. Ray Dobbins

Reverence for life is more than solicitude or sensitivity for life. It is a sense of the whole, a capacity for wonder, respect for the intricate universe of individual life. It is the supreme awareness of awareness itself. It is pride in being.
Norman Cousins

A wise man's path winds upward to life; he shuns the downward path to death.
Megiddo Message

I went to the woods because I wished to live deliberately, to front only the essential facts of life, and see if I could not learn what it had to teach, and not, when I come to die, discover that I had not lived.
Henry David Thoreau

I was discussing life with my elderly father and he asked me if I took care of myself so that I could look forward to a long life.
"No," I said, "I don't think it would be too attractive to live a long time."
"Why not?" he asked.
"Well," I said, "You don't seem to be enjoying yourself so much at the age of 89."
"Oh," he said, and then, very emphatically: "I'll tell you this: I'm enjoying it a lot more than if I were dead."
Fred Graeser

If I had one year to live I would like to leave this message to those left behind: "Remember that I lived. Forget that I died."
Bernard Harrison

He always said he would retire
When he had made a million clear,
And so he toiled into the dusk
From day to day, from year to year.
At last he put his ledgers up
And laid his stock reports aside—
But when he started out to live
He found he had already died.
Author Unknown

A man should so live that at the close of every day he can repeat: "I have not wasted my day."
The Zohar

If God gave me my choice of the whole planet or my little farm, I should certainly take my farm.
Ralph Waldo Emerson

"Must you go?" pleaded an infatuated baroness who had thrown a splendid party for Johannes Brahms. "Not at all," replied the composer, putting on his hat and heading for the door, "It's entirely a matter of choice."
Tit-Bits

Nobody grows old by merely living a number of years. People grow old by deserting their ideals. You are as young as your faith, as old as your doubt; as young as your self-confidence, as old as your fear; as young as your hopes, as old as your despair. In the central place of every heart there is a recording chamber; so long as it receives messages of beauty, hope, cheer, and courage, so long you are young. When the wires are all down and your heart is covered with the snows of pessimism and the ices of cynicism, then, and then only, are you grown old.
Douglas MacArthur

I will leave man to make the fateful guess,
Will leave him torn between the No and Yes;
Leave him in tragic loneliness to choose,
With all in life to win and all to lose.
Edwin Markham

Man becomes truly human only at the time of decision.
Paul Tillich

13

Improving the quality of life

121 With liberty for all

Liberty means responsibilities. That is why so many men dread it.
Personnel Journal

For what avail the plow or soil,
Or land, or life, if freedom fail?
Ralph Waldo Emerson

Freedom is like a bag of sand. If there is a hole anywhere in the bag, all the sand will run out. If any group of our people are denied their rights, sooner or later all groups stand to lose their rights. All the freedom will run out.
Robert K. Patterson

Be thankful you're living in a land where you can say what you think without thinking.
Arnold H. Glasow

Proclaim liberty throughout the land unto all the inhabitants thereof.
Leviticus 25:10

Liberty is the only thing you cannot have unless you are willing to give it to others.
William Allen White

American liberty is a religion. It is a thing of the spirit. It is an aspiration on the part of the people for not alone a free life but a better life; and so I say to you people of the world, I think I know the heart of the American people. I have lived among them; I know them well. And despite the occasional hesitation and doubts, the American people will reach out, will give

their utmost to see that this precious thing we call liberty shall not disappear from the world, either in Europe, or in Asia or in America.
Wendell L. Willkie

Faith in God is the strongest bulwark of a free society. Human freedom began when men became conscious that over and above society and nature there is a God who created them . . . who fashioned them in His likeness, and that they are, therefore, possessed of intrinsic and independent significance and are endowed, as individuals, with original and irrevocable rights and authority.
Abba Hillel Silver

The cause of freedom is identified with the destinies of humanity, and in whatever part of the world it gains ground, by and by it will be a common gain to all who desire it.
Louis Kossuth

Freedom is not something man can give us. God has already given it. But it is something that we can easily lose by failing to understand and appreciate it.
Kenneth W. Sollitt

No matter how we defend free speech—and I would defend it with the passion of Voltaire—I think we must also agree that it carries with it an obligation to be fair, to be informed, and to be sincerely motivated.
Adlai E. Stevenson

Man is most free in the discovery that he is not free.
Reinhold Niebuhr

Freedoms are *always* lost unless they are continually fought for.
Leavitt C. Parsons

The God who gave us life gave us liberty at the same time.
Thomas Jefferson

122 By teachers we are taught

A teacher affects eternity. He can never tell where his influence stops.
Henry Adams

Every great teacher develops a style that is distinctively his own. He is never content to be an imitator, a faddist, a cultist, a goosestepper. Indeed, he seldom if ever thinks in such terms. Rather, he has so developed his teaching craft that what he does with his students is discriminating, unique, original. In his own way, he "makes you want to do or be."
Leland B. Jacobs

Carlyle once received a letter from a young man which read like this: "Mr. Carlyle, I wish to be a teacher. Will you tell me the secret of successful teaching?" Carlyle immediately wrote back: "Be what you would have your pupils be. All other teaching is unblessed mockery and apery."

F. Russell Purdy

Teachers are our greatest servants. They mold the nation by molding the plastic clay of youth. They do more than fill minds, they free minds. They do more than teach facts, they inspire growth. They do more than teach boys and girls to make a living, they stimulate them to build great lives. They teach them how to think. They teach them to seek, to find, to expand their horizons. They teach them to discover the world and they teach them to live in it as world citizens.

Unknown, unsung, the teacher does the noblest work on earth. She discovers the tiny seeds of genius, and cultivates them so that they may blossom in all their glory.

Good Reading

Teaching is not lecturing or telling things. Teaching is devising a sequence of questions which enables kids to become aware of generalization themselves.

Max Beherman

The teacher is often the first to discover the talented and unusual scholar. How he handles and encourages, or discourages, such a child may make all the difference in the world to that child's future—and to the world.

Loren Eiseley

A teacher who can arouse a feeling for one single good action, for one single good poem, accomplishes more than he who fills our memory with rows and rows of natural objects, classified with name and form.

Goethe

No printed word nor spoken plea
Can teach young hearts what men should be,
Not all the books on all the shelves,
But what the teachers are themselves.

Arthur Guiterman

As a former teacher with a life-long interest in public affairs, I'm glad to see teachers playing a growing role in our society. I am convinced that the classroom teacher is the most important transmitter of what we call the American dream.

Lyndon B. Johnson

If we work upon marble it will perish; if we work upon stone it will crumble to dust; but if we take a child and train it well, we rear a monument which time can never efface.

Dean Farrar

The object of teaching a child is to enable him to get along without his teacher.

Elbert Hubbard

The difference between the person who instructs and the person who is a real teacher lies in the ability to recognize the importance of a child's feelings about himself. We are really teaching if each child can leave our group holding his head high with self-respect and feeling that he is a person of worth.

Gladys Gardner Jenkins

Teachers are many things all of which are important. To the child, the teacher is the key to knowledge, understanding, and wisdom. To the community, the teacher represents the voice of wide understanding needed in the solution of problems in and out of the classroom. To the nation, the teacher is necessary for he instills the basic knowledge about the rights and responsibilities of government so that free citizens can govern themselves. A nation's economic strength, too, stems from the teacher who conveys not only the skills that advance the nation but which enable her citizens to think and reason.
Robert H. Wyatt

Although a teacher cannot teach what he does not know, he can sure enough inspire students to learn what he doesn't know. A great teacher has always been measured by the number of his students who have surpassed him.
Don Robinson

What the teacher is is more important than what she teaches.
Karl Menninger

The mediocre teacher tells. The good teacher explains. The superior teacher demonstrates. The great teacher inspires.
William Arthur Ward

There is no office higher than that of a teacher of youth, for there is nothing on earth so precious as the mind, soul, character of the child. No office should be regarded with greater respect.
William Ellery Channing

123 For the sake of humanity

Men are sometimes cruel, but Man is kind. Men are sometimes greedy, but Man is generous. Men are mortal, but Man is immortal.
Adlai E. Stevenson

I am a human being, and I consider nothing human alien to me.
Terence

Men are more important than tools. If you don't believe so, put a good tool into the hands of a poor workman.
John J. Bernet

Man has indeed learned to master his physical world far beyond what his forefathers could ever have imagined. He has greatly improved the condition of his life, raised the standard of living, but he himself as a human being has not been affected by all these advances or by this so-called progress, because when the recent wars broke out a very primitive human being, full of cruelty and brutality and selfishness came to the fore and proved that man after all has not changed.
Rudolph Allers

The greatest danger in nuclear technology is not that the machines will begin to think like men but that men will begin to think like machines.
Edward H. Weiss

Man imperishably stands
Through his thousand destinies.
There are planets in his eyes
There are aeons in his hands.

Time in him is ever now;
Yesterday is in his veins
And tomorrow in his loins.
And forever on his brow.
Dilys Bennett Laing

It is better to be a man for ten minutes than to be a tortoise for a hundred years.
Italian Proverb

We are all blind—until we see
That in the human plan
Nothing is worth the making
If it does not make the man.

Why build these cities glorious,
If man unbuilded goes?
In vain we build the world, unless
The builder also grows.

Edwin Markham

Be ashamed to die until you have won some victory for humanity.
Horace Mann

Man is a creature who hangs between his grandeur and his misery, poised between his finitude and his transcendence.
Alexander Pope

Man was made to stand on the shore, to celebrate the sun and the sky, to use the wind and master the water, to care passionately for the children tumbling about the sand. He was made to grow in the image of his Father, to embrace his fellows everywhere, to open the doors, to feed the hungry, to return good for evil. Nothing is harder, but anything else is sure damnation.
Sidney J. Harris

You must not lose faith in humanity. Humanity is an ocean; if a few drops of the ocean are dirty, the ocean does not become dirty.
Mohandas Gandhi

In China a man was watching a nun cleaning the gangrenous sores of wounded soldiers. "I wouldn't do that for a million dollars," he said. Without a pause in her work, the sister replied, "Neither would I."
Source Unknown

Whenever there is conflict between property rights and human rights, human rights must prevail.
Abraham Lincoln

One man is equal to the whole creation.
The Talmud

Big things show what a man can do; little things show what a man is.
Megiddo Message

The supreme task of our age is not to make things easy but man nobler.
B. G. Kher

124 Training ourselves for sensitivity

We should listen, not to avoid riots, but because there is so much truth in the charges they are leveling.
Harry E. Smith

Most of us live too near the surface of our abilities, dreading to call upon our deeper resources. It is as if a strong man were to do his work with only one finger.
John Charles Wynn

1. Do more than exist . . . live.
2. Do more than look . . . observe.
3. Do more than read . . . absorb.
4. Do more than hear . . . listen.
5. Do more than listen . . . understand.
6. Do more than think . . . ponder.
7. Do more than talk . . . say something.
NYLIC Review

Life is found in becoming something rather than in having something, in an inward condition of the mind and spirit, not in an outward set of circumstances.
Matthew Arnold

No sensitive person can look at the sky on a cloudless night without asking himself where the stars came from, where they go, and what keeps the universe in order. The same questions arise when we look at the internal universe within the human body, or even just at that pair of sensitive and searching human eyes which constantly strives to bridge the gap between these two universes.
Source Unknown

Sensitivity to fellow human beings is the first quality of leadership. This means that we need not only response from others, but we need the capacity in ourselves to respond naturally and intimately to others. We simply can't go it alone. We learn to be responsive by concerning ourselves with others, not by trying to persuade others to be concerned with us.
James F. Oates, Jr.

Observation is the most vital part of my life, but not any sort of observation. I have trained myself to let nothing pass by: "One never pays enough attention," Cezanne used to say, and I have made his word mine.
Pablo Picasso

I called the devil, and he came;
With wonder his form did I close scan;
He is not ugly, and he is not lame;
But really a handsome and charming man.
Heinrich Heine

Pride is an exaggerated sense of our own importance and an inward belief that we deserve praise. Whoever would attain the trait of cleanness must be free from the taint of pride. He must realize that pride is a form of blindness which prevents even a man of understanding from seeing his own shortcomings.
Moses Hayyim Luzzatto

Prayer is opening the heart to God. It is not all petition. It has its listening side. Prayer is more than speaking to God; it is giving God an opportunity to speak to us.

Costen J. Harrell

Throw yourself into a furnace rather than shame a fellow man in public.

The Talmud

It is the individual who knows how little he knows about himself who stands a reasonable chance of finding out something about himself before he dies.

S. I. Hayakawa

Only that day dawns to which we are awake.

Henry David Thoreau

Art is the difference between seeing and just identifying.

Jean Mary Morman

A little girl danced into the kitchen where her mother was busy preparing dinner. "Mother," she cried, "guess what!"

"I don't know—what?" the mother asked, not looking up from the potato she was peeling.

"Mother, you're not listening."

"Yes, I am, honey." She pushed the peelings into the garbage disposal.

"But, Mother, you're not listening with your eyes."

Agnes White Thomas

Compassion is a sign of a truly great and generous heart. Compassion is understanding the troubles of others, coupled with an urgent desire to help. Man naturally is not compassionate. It is cultivating an ability to put himself in the other fellow's shoes, remembering that all facts and circumstances influencing the other fellow cannot be known to him.

Megiddo Message

A little boy once asked how he might become a good conversationalist (what he meant was to be effective in human relations). The wise old sage, who was asked the question, responded, "Listen my son . . ." and paused then momentarily. "Yes, yes," cried the boy, "Go on." "That is all. Listen, my son," responded the wise man.

Source Unknown

Margaret Fishback reported that she recently watched a crowd on Fifth Avenue gather around some policemen who were trying to shield a prostrate figure on the sidewalk from the gaze of the curious. One woman looked for a moment and then said to a friend, "He's probably only dead."

Jerome Beatty, Jr.

Two monks were required to do penance. For one day they were to walk about with peas in their shoes.

All day long one monk limped. The other walked with ease.

The sufferer said to his fellow: "How can you endure the agony of tender feet, walking on hard dry peas?"

The other replied: "I boiled my peas."

Personnel Administration

125 Rest and recreation

Working hours are for making a living. Leisure hours are for making a life.
J. Gustav White

Time you enjoy wasting is not wasted time.
Anonymous

If today's average American is confronted with an hour of leisure, he is likely to palpitate with panic. An hour with nothing to do? He jumps into a dither and into a car, and drives off fiercely in pursuit of diversion . . . We "catch" a train. We "grab" a bite of lunch. We "contact" a client. Everything has to be active and electric . . . We need less leg action and more acute observation as we go. Slow down the muscle and stir up the mind.
Author Unknown

Who has not shown his high respect for that sacred seventh day, by giving rest and relaxation from labor to himself and his neighbors, freemen and slaves alike, and beyond these to his beasts? For the holiday extends also to every herd, and to all creatures made to minister to man, who serve like slaves their natural master. It extends also to every kind of trees and plants; for it is not permitted to cut any shoot or branch, or even a leaf, or to pluck any fruit whatsoever. All such are set at liberty on that day, and live as it were in freedom, under the general edict that proclaims that none should touch them.
Philo

Tell me what a man does with his spare time and I'll tell you what kind of person he is.
Author Unknown

Recreation's purpose is not to kill time, but rather to make time live; not to help the individual serve time but to make time serve him; not to encourage people to hide from themselves but to help them find themselves.
Good Reading

Recreation is not the highest kind of enjoyment, but in its time and place is quite as proper as prayer.
Samuel I. Prime

We do well to recognize that the problem of leisure is related to the ultimate concern of life itself; it runs throughout the search for meaning. If contemporary man has problems of fear, anxiety, boredom, these may be related to his alienation from God and from his fellowman. The depth of this alienation may show nowhere as much as it does in the use he makes of his unstructured hours; here is where true despair and lack of creativity will show first and in greatest depth.
G. Willis Bennett

Leisure is like an empty bottle. It depends on what you put into it. More leisure does not automatically mean more culture, more happiness. It may mean more crime, more boredom, more time-killing activities.
Krastyu Krasteff

Some puritan perversity in the American character makes us hate the nothing-doers of the world. A man quietly doing nothing is a challenge to the American system. He must be cajoled, badgered and, if necessary, blackguarded into purposeful living. Every once in a while it is important to do nothing.
Russell Baker

I think recreation is terribly important in the lives of people, because it is re-creation, if it is used rightly. I don't care whether it is making artificial flies or casting or working on a stamp collection or swatting a baseball or golf ball—it can be the change of pace that seems to me so very, very important in the lives of all of us. It becomes more important as tensions increase—an opportunity to totally shift gears, even though we work harder in our recreational activities than we do possibly in our business. It isn't the intensity. In fact I have always said that if a recreational activity is going to do any good for a person, he has to take it seriously and really work at it—in contrast to being a dilettante.
William C. Menninger

All the evils of life have fallen upon us because men will not sit quietly alone in a room.
Blaise Pascal

In the Indian story when the King asks, "How shall I find the truth?" the sage replies, "When you have stopped looking for it."
Indian Legends

Leisure is not only the occasion but also the capacity for steeping oneself in the whole of creation.
Josef Pieper

Two women were stretched out on adjacent cots in a Red Cross blood center. The nurse congratulated one of them, a weary-looking young housewife, on contributing her eighth pint, making her a Gallon Donor.
"You come here often?" the other woman asked, making conversation.
"Yes," the tired-looking one replied with a sigh. "It's the only volunteer work I know of that I can do lying down."
Catholic Digest

I have always believed that one of the most overlooked and underrated treasures in our common religious heritage is the Sabbath, the setting aside of one day in seven so that man might restore his soul.
Arthur J. Goldberg

The purpose of any vacation should be to refresh our shaken spirits and renew our forgotten purposes, but so often this is lost. These days should be the most carefully planned (not just scheduled) days of the year. This is the time to guide yourself back in purpose and put yourself at peace. During these days, the mind more than the body needs refreshing, so plan your two or three weeks to fit that purpose—and you will find God.
Patrick R. Buth

126　The power of speech

Words can bruise and break hearts, and minds as well. There are no black and blue marks, no broken bones to put in a plaster cast, and therefore no prison bars for the offender.
Marlene Dietrich

The true meaning of a word is to be found by observing what a man does with it, not by what he says about it.
Percy Williams Bridgman

Human speech is a sacrament; it is at the root of all human life and we do not ponder enough the mystery whereby words pass from one human mind to another, bringing communion between men and nations. Marvelous too is the way in which words, as tools, come out of the changing life of men.
Gordon Rupp

Words at great moments of history are deeds.
Clement Atlee

While a great speech can never move mountains, it can move people to the mountains and stir them to begin their necessary tasks.
Richard H. Hunt

Words have power. They sing. They hurt. They teach. They sanctify. They were man's first immeasurable feat of magic. They liberated us from ignorance and our barbarous past. For without these marvelous scribbles which build letters into words, words into sentences, sentences into systems and sciences and creeds, man would be forever confined to the self-isolated prison of the scuttlefish or the chimpanzee.
Look Editorial

If you are tempted to reveal
A tale to you someone has told
About another, make it pass,
Before you speak, three gates of gold.

These narrow gates: First, "Is it true?"
Then, "Is it needful?" In your mind
Give truthful answer. And the next
Is last and narrowest, "Is it kind?"
And if to reach your lips at last
It passes through these gateways three,
Then you may tell the tale, nor fear
What the result of speech may be.
Beth Day

The minister was whaling away with his golf club trying to get out of the sand trap. Finally he lifted his ball only to have it go over the green into a trap on the other side.

Red-faced and exasperated, he turned to the other members of the foursome. "Won't one of you laymen please say a few appropriate words?"
S. C. Easley

A torn jacket is soon mended, but hard words bruise the heart of a child.
Henry Wadsworth Longfellow

A study of 4,993 industrial advertisements showed that ads with four to ten words in their headlines got about the same readership as those with more than ten words. Don't count the words; make the words count.
Crumbley

Is not *My* word like fire, says the Lord, and like a hammer which breaks the rock in pieces?
Jeremiah 23:29

I do not want of you sacrifices and offerings, but words of contrition; as it said: "Take with you words and turn to the Lord." (Hosea 14:2)
The Midrash

If has been held in some quarters that conferences are nothing but talk. The answer is that in an honest and accurate sense, they *are* talk. But so too, was the Sermon on the Mount. So were the Lincoln-Douglas debates. What were the lamentations of the ancient Hebrews but talk to revive their people and to restore their relationship to God and to hope? What, indeed, were the spirituals of the slaves of our own South but talk set to the chants for a new day of freedom and dignity?
Roy Wilkins

It is with a word as with an arrow— once loose it does not return.
Megiddo Message

Speech is civilization itself. The word, even the most contradictory word, preserves contact—it is silence which isolates.
Thomas Mann

A speaker, nearing the close of a long, long oration, said, "I'm pleading for the next generation!"
"If you talk much longer," interrupted an impatient hearer, "you can plead *to* the next generation!"
Source Unknown

127 Balm for the suffering

The secret of your life and the meaning of your life—its priorities, its values, its orientation—may be found in what you are willing to suffer for: for what purpose or for what person.
Harry Chase

We so often ask when things go wrong with us, "Why should this happen to me?" and forget all the good things that have come our way through the love and labor of others that we had neither earned nor deserved, but just taken for granted.
A. Graham Ikin

To suffer is not the worst thing that can happen to us; the worst thing is not to believe in anything worth suffering for.
Sarah Patton Boyle

How singular is this thing called pleasure! And, curiously, it is related to pain. Pleasure and pain never come to a man together. Yet, he who pursues either of them, is usually compelled to take the other. They are two, and yet they grow together, and of one head and stem.
Socrates

Faith has always been an essential factor in all medical treatment. As a profession, consciously or unconsciously, more often the latter, faith has been one of our most valuable assets.
William Osler

The true way to mourn the dead is to take care of the living who belong to them.
Edmund Burke

To heal sometimes
To relieve often.
Edward Livingston Trudeau

Some people never look up until they are flat on their backs; they never think of God until they are face to face with some disaster. A great deal of rust requires a sharp file. Many a person would never think upon the meaning of life unless sickness had detached him from too great love of the foibles of this life.
Fulton J. Sheen

Grief never disappears when it is supposed... The more you grieve in the aftermath of your tragedy, the better your emotional health will be. You must find the reason for your own living and accept the fact God has a very definite purpose for your life. That is the reason you are still here. Exercise, work, and faith are three great helps to anyone.
Cort R. Flint

What does not destroy me, makes me stronger.
Friedrich Nietzsche

Who best can suffer, best can do.
John Milton

A man busy nursing his own wounds has no time to inflict them on others.
Peter de Vries

Real strength comes from the endurance of sorrow and even a nodding acquaintance with suffering.
Art Linkletter

The wounded oyster mends his shell with pearl.
Ralph Waldo Emerson

There is no question of competing. The amount of human suffering is so great that all our combined efforts are weak in comparison to the need.
Dana Farnsworth

When two people are sick, and one is rich and the other poor, it is the duty to visit the poor one, for many will visit the rich person, while few will visit the poor one.
Book of the Pious

From out the throng and stress of lies,
From out the painful noise of sighs,
One voice of comfort seems to rise:
"It is the meaner part that dies."
William Morris

Billie Bray, when he heard someone telling a long story of troubles endured and sorrowings suffered, exclaimed: "I've had my trials and troubles. The Lord has given me both vinegar and honey, but He has given me the vinegar with a teaspoon and the honey with a ladle."

Robert G. Lee

When I was brought to the concentration camp of Auschwitz, a manuscript ready to be printed was confiscated from my pocket. Certainly my wish to write this manuscript anew helped me to survive. When I fell ill one day from typhus fever, I jotted down on little scraps of paper a lot of notes destined to help me reconstruct the manuscript, should I live to the day of liberation.

One night, I remember, it seemed to me that I would have to die. It was then I underwent perhaps the deepest experience of my time in concentration camp. While the concern of most of the camp was: "Will we survive the camp? For, if not, all this suffering will have no sense," the question for me was: "Has all this suffering, this dying around us a meaning? For, if not, then ultimately, there is no sense to surviving."

Viktor E. Frankl

If you are melancholy for the first time, you will find upon a little inquiry that others have been melancholy many times and yet are cheerful now.

Leigh Hunt

---

128 The open mind

A well-known artist noticed a drawing of a fish by a pavement artist and asked what sort of a fish it was supposed to be.

"A shark, sir," said the artist.

"But you've never seen a shark."

"That's true," said the pavement artist, "but don't some of you Academy fellows paint angels?"

Source Unknown

A flash of lightning from the clouds might be compared to a flash of insight in the mind; in each case a high potential seems to be built up from feeble beginnings.

Merl Ruskin Wolfard

Time was invented by Almighty God in order to give ideas a chance.

Nicholas Murray Butler

There are two ways of getting through the world—one is to stop thinking, and the other is to stop and think.

Megiddo Message

The most distinctive mark of a cultivated mind is the ability to take another's point of view; to put one's self in another's place, and see life and its problems from a point of view different from one's own.

A. H. R. Fairchild

Somebody once asked Newton, "How did you discover the law of gravitation?" "By thinking about it all the time," was his answer.
Herman A. Moench

The next time your students look for an analogy to thinking, tell them the one about the parachute instructor who said: "Minds are like parachutes; they function only when open."
Joseph Crescimbeni

It is better to debate a question without settling it than to settle it without debate.
Joseph Joubert

Shortly after I began my work in Bedford-Stuyvesant, I received an unexpected visit from Senator Kennedy in my office. I happened to have my jacket off, my tie loosened and my feet on the desk. "What are you doing?" the Senator asked. "I'm thinking," I replied. "Fine," said the Senator. "But what are you going to do when you put your feet down?"
William M. Birenbaum

Intuition is reason in a hurry.
Holbrook Jackson

Prejudice is emotion without mind. Conviction is emotion with mind.
H. W. Rupp

Our country is not so rich in intellectual and inspirational leadership, or so certain of its course in the world, or so perfect in the treatment of its citizens, that it can afford the suppression of any thoughtful view or voice . . . We cannot afford to listen merely to the spokesmen for the state and the status quo, for the comfortable and the conformed. We have enough timidity and stupidity in our midst without telling those clergymen who are willing to stand up and be counted to sit down.
Theodore Sorensen

It's a good thing to have an open mind—but not so open that your brains fall out.
Neilson

A meddling old woman accused one of the contractor's workmen of having reverted to drink because "with her own eyes" she had seen his wheelbarrow standing outside the tavern.

The accused man made no verbal defense but that evening he placed his wheelbarrow outside her door and left it there all night.
Future

A young Sunday school teacher asked one of her pupils what prejudice is. With singular wisdom the lad answered, "I think it's when you decide some fellow is a stinker before you even meet him."
Oren Arnold

Too many people seem to be saying by their attitudes, "I have made up my mind. Do not confuse me with facts."
Anonymous

129 Worry wears one down

Worry about the future doesn't improve the future—it only ruins the present.
The Country Parson

Worry is a thin stream of fear trickling through the mind. If encouraged, it cuts a channel into which all other thoughts are drained.
A. S. Roche

Eight percent of a person's worries are "legitimate."
 Forty per cent will never happen.
 Thirty per cent over people's criticisms of us.
 Twelve per cent over old decisions.
 Ten per cent over our health.
 Thus 92 per cent of our worries are proved foolish.
Thomas S. Kepler

The legs of the stork are long, the legs of the duck are short: you cannot make the legs of the stork short, neither can you make the legs of the duck long. Why worry?
Chinese Proverb

Worry is like a rocking chair. It will give you something to do, but it won't get you anywhere.
Anonymous

A day of worry is more exhausting than a week of work.
John Lubbock

If you want to test your memory, try to recall what you were worrying about one year ago today.
Rotarian

The old Irish mother may have been wiser than funny when she said to her son who would have to cross a swollen stream on his way home one night, "Tell me exactly when you expect to cross, so that I'll know when to worry."
Erwin L. McDonald

If there is worry in the heart of man, let him talk it away. Yea, a good word will even make it glad.
Proverbs 12:25

Never bear more than one kind of trouble at a time. Some people bear three—all they have now; all they ever had; and all they expect to have.
Catholic Digest

You cannot prevent the birds of sadness from flying over your head, but you can prevent them from nesting in your hair.
Chinese Proverb

Officials at the Hayden Planetarium in New York, where a show on the subject was given, love to recall the aged lady spectator who came up to the narrator after a performance and asked, "How many years before the sun blows up?"
 "Twenty billion," said the man.
 "Thank heavens!" replied the old girl with a sigh of relief. "thought you said twenty million."
Richard F. Dempewolff

When Bulstrode Whitelocke was ambassador to the Hague he was tossing about through the night in anxiety concerning some of the problems that faced him the day before. It seemed to him that he could do nothing about them—except worry. An old servant lying in the same room said to him, "Sir, may I ask a question?" "Certainly," replied the ambassador. "Sir, did God govern the world before you came into it?" "Undoubtedly," replied Whitelocke. "And will He rule the world when you have gone out of it?" "Of course, He will," said the ambassador. "Then, sir, can you trust Him to rule the world while you are in it?"

The ambassador sensed the faith behind the question, and quickly adopted it by turning on his side and going to sleep!

A. Purnell Bailey

"The newspapers are so full of items concerning another war that I cannot help worrying," said a mother to a teacher.

"There is no cause for worry, madam," the teacher said. "We must disregard half of what we read in the newspapers."

The woman pondered his statement for a moment and then said, "Yes, I know, but which half must we disregard?"

Dave J. Teter

Our greatest pretenses are built up not to hide the evil and ugly in us, but our emptiness. The hardest thing to hide is something that is not there.

Eric Hoffer

I got my ulcers
And numerous ills
From mountain climbing
On molehills.

Fred W. Norman

Some of your hurts you have cured,
And the sharpest you still have survived;
But what torments of grief you endured,
From evils that never arrived.

Ralph Waldo Emerson

---

130 Growing a soul

Some years ago a white explorer was conducting a safari in darkest Africa, and for four days he had driven his native bearers unmercifully. They covered perhaps twice as much mileage as usual on such a trip. But the fifth day he got up all ready to go early in the morning, and the natives were all squatting on their haunches, and they refused to move. Well, he berated them and urged them to no avail. And finally the leader spoke up and he said, "My men say that for the last four days they have traveled so rapidly and so far that they have left their souls behind. They are just going to sit here and wait until their souls catch up to their bodies."

W. D. Snively, Jr.

The eye is the window of the soul.
Czechoslovakian Proverb

Develop the mind at the expense of the soul and you father a monster.
Willie Mae Cary

We might best compare "soul" to electrical power. Electricity exists. When the lamp is plugged in, the light glows; when the lamp is turned off, it ceases to glow. Where did the electricity go? It didn't go anywhere. It simply continues to exist, even though it no longer sends its power into that particular bulb.
Harold Krantzler

We have been brainwashed into accepting the material and physical values in life as the answers to the hunger of our souls.
Harrison R. Thompson

It takes a soul
To move a body: it takes a high-souled man
To move the masses, even to a cleaner stye;
It takes the ideal to blow a hair's breadth off
The dust of the actual.
Elizabeth Barrett Browning

We are rather tired of the fraudulent way in which we talk of "personality" instead of "character," personality without moral worth, valued only for attractiveness or impressiveness. Multitudes of people want to know how to glitter, how to be glib. We have been more interested in "oomphiness" and "itness" than in wholesomeness and righteousness. Too few times do we hear it said of anybody, "He is a splendid character." We only hear, "He has a marvelous personality." It is all very shabby, very shoddy, very fraudulent—and now it is becoming very tiresome.
A. Powell Davies

We need solitude to look into the mirror of our souls. Izaak Walton, the great fisherman, recommended fishing to quiet the inner man. We all need to meditate and invite the soul.
A. Devaney

Many moderns have forgotten that they are also spiritual beings. To deny the spiritual side of one's nature does it great violence.
Viktor E. Frankl

The secret of youthful looks in an aged face is easy shoes, easy corsets and an easy conscience.
Anonymous

Dean Hayes of Duquesne University in Pittsburgh tells the story of a group of women who gathered once each week at a bridge club. Every now and then, instead of bridge, they would have a guest speaker. This one day they had a surgeon as speaker. "You know," he said, "I have operated on many people over a number of years. I have performed thousands of operations on every part of the human anatomy. And this forces you to some very difficult conclusions. After looking at every part of man, I have come to the conclusion that man has no soul. I have never seen one."

Martha raised her hand and said, "Doctor, have you operated on any brains?"

He replied: "Thousands of them."
She asked: "Did you ever find a thought?"
James E. Gates

Our ideals are our better selves.
A. Bronson Alcott

A nation is a soul, a spiritual principle. To have a common glory in the past, a common will in the present; to have done great things together, to want to do them again —these are the conditions for the existence of a nation.
Abba Eban

Just as the soul fills the body, so God fills the world. Just as the soul carries the body, so God carries the world.
The Talmud

14
Marks of maturity

131 According to the effort so is the reward

At the age of 75, his international reputation as a virtuoso long since assured, Pablo Casals was asked why he continued to practice the cello four hours daily. "Because," he answered, "I think I'm making some progress."
Instrumentalist

Miracles sometimes occur, but one has to work terribly hard for them.
Chaim Weizmann

Those who expect to reap the blessings of freedom must, like men, undergo the fatigue of supporting it.
Thomas Paine

It takes twenty years to be an overnight success.
Eddie Cantor

A girl said to Marion Anderson, "I would give anything in the world if I could sing like that." The singer replied: "Would you give eight hours a day practice?"
Source Unknown

A Marine lieutenant, straight from the platoon leader course at Quantico, took over a battle-experienced platoon on the main line of resistance in Korea. On the first night of his command he saw that his men were beginning to dig their foxholes, and the green lieutenant asked the platoon sergeant, "Sergeant, where is my foxhole?"
Replied the sergeant, "You're standing on it, sir, you just have to move the dirt."
Thomas Gallagher

Victory won't come to me unless I go to it.

Marianne Moore

He had delivered the master oration of the conference. When finally the applause subsided, a cocky young doctor of divinity strolled up to him. "That was a masterly address you delivered extemporaneously. Yet you must have had some preparation to have done it so well. How long did it take you to prepare it?"

The older man looked gently for some time at the younger one before he answered. And then: "Sixty years, young man, sixty years!"

Highways of Happiness

For Betty Corstorphine, blind 18 years, the sacrifice was this:

She would have to travel across the country, submit to delicate surgery, allow two stainless steel wires to be inserted into the depths of her brain and undergo the unmeasured pain of electricity in her optic nerve.

The reward? Five, perhaps six, flashes of light—and the hope that someday persons who cannot see through their own eyes might see through the eyes of electronics.

Betty Corstorphine heard the proposal and told her doctor:

"I'll take the honor."

The wires, about half the thickness of a human hair, were inserted into her brain under local anaesthetic by Dr. Tracy Putnam, chief neurosurgeon at the hospital. They were pushed about two inches deep into the convolutions at the back of the head to the centers of vision, and they were attached to a transistor amplifier and a photoelectric cell.

Miss Corstorphine held the photoelectric cell and pointed it about a darkened room. It was when she pointed it toward the light that she saw the flashes.

"Whenever the voltage got to a certain height I felt a pressure—an ache," said Miss Corstorphine, "and could see the light. It changed the darkness into gray and the grayness into light.

"And whenever it reached a certain voltage I felt a pain.

"But as I felt the pain"—and here, Miss Corstorphine's face brightened into a glow—"I saw the light."

The New York Times

When the method and discipline of knowledge are added to talent, the result is usually altogether outstanding.

Marcus Tullius Cicero

The saints are the sinners who keep on trying.

Robert Louis Stevenson

Men try in two ways to reach the treetops and the mountain tops. One is by gazing and dreaming at them; the other is by climbing to them. Men try by those same two ways to reach the highest places in their lives.

Nuggets

He who would eat the kernel must crack the shell.

Titus Maccius Plautus

14

Marks of maturity

131 According to the effort so is the reward

At the age of 75, his international reputation as a virtuoso long since assured, Pablo Casals was asked why he continued to practice the cello four hours daily. "Because," he answered, "I think I'm making some progress."

Instrumentalist

Miracles sometimes occur, but one has to work terribly hard for them.

Chaim Weizmann

Those who expect to reap the blessings of freedom must, like men, undergo the fatigue of supporting it.

Thomas Paine

It takes twenty years to be an overnight success.

Eddie Cantor

A girl said to Marion Anderson, "I would give anything in the world if I could sing like that." The singer replied: "Would you give eight hours a day practice?"

Source Unknown

A Marine lieutenant, straight from the platoon leader course at Quantico, took over a battle-experienced platoon on the main line of resistance in Korea. On the first night of his command he saw that his men were beginning to dig their foxholes, and the green lieutenant asked the platoon sergeant, "Sergeant, where is my foxhole?"

Replied the sergeant, "You're standing on it, sir, you just have to move the dirt."

Thomas Gallagher

Victory won't come to me unless I go to it.

Marianne Moore

He had delivered the master oration of the conference. When finally the applause subsided, a cocky young doctor of divinity strolled up to him. "That was a masterly address you delivered extemporaneously. Yet you must have had some preparation to have done it so well. How long did it take you to prepare it?"

The older man looked gently for some time at the younger one before he answered. And then: "Sixty years, young man, sixty years!"

Highways of Happiness

For Betty Corstorphine, blind 18 years, the sacrifice was this:

She would have to travel across the country, submit to delicate surgery, allow two stainless steel wires to be inserted into the depths of her brain and undergo the unmeasured pain of electricity in her optic nerve.

The reward? Five, perhaps six, flashes of light—and the hope that someday persons who cannot see through their own eyes might see through the eyes of electronics.

Betty Corstorphine heard the proposal and told her doctor:

"I'll take the honor."

The wires, about half the thickness of a human hair, were inserted into her brain under local anaesthetic by Dr. Tracy Putnam, chief neurosurgeon at the hospital. They were pushed about two inches deep into the convolutions at the back of the head to the centers of vision, and they were attached to a transistor amplifier and a photoelectric cell.

Miss Corstorphine held the photoelectric cell and pointed it about a darkened room. It was when she pointed it toward the light that she saw the flashes.

"Whenever the voltage got to a certain height I felt a pressure—an ache," said Miss Corstorphine, "and could see the light. It changed the darkness into gray and the grayness into light.

"And whenever it reached a certain voltage I felt a pain.

"But as I felt the pain"—and here, Miss Corstorphine's face brightened into a glow—"I saw the light."

The New York Times

When the method and discipline of knowledge are added to talent, the result is usually altogether outstanding.

Marcus Tullius Cicero

The saints are the sinners who keep on trying.

Robert Louis Stevenson

Men try in two ways to reach the treetops and the mountain tops. One is by gazing and dreaming at them; the other is by climbing to them. Men try by those same two ways to reach the highest places in their lives.

Nuggets

He who would eat the kernel must crack the shell.

Titus Maccius Plautus

132 Health and the art of healing

Look to your health; and if you have it, praise God, and value it next to a good conscience.
Izaak Walton

It is not an overstatement to say that fully 50 per cent of the problems of the acute stages of an illness and 75 per cent of the difficulties of convalescence have their primary origin not in the body, but in the mind of the patient.
Medical Scientist

Health lies in labor, and there is no royal road to it but through toil.
Wendell Phillips

Dr. Melvin Casberg, a Long Beach physician and former Dean of the St. Louis School of Medicine, expressed concern over the loss of the personal touch in medicine. It is giving way to mechanical gadgetry. Cold metal is replacing the feel of the doctor's hand. One disadvantage to specialization is a loss of focus on the whole man.
Source Unknown

There is no herb that is not a medicine... what is rare is the man who knows how to put it to right use.
Sanskrit Proverb

Some years ago a fascinating report written by specialists of forestry was published, concerning the examination of a giant sequoia tree that had been felled in California. The tree was a seedling in the third century before the calendar. It was severely damaged by a forest fire five hundred and sixteen years later, but nature, immediately setting to work to repair the damage, slowly began to create successive layers of living tissue over the giant scar left by the flames.

The process of healing continued, according to the authorities, for more than a century, and by 350 the wounds had been completely healed.

"In later centuries," the report continued, "two fires damaged the tree badly. But when the tree was finally cut down, the scar left by the first of these fires had been completely obliterated, and the scar left by the second was in process of being covered. That last scar was a gigantic wound eighteen feet wide and thirty feet high, but had Nature been given a chance even that wound would have been entirely healed."
Source Unknown

Ill health of body or of mind is defeat. Health alone is victory. Let all men, if they can manage it, contrive to be healthy!
Walter Scott

The art of medicine is to see people, not as problems to be solved, but as sensitive human beings to be helped.
Francis J. Braceland

Psychiatrists who ignore the spiritual side of mental disorders are like doctors who pretend a patient has no body above the neck.
Viktor E. Frankl

It is better to treat at the beginning than at the end.
Desiderius Erasmus

Only the physician who believes in a potential power for healing that exists within his patient can treat his patient. Whether he calls this power the "vis medicatrix naturae" (healing power of nature) or the "vis medicatrix dei" (healing power of God), the worthy physician has faith that the patient is fighting alongside him for health and against sickness. In a sense the physician can be only the assistant to this power, saying with Ambroise Pare, the father of French surgery, "I dressed his wounds and God healed him," or with Sigmund Freud, the father of psychoanalysis, that we are the midwives participating in the birth of the healthy self.
Source Unknown

What constitutes being human? Personhood. The ability to be concerned for other human beings. Animals are concerned for their own instinctive needs; the degree of our being human stands in direct proportion to the degree in which we care for others. The word cure comes from the word care.
Abraham Joshua Heschel

Dr. Ruget, late president of the National Urological Society and a splendid churchman, said some time ago that "in the pursuit of scientific wizardry we (doctors) may have lost some of the heart and soul of our profession. Men of science are unbelievably intolerant and narrow when they fail to recognize that it is God's creative power, working through us, that brings success to our efforts; that the healing resources of this universe were not invented by us. Whether or not we admit it, we are always dependent upon that Power which is greater than ourselves."
Louis H. Evans

When a finger is cut, the cells in the skin and flesh around the wound are more or less severely damaged. Through the nervous system, the rest of the body is notified of the emergency, and immediately the proper measures are taken to repair the injured cells. The blood rushes antibodies to combat possible infection from invading bacteria. Other organs of the body send additional substances required for healing purposes. By cooperative action of the rest of the body, in short, the injured cells in the finger are restored to their original, intact state.
Smiley Blanton

Someone once said to Walter B. Cannon, M.D., Harvard Medical School's late great physiologist, "When you see how many diseases there are, you wonder how anyone is ever well." (There are 999 different diseases, according to a recent World Health Congress report.) Dr. Cannon is reported to have answered, "Oh, no, when you know something about the human body and its tremendous resources for health, you wonder why anyone is ever sick."
Author Unknown

133 Serenity in the face of sorrow

Never allow your own sorrow to absorb you, but seek out another to console, and you will find consolation.
J.C. Macaulay

Experiencing a great sorrow is like entering a cave. We are overwhelmed by the darkness and the loneliness. We feel that there is no escape from the prison-house of pain. But God in His lovingkindness has placed on the invisible wall the lamp of faith, whose beams shall lead us back to the sunlit world, where work and friends and service await us.
Helen Keller

I walked a mile with Pleasure
She chattered all the way
But left me none the wiser
For all she had to say.

I walked a mile with Sorrow
And ne'er a word said she
But oh the things I learned from her
When Sorrow walked with me.
Robert Browning Hamilton

I smiled to think God's greatness flowed around our incompleteness-
Round our restlessness, His rest.
Elizabeth Barrett Browning

A charwoman could sleep between her mop and bucket during a bombing raid on London. When asked how she could do it, she said. "The good Lord says that He stays awake and watches over His own. There is no use of both of us being awake!"
Author Unknown

Our educational system is too much a matter of words. We do not do enough to sharpen the perception, the sensations, the imagination of the young. To indicate sorrow, for instance, we employ only one word—"sorrow." Yet there are three thousand million conscious human beings, and there are three thousand million different kinds of sorrow.
Aldous Huxley

There are sorrows, it is true, so great that to give them some of the ordinary vents is to run a hazard of being overthrown. These we must strengthen ourselves to resist or bow quickly and drily down, as the traveler does the wind in the desert. But when we feel that tears will relieve us, it is false philosophy to deny ourselves at least refreshment.
Leigh Hunt

Sorrow, like rain, makes roses and mud.
Austin O'Malley

Out through the fields and woods
And over the walls I have wended;
I have climbed the hills of view
And looked at the world, and descended;
I have come by the highway home,
And lo, it is ended.

Ah, when to the heart of man
Was it ever less than a treason
To go with the drift of things,
To yield with a grace to reason,
And bow and accept the end
Of a love or a season?
Robert Frost

When a noted astronomer was dying he was asked if he feared to go out into the unknown. He calmly replied, "I have loved the stars too fondly to be fearful of the night."
W. Lynn Crowding

Simply being with a person who is bereaved will give him more solace and comfort than you know.
Norman Vincent Peale

It takes the night to bring out the stars.
Anonymous

We must face grief without any expectation of miraculous healing, but with the knowledge that if we are courageous and resolute we can live as our loved ones would wish us to live, not empty, morose, self-centered, and self-pitying, but as brave and undismayed servants of the greater life.
Joshua Loth Liebman

O God, give us serenity to accept what cannot be changed, courage to change what should be changed, and wisdom to distinguish the one from the other.
Reinhold Niebuhr

Acceptance of what has happened is the first step to overcoming the consequences of any misfortune.
William James

---

134 Mentally awake

You cannot reach out and touch an idea; it reaches out and touches you. It reaches inside you and grasps you with a mightly power and force. An idea is God touching you, speaking to you, telling you the earth-shaking secret that you need to know in order to achieve, to do, to be.
James A. Decker

As one scientist put it, "I can schedule my lab hours, but I can't schedule my best ideas."
Source Unknown

Ideas are precious. An idea is the only lever which really moves the world.
Arthur F. Corey

Ideas cross mountains, borders and seas. They go anywhere a man can go and endure long after he is gone. Ideas are indestructible because of their very nature There is no defense on earth against them.
Walter Goldstein

Ideas come from the bottomless pit of the soul and off the surface of the mind. They may be the result of a painstaking scientific investigation or the outcome of a flash of insight into the realm of the unknown. Ideas can come from joining one fact with another as well as from butting one idea headlong into its opposite. Throw an idea into a cauldron and it may emerge as refined gold or escape as a jet of vanishing steam.

Ideas are born in the desert, the jungle, the slum, the suburb, and the paradise of the mind. While some climates are more conducive to the growth and development of ideas than others, wherever you find men you come in contact immediately with a creature in whom an idea can originate.

We define and an idea is born. We distinguish and an idea is born. We combine and an idea is born. We examine and an idea is born. We break what we know into parts and reassemble the parts and an idea is born...

Ideas are born by selecting at random from an assortment of a zillion situations into which it is man's lot to find himself. We meet people and an idea is born. We ask a question and an idea is born...

Ideas stop when we die.
Lasalle Woelfel

We learn to do neither by thinking nor by doing; we learn to do by thinking about what we are doing.
George D. Stoddard

The human mind is not a deep freeze for storage; but a forge for production.
W. A. Donaghy

Diamonds are only found in the darkness of the earth. Truths are only found in the depths of thought.
Construction Digest

It helps to reflect that the best writers have always been criticized. Anyone who expresses himself forthrightly, will one day encounter opposition to his views. This need not necessarily be hostility. Theodore Leschetizky put it succinctly: "We learn much from the disagreeable things people say, for they make us *think*; whereas the good things only make us glad."
Alma Boice Holland

Let us not be too quick to condemn the "arm-chair" philosopher; nor is it shameful for man to sit down when he thinks. The scholar, after all is not Man using the calculator, or Man using footnotes. He is, as Emerson said, Man Thinking.
Otis M. Walter

Quiet minds cannot be perplexed or frightened, but go on in fortune or misfortune at their own private pace like the ticking of a clock during a thunderstorm.
Robert Louis Stevenson

Why should we think upon things that are lovely? Because thinking determines life. It is a common habit to blame life upon environment. Environment modifies life but does not govern life. The soul is stronger than its surroundings.
William James

The human spirit dances beyond neatness and logic.
Anonymous

The purpose of the mind is to cultivate itself, to steep itself in great books, great music, great literature, great ideas—not because these great things will improve one's health or house or pocketbook, but because they are intrinsically good. The mind is not a monkey wrench; it is a greenhouse, whose purpose is that of creating and preserving lovely things within itself no matter how violent the storms or bleak the winter outside.

Source Unknown

A high-school boy went out for the football team, but he proved too adept at broken-field running. After one day, he eluded all tacklers and went scooting down the field. Just before he reached the goal line, he crashed into a steel pole that stood out of bounds, When he regained consciousness, his worried coach asked what had happened. "I run faster," replied the young man, "with my eyes shut."

Giles H. Runyon

The only way to keep trouble out of the mind is to have something better inside it.

David Johnson

Mind is the foundation of man. If that be solid, the building will stand.

Baal Shem Tov

135 The vital balance

A fanatic is a fellow with such a large chip on his shoulder that it makes him lose his balance.

Cyrus N. Peace

To get the most out of life, it's best to ask for less than you know you can get. Even prayers should be reasonable.

William Feather

The gem cannot be polished without friction, nor man perfected without trials.

Confucius

A newspaperman, traveling through the backwoods, saw a gnarled, wrinkled, bent old man sitting in a rocking chair on the porch of his house. Sensing a human interest story, the reporter decided to interview the ancient fellow.

"Sir, I'd like to know the secret of your long life," said the reporter.

"Well, I drink a gallon of whiskey, smoke 50 cigars and go out dancing every day of my life," said the man.

"Remarkable!" exclaimed the reporter. "Exactly how old are you?"

The reply: "Twenty-seven."

Bill Cullen

All empty souls tend to extreme opinion. It is only in those who have built up a rich world of memories and habits of thought that extreme opinions affront the sense of probability. Propositions, for instance, which set all the truth upon one side can only enter rich minds to dislocate and strain, if they can enter at all, and sooner or later the mind expels them by instinct.

William Butler Yeats

Progress in art does not consist in extending one's limitations, but in knowing them better.
Georges Braque

The search for bread without the restraints of faith led to a dehumanizing materialism which Marx rationalized into a colossal economic and political philosophy while the search for the soul without concern for bread made religion peripheral to the real issues of society. And so, swinging from one partial extreme to the other, mankind was despoiled of wholeness and fulfillment.
Feodor Dostoevski

It was said that Frederick the Great of Prussia was walking along a road on the outskirts of Berlin one day, when he accidentally brushed against a very old man.

"Who are you?" the king asked out of idle curiosity as the walk came to an abrupt halt.

"I am a king," the old man answered.

"A king? Over what principality do you reign?" asked the amazed Frederick.

"Over myself. I rule myself because I control myself. I am my own subject to command," replied the elderly one proudly.
Source Unknown

It isn't so hard to become mature, but you've got to work at it. Dr. James F. Bender, of New York City, says there are three marks of maturity. The first is ability to inhibit temper tantrums, which he calls infantilisms that are costly indeed in terms of human relations." Second, he puts the capacity for keeping a confidence, and says no individual who cannot resist the impulse to break a secrecy is grown up. Finally: "I would place an attitude of imperviousness to those twin imposters—blame and fame. A hysterical person is thrown off balance by words of condemnation or praise."
Charles B. Roth

The web of our life is of a mingled yarn, good and ill together.
William Shakespeare

No man is free who cannot command himself.
Pythagoras

All sunshine makes Sahara.
Arab Proverb

Extremists, to whatever camp they belong, are the disease germs in the body politic. They can never create, but when the general health of the body is weak, they can bring destruction. They are reckless as to the means they employ, and because their passion-blinded eyes can discern no difference between the most moderate and the most violent of those who differ from them, they are ready to combine with the latter in order to defeat the former.
Duff Cooper

The size of a man can be measured by the size of the thing that makes him angry.
John Morley

136 The high price of hate

Hate or a deep-seated hostility is the most inefficient use a person can make of his mind.
Ross L. Holman

When you fight a monster, beware lest you become a monster.
Friedrich Nietzsche

Two cats of Kilkenny.
Each thought there was one cat too many;
So they fought and they spit,
And they scratched and they bit,
Till, excepting their nails and the tip of their tails,
Instead of two cats, there weren't any.
Anonymous

In every war we give our best men and women, not our worst. Only those who can pass the physical and mental tests are crippled and slain. Only those capable of dreaming great dreams and achieving great goals are sent to the sacrifice.
Harold E. Kohn

Men and women are constantly trapped by this circle of self-defeat rising from buried hatreds.
Smiley Blanton

Violence of any kind is in effect a social fever. It indicates that something is wrong in society. Yet even though it is a symptom of a deeper malaise, violence has effects of its own. Actually, if it is too frequent and widespread, society becomes an anarchy in which man is a wolf to man. Both the fever and its causes must be treated. Or, to put it in the current political argot, we need both order and justice.
Amitai Etzioni

If you want to travel fast, travel light—take off all your jealousies, prejudices, selfishness and fears.
Glenn Clark

Hate hurts the hater as well as the hated, but it keeps a person so intent upon seeing and punishing the evil in another that one is oblivious to what is happening to oneself.
Harold E. Kohn

Bitterness paralyzes life; love gives it power. Bitterness imprisons life; love releases it. Bitterness sours life; love makes it sweet. Bitterness sickens life; love heals it. Bitterness blinds life; love anoints its eyes.
Harry Emerson Fosdick

We can no longer turn away from the fact of violence for it is before our eyes wherever we look. A man risks his life by running for political office. A man risks his life by standing up against entrenched bigotry. A man risks his life simply by trying to live his life, by exercising the liberty that is rightfully his, by attempting to pursue happiness as he sees it. The cure to the virus of violence that infects America will not be found in stiffer laws, more police or a National Guard armed with helicopters and rockets. The cure will be found only in the heart.
Don Oakley

Hatred and violence are self-defeating . . . they are self-defeating, for they strike at the very heart of obedience to law, peaceful process and political cooperation which are man's last best hopes for a decent world.
Robert F. Kennedy

A person who does not have a proper regard for himself can have no respect for others. He hates in others what he hates in himself.
Paul William Schubert

You can't shoot sense or religion into a man any more than you can beat daylight into a cellar with a club.
Abraham Lincoln

It is setting a very high price on one's conjectures to burn a man alive for them.
Montaigne

The way to stop fighting is for everybody to stop fighting. All violence must stop.
Arthur J. Goldberg

Some of our sweet little suburbs are concentrations of people of one race, one religion, and one batch of prejudices. The people there spend all their time figuring ways to keep other people out.
Margaret Mead

There is nothing big in bigotry.
Anonymous

137 Problems must be seen in perspective

A true cessation of problems would be the beginning of death for a society or individual. We aren't constructed to live in that kind of world. We are problem-solvers by nature . . . so much so that when problems of the real world aren't pressing in upon us, we invent artificial ones such as how to reduce our golf score.
Civil Service Journal

A problem well stated is a problem half solved.
Armstrong Journal

The truest help we can render an afflicted man is not to take his burden from him, but to call out his best energy, that he may be able to bear the burden.
Phillips Brooks

The little girl standing by the elevator in a department store was crying, and the floorwalker asked her, "What's the matter, little girl? Are you lost?"

"No," she said between sobs. "I'm here; my mother's lost."
C. Kennedy

Where there is no anguish in the heart, there will be no great music on the lips.
Karl Barth

A biologist one day observed an ant carrying a piece of straw which seemed a big burden for it. The ant came to a crack in the earth, which was too wide for it to cross. It stood for a time, as though pondering the situation. Then it put the straw across the crack and walked across it as a span.

"What a lesson for us!" the impressed biologist said. "The burden can become the bridge for progress."
Grit

Did you ever look at another person and think: "He really has it made. If I had his position or wealth or ability, look what I could do?" But the truth is that person may then be going through the most trying time of his life. No person has ever escaped the struggle to live rather than just exist. Those who survive are always the ones who face their difficulties and go on.
C. W. Brockwell

For twenty years Professor Edwin R. Keedy of the University of Pennsylvania's Law School used to start his first class by putting two figures on the blackboard: 4 and 2. "What's the solution?" he would ask. A student would call out, "six." Another would say, "two," but Keedy would pass them by. Several men would shout the final possibility, "eight" and the teacher would shake his head. Finally Keedy would point out their collective error. "All of you failed to ask the key question, what is the problem? Gentlemen, unless you know what the problem is, you cannot possibly find the answer." Dr. Keedy's classroom gambit was deadly serious. He knew that in law, as in everyday life, too much time is spent trying to solve the wrong problem—like polishing brass on a sinking ship.
Murray Teigh Bloom

Sheldon phoned an old friend whom he hadn't seen in years. The conversation went as follows:
Sheldon: "Hello, Irving. Long time no see. Tell me, what's new?"
Irving: "What can I tell you? I can't kick."
Sheldon: "You don't sound so good. What happened?"
Irving: "Well, my business just failed."
Sheldon: "Oh, I'm sorry to hear that. What else?"
Irving: "My wife just left me."
Sheldon: "Oh, I'm sorry to hear that. What else?"
Irving: "I was just in a terrible automobile crash; the car was completely demolished."
Sheldon: "My, oh my! Let me ask you then, Irving, why do you say you can't kick?"
Irving: "Because (sigh) I'm in a cast from the waist down!"
Source Unknown

There are really no problem children; only children with problems.
Joseph Crescimbeni

"Dad, what is a traitor in politics?"
"A traitor, my son, is a man who leaves our party and goes over to the other side."
"Well, then, what is a man who leaves his party and comes over to our side?"
"A convert, my son."
Elberton Star

Waitress: "The client complains that his sandwich is small."
Manager: "Put it on a smaller plate and take it back."
Swedish Newspaper

In every age of anxiety there must be those who lift themselves above the despair of their day. In every period of history there must be dreamers who refuse to surrender to defeatism. In every age of crises, religiously mature men and women must separate themselves from the doleful majority and lift their eyes on high. They resist the onrushing tidal wave of pessimism that threatens to engulf their dreams, and insist that it was out of the black threads of darkness that a pattern of light was woven into the texture of the universe. They see beyond tragedy to the light and hope of a new tomorrow. These are the pioneers of spiritual frontiers.
William B. Silverman

It is not given to human beings to foresee or to predict to any large extent the unfolding course of events. In one phase men seem to have been right, in another they seem to have been wrong. Then again, a few years later, when the perspective of time has lengthened, all stands in a different light. There is a new proposition. There is another scale of values.
Winston Churchill

---

138 Pathways to spirituality

Religion must justify itself through the moral action.
Ismar Elbogen

To educate a man in mind and not in morals is to educate a menace to society.
Theodore Roosevelt

The Bible is like a telescope; it is not to look at but to look through.
Merlin Schwein

Democracy cannot live in hate and fear. Prejudice and bigotry are the advance guard of failure. Let us hear again the faith of our forebears; let us listen again to the inspired hopes of our national conscience; let us obey again the word of our religions.
Lyndon B. Johnson

In the sphere of morality it is the same as in the sphere of knowledge. The more knowledge we acquire, the more we learn how much we do not know. The more good we do, the more urgently obvious it becomes to us how much good there remains to be done, and how far we lag behind.
Leo Baeck

The present tendency is to suppose that God is served by our bestowing upon Him our approval. But God is

served only when men's lives are transformed by Him. This transformation is marked by a turning away from the worship of material success, selfish comfort and superficial security toward the adventure of a life fixed and directed toward high human good for all mankind.
Eugene Carson Blake

"What you're tryin' to tell me," said my sharp young son after my lecture on morals, "is that I have to walk straight if I aim to get into the best circles."
Burton Hillis

Love means to love that which is unlovable, or it is no virtue at all; forgiving means to pardon that which is unforgivable, or it is no virtue at all; and to hope means hoping when things are hopeless, or it is no virtue at all.
G. K. Chesterton

The great act of faith is when man decides that he is not God.
Oliver Wendell Holmes

Protest is a powerful weapon of change. But it is a negative weapon. Religion's main task is to create new life, not just to protest the old.
R. N. Usher-Wilson

A young machinist and his bride, honeymooning on the shore of a New Hampshire lake, were caught in a canoe in a sudden violent squall. The machinist, scared within an inch of his life, resorted to prayer.

"Save us," he implored, "and I vow to give up smoking, drinking, gambling..."

"Don't go too far, darling," interrupted his bride hastily. "I think I hear a motorboat coming to rescue us."
Bennett Cerf

As they were leaving church, the wife turned to her husband. "Did you see that new hat Mrs. Lambert was wearing?"

"No, I didn't," he answered.

"Well, did you notice the new velvet dress Mrs. Frawley had on?" she asked.

"No, I don't think I noticed that, either."

"Oh, for goodness sakes," the wife snapped. "A lot of good it does you to go to church!"
Frances Benson

A religious institution is a hospital for sinners; not a club for saints.
Russell Blowers

I would think of my religion as a gamble rather than think of it as an insurance premium.
Stephen S. Wise

Perhaps the most urgent reason why the quality of moral response has become the decisive issue in politics is quite simply that most of the major problems of our day present themselves in moral terms, and are probably insoluble without some stirring of generosity, some measure of vision.
Adlai E. Stevenson

139 Loyalty is more than an oath

We believe it is more important for men to speak their minds than to mind their speech.
Louis Jacobs

The first requisite of a good citizen in this republic of ours is that he shall be able and willing to pull his weight.
Theodore Roosevelt

You can never buy an employee's loyalty—this you have to earn.
Clarence Frances

How many homes have started in romance and ended in recrimination and wretchedness because neither husband nor wife had a loyalty higher and more controlling than his or her desires.
Glenn B. Ogden

We will never bring disgrace to this our city by any act of disloyalty or cowardice, nor ever desert our suffering comrades in the ranks.
Old Athenian Oath

They who would initiate and carry through a revolution have got to give more than their spare evening to it.
Vladimir I. Lenin

I think the relationship between a person and his country is something like that between a person and his parents. There is kinship, but the amount of love and affection and concern varies according to your experiences with them and on how you react to these experiences. To command that all children love their parents or their country, no matter what, is unwise; and it won't work anyway. Love, affection, loyalty are given. They cannot be commanded by law or oath. We cannot expect everyone to show the same amount of patriotism, nor to show it in uniform ways.
Philip A. Silk

When the late Mr. and Mrs. Henry Ford celebrated their golden wedding anniversary, a reporter asked them, "To what do you attribute your 50 years of successful married life?"

"The formula," said Ford, "is the same formula I have always used in making cars—just stick to one model."
The International Teamster

When the Titanic went down in 1912, Mrs. Oscar Stous was offered safety in a lifeboat. She refused it because there was not room for her husband in the boats. She said: "We have been together through a great many experiences over the years and I will not leave him now. Where he goes, I will go."
Source Unknown

Those who are demanding freedom from responsibility have yet to discover there is only freedom for the responsible.
Paul L. Fisher

A man is a little like a tree. A tree has to be planted before it can spread its branches. A man has to be rooted in something before he can reach for the moon. In fact, you never find a world-wide interest that is not grounded in some local loyalty. You never find a man who loves the world in general who does not love some little spot of the world in particular. You never find, I think, a man or a woman who loves family life in general who is not committed to some one family for whom he would gladly die. You never find a man who is interested in world politics who is not interested in the political life and social life of his own town. You might almost say that a man becomes universal to the degree to which he is willing to be provincial.

Source Unknown

The story runs that an applicant for a position at a customs office once tried a civil service examination, in which he faced this question: "How far is the sun from the earth?" He answered, "I do not know how far the sun is from the earth, but it is far enough so that it will not interfere with the proper performance of my duties at the customs office."

Anonymous

There is only one way to be an ethical individual, that is to choose your cause and serve it.

Josiah Royce

The strength of a country or a code lies in the true sense of loyalty it can arouse in the hearts of its people.

Louis C. Gerstein

Love and loyalty toward a person is the very substance on which society thrives. It was this attitude toward Robert E. Lee which held a ragged and dwindling army of Confederate soldiers together to the last despairing days of Appomattox. The healing art of the physician is itself based on such confidence and faith, and many cures spring wholly from it.

Smiley Blanton

---

140 The calm within the storm

One night Abraham Lincoln, on a camping trip, was awakened by a companion who, alarmed by some shooting stars which he saw streaking across the skies, cried, "Abe, Abe, the world is coming to an end." Lincoln peered beyond the shooting stars. "Be calm," he said, "the constellations are still in their places."

Robert W. Youngs

O Lord, give me beauty in the inner soul and may the outward man and the inward man be at one!

Socrates

When the water in a pot is agitated the moon reflected there looks distorted. The moving water disturbs any reflected image. Similarly, when the calm waters of a man's heart are stirred by likes and dis-

likes, he is unable to solve his problems and to make wise decisions. Nor can a restless heart reflect the inward presence of the blissful soul.
Paramhansa Yoganda

Drop Thy still dews of quietness,
Till all our strivings cease;
Take from our souls the strain and stress,
And let our ordered lives confess
The beauty of Thy peace.
John Greenleaf Whittier

No other choice is left to man; he has to find
His way between sensual pleasure and peace of mind.
Friedrich von Schiller

Integrity is the harmony between a man's inner purposes and his outer actions.
John Bennett

One ship drives East, another West
While the selfsame breezes blow.
'Tis the set of the sail and not the angle
That bids them where to go.
Like the winds of the sea are the ways of fate
As we journey along through life.
'Tis the set of the soul that decides the goal,
And not the calm or the strife.
Ella Wheeler Wilcox

Although he was never considered a churchman, Le Corbusier, the French architect, created two of the most beautfiul religious buildings that have been seen in this century; the monastery near Lyons and the chapel at Ranchamps, France.

When asked about his perception and grasp of the spiritual needs of others, he said, "I have worked for what men today most need: silence and peace."
David Poling

Teach me, Father how to go
Softly as the grasses grow;
Hush my soul to meet the shock
Of the wild world as a rock;
But my spirit, propt with power,
Make as simple as a flower;
Let the dry heart fill its cup,
Like a poppy looking up;
Let life lightly wear her crown,
Like a poppy looking down.

Teach me, Father, how to be
Kind and patient as a tree.
Joyfully the crickets croon
Under shady oak at noon,
Beetle on his mission bent,
Tarries in that cooling tent.
Let me also cheer a spot,
Hidden field or garden grot—
Place where passing souls can rest
On the way and be their best.
Edwin Markham

No one could tell me what my soul might be:
I searched for God, and God eluded me;
I sought my brother out, and found all three,
My soul, my God and all humanity.
Abdul Mansur

Only when a man is at peace within himself can he find the inclination to relax. It is inner security, not the golf course or the vacation paradise, that releases a man from the tension of the daily round.
Ellsworth Kalas

If anyone is searching for peace of mind today, he's searching for a will-o'-the-wisp. Anxiety is a healthy phenomenon—the motivating factor by which we get things done.

Donald W. Hastings

Therefore I thank my God,
   and joy to do His will;
I know, whate'er befalls,
   His love doth lead me still.
So like a little child,
   who clasps his father's hand,
Serene I take my way;
   in faith untroubled stand.

Johann Sebastian Bach

After all, the lives that do the most in the world are the quiet, steady lives. They are like the stars, they just stay in their appointed place and shine with the light of God, who gave them life. Meteors shoot brilliantly across the sky, and we exclaim and wonder, but long after they have finished the stars shine on to guide us.

This Day

He who created the day has also provided for it.

The Midrash

If a man would make his record true
The following things he must do,
Think without confusion clearly,
Love your fellow man securely,
Act from honest motives purely
Trust in heaven and God securely.

Henry van Dyke

Courage is the price that life exacts for granting peace.

Amelia Earhart Putnam

15

Toward the future

141 Hope springs eternal

The optimist pleasantly ponders how high his kite will fly; the pessimist woefully wonders how soon his kite will fall.
William Arthur Ward

Little Emma was taking an examination in school; one of the questions asked was this: "Upon what do hibernating animals subsist during the winter?" Emma thought about that one for a long time; then she wrote: "On the hope of a coming spring."
Author Unknown

What, then, is man? Hope turned to dust. But the opposite is equally true. What is man? Dust turned to hope.
Elie Wiesel

You could cover the whole world with asphalt but sooner or later green grass would break through.
Ilya Ehrenburg

Hope is the dream of a man awake.
Matthew Prior

I believe that man will not merely endure, he will prevail. He is immortal, not because he alone among creatures has an inexhaustible voice, but because he has a soul, a spirit capable of compassion and sacrifice and endurance.
William Faulkner

Memories are short, and appetites for power and glory are insatiable. Old tyrants depart. New ones take their places. Old differences are

255

composed, new differences arise. Old allies become the foe. The recent enemy becomes the friend. It is all very baffling and trying but we cannot lose hope, we cannot despair. For it is too obvious that if we do not abolish war on this earth, then surely, one day, war will abolish us from the earth.
Harry S. Truman

One of the signs of maturity is a healthy respect for reality—a respect that manifests itself in the level of one's aspirations and in the accuracy of one's assessment of the difficulties which separate the facts of today from the bright hopes of tomorrow.
Robert H. Davis

Religion has emerged into human experience mixed with the crudest fancies of barbaric imagination. Gradually, slowly, steadily, the vision recurs in history under nobler form and with clearer expression. It is the one element in human experience which persistently shows an upward trend. It fades and then recurs. But when it renews its force, it recurs with an added richness and purity of content. The fact of the religious vision and its history of persistent expansion is our one ground for optimism.
Alfred North Whitehead

In spite of the tensions and uncertainties of our time, something profoundly meaningful is taking place. Old systems of exploitation and oppression are passing away; new systems of justice and equality are being born. In a real sense this is a great time to be alive. Granted that we face a world crisis which leaves us standing so often amid the surging murmur of life's restless sea. But every crisis has both its dangers and its opportunities. It can spell either salvation or doom. In a dark, confused world the Kingdom of God may yet reign in the hearts of men.
Martin Luther King

To suffer woes which hope thinks infinite;
To forgive wrongs darker than death or night;
To defy power which seems omnipotent;
To love and bear; to hope till hope creates
From its own wreck the thing it contemplates.
Robert Browning

The human heart refuses to believe in a universe without a purpose.
Immanuel Kant

We travel the dusty road till the light of day is dim,
And sunset shows us spires away on the world's rim.
We travel from dawn to dusk, till the day is past and by,
Seeking the Holy City beyond the rim of sky.
Friends and loves we have none, nor wealth nor blest abode.
But the hope, the burning hope, and the road, the lonely road.
John Masefield

142 Improving our vision

The American people cannot afford to trust their future to men of little vision. The Bible warns us that where there is no vision the people perish.
Harry S. Truman

We have followed the so-called practical way for too long a time now, and it has led inexorably to deeper confusion and chaos. Time is cluttered with the wreckage of communities which surrendered to hatred and violence. For the salvation of our nation and the salvation of mankind, we must follow another way...
Martin Luther King

When I look into the human future I see
scientists still struggling with problems, but
they are the problems of wresting the truth
from nature, not of wasting time fighting for
freedom of the intellect.

I see artists still working day and night at their
canvases and marble, but to incarnate their
vision of beauty, not to keep the wolves from
their doors.

I see all men laboring not to ward off hunger,
disease, and enslavement, but for self-fulfillment
and mutual aid.

I see each religion and culture exerting its fullest
energies but for the purpose not of fighting off the
assault of other faiths and traditions but so as to
make the most of its own resources for its own sake
and that of the world.

I see each polity, each economy hard at work but with
one problem only—to give to each person the maximum
of freedom, the most generous access to the good things
of living.

I see each national state very very busy not in
defending itself against its neighbors but in doing
its best for its citizens and its sister national states.

This to me will be heaven on earth.
Milton Steinberg

The eye of a man will still be sharper than the eye of a TV camera because it is linked to a brain and a heart.
Saul Pett

I submit we are not seeing the loss of values, but a creation of values. My plea is don't damn the protesters but say a prayer and bear with them. I think out of this will come a greater set of values than we have had before.
Robert H. Felix

What most narrows the range of our thoughts and lowers our standards is the Mere Present, the great jailer of men's minds.
Gilbert Murray

No one can walk backward into the future.
Proverb

It is a peculiarity of man that he can only live by looking to the future. And this is his salvation in the most difficult moments of his existence, although he sometimes has to force his mind to the task.
Viktor E. Frankl

It is the dream within the person that counts more than anything else. If a parent can give a child a vision, he has given him one of the best gifts. If a teacher can create an idea of what life might be, she has done her part.
Gerald Kennedy

Someone shoves a waste block of marble aside as useless. Michelangelo says, "Bring it into my studio. An angel is imprisoned in that marble and I intend to set it free."
Source Unknown

The unexamined life is not worth living.
Socrates

A vision without a task is a dream;
A task without a vision is drudgery;
A vision and a task is the hope of the world.
Source Unknown

One evening at dusk, Robert Louis Stevenson stood as a boy at the window of his home and watched the darkness envelop the city. "Robert," his nurse said to him, "come and sit down. You can't see anything out there."

But young Stevenson insisted, "I can see something wonderful. There is a man coming up the street making holes in the darkness." It was the lamplighter.
Gwynne W. Davidson

Moral education is impossible apart from the habitual vision of greatness.
Alfred North Whitehead

When you're thirsty it's too late to think about digging a well.
Japanese Proverb

All of us are standing in the mud, but a few of us are looking at the stars.
Oscar Wilde

Where did the steamboat, the locomotive, the automobile, the electric light, the typewriter, the sewing machine, the airplane, the radio, television, spaceships and a million other objects and conveniences come from? All were thoughts or mental pictures in the minds of men before these things became realities. Everything on this earth, except that which nature creates or has provided, is the result of sustained thought.
Harold Sherman

Spirit is first of all a questing and aspiring thing, seeking in the world outside for something to satisfy its inner longing.
Edmund W. Sinnott

143 Thoughts on immortality

Hour by hour and day by day fresh beauties burst upon our sight.
The trees once dark against the sky are caught in webs of golden light.
Outlines soften, colors deepen, New songs echo down the lane.
A miracle is happening. The world is being born again.
Patience Strong

The pious men of all the nations share in the world to come.
The Talmud

The past is what we have; the present is what we make; and the future is what we bequeath.
N. Shanmugam

Lives of great men all remind us
We can make our lives sublime,
And, departing, leave behind us
Footprints on the sands of time.
Henry Wadsworth Longfellow

The great use of life is to spend it for something that will outlast it.
William James

Everything that lives must die, but life itself is undying.
Jacob Gordon

We do not believe in immortality, because we have proved it. We forever try to prove it, because we believe it.
James Martineau

Confident belief in immortality is important for this fundamental reason; that upon it depends the practice of immortality now. No man will really live as though he were an eternal person until he is assured that such an interpretation of his life is true.
Harry Emerson Fosdick

If what never before existed, exists, why cannot that which once existed, exist again?
Gabiha ben Pasissa

I believe that the soul of Man is immortal and will be treated with justice in another life respecting its conduct in this.
Benjamin Franklin

Place then a cap upon thy head
Adorn thyself with a Tallit and pray.
The day is waning and the darkness thickens.
A moment more and hidden gates will open
With steps of prayer approach, glance within.
Strange sounds in unknown tongue will encompass thee.
A new—another light will flash and embrace thee
And lo—you will begin to see, to hear, to understand
The secret of the life you lived upon the earth,
The trembling and the pain,
The yearning for the hidden.
Then you will know that only life's reflection did you see,
Only the dim shadow of existence.
But here, in the dwelling place of light,
Here there are no mysteries and no doubts.
Here is the final answer!

And, as this revelation is diffused within thee
You will be born anew
And you will dwell secure
Within the radiance of the truest reality.

Hillel Ha-Bavli

Who knows but life be that which men call death; and death what men call life?

Euripides

At bottom no one believes in his own death. Or, to put the same thing in another way, in the unconscious every one of us is convinced of his own immortality.

Sigmund Freud

The best argument I know for immortal life is the existence of a man who deserves one.

William James

Women keep the central core of religion in the face of man's combativeness. Women believe in survival beyond the grave. No woman believes for one moment that the child she bears is not established for all of what life there is to be, and in her endowment of her child she feels it is forever to live, advancing from perfection to perfection through eternity.

Harry Golden

For each one of us the moment comes when the great nurse, death, takes man, the child, by the hand and quietly says, "It is time to go home. Night is coming. It is your bedtime, child of earth. Come; you're tired. Lie down at last in the quiet nursery of nature and sleep. Sleep well. The day is gone. Stars shine in the canopy of eternity."

Joshua Loth Liebman

Man is pleased to know that he will rest near his fathers.

The Talmud

People clamor for immortality when they have not shown ability to use this life.

Ralph Waldo Emerson

---

144   The possible dream

When you plant for a year, plant grass; when you plant for ten years, plant trees; when you plant for centuries, plant men.

Chinese Proverb

Every act of progress the world has ever known began first with a dreamer. After him came the scientist or the statesman, the expert or the technician. But first came the dreamer.

Maurice Davis

There is one thing stronger than all the armies of the world, and that is an idea whose time has come.

Voltaire

And man is mind and evermore he takes the toil of thought.
And shaping what he wills,
Brings forth a thousand joys, a thousand ills,
He thinks in secret and it comes to pass,
Environment is but his looking glass.
S. Shepard Levy

We all know and love the word "landscape," Someone has proposed a similar word, "mindscape." That would mean a view of the mind, what a mind thinks about, what it desires most, the language it uses the visions it has.
Halford E. Luccock

Two men look through the same bars
One sees the mud, and one the stars.
Eugene P. Berlin

What they undertood to do
They brought to pass;
All things hang like a drop of dew
Upon a blade of grass.
William Butler Yeats

Whatsoever road you may explore, you will not reach the limits of the soul, for the soul has no limits.
Heraclitus

The world is full of things for man *to fight against:* war, ignorance, tyranny, injustice, self-seeking, racial discrimination, the population explosion, destruction of natural resources, man's inhumanity to man, and many other forms of suffering and evil in the modern world. Fortunately, the world is also full of things *to fight for:* truth, goodness, beauty, freedom, justice, peace, joy and delight, social well-being, human dignity, and man's humanity to man.
Howard S. Hoyman

Research is to see what everybody else has seen, and to think what nobody else has thought.
Albert Szent-Gyorgyi

There is a divine dream which the prophets and rabbis have cherished and which fills our prayers, and permeates the acts of true piety. It is the dream of a world, rid of evil by the grace of God as well as by the efforts of man, by his dedication to the task of establishing the kingship of God in the world. God is waiting for us to redeem the world. We should not spend our life hunting for trivial satisfactions while God is waiting constantly and keenly for our effort and devotion.
Abraham Joshua Heschel

Some men see things as they are, and say why. I dream things that never were, and say why not.
Robert F. Kennedy

As long as man has a dream in his heart he cannot lose the significance of living. It is a part of the pretensions of modern life to traffic in what is called realism—being practical and down to earth. Men cannot continue long to live if the dream in the heart has perished . . . and the last embers of their hope fade away.
Howard Thurman

I think the greatest thing in life is to be able to dream, to have great

aspirations; but I think it equally important that you have a will that can turn that dream into reality.
Bob Richards

What happens to a dream deferred?
Does it dry up
Like a raisin in the sun?
Or does it explode?
Langston Hughes

Man in this moment of history has emerged in greater supremacy over the forces of nature than has ever been dreamed of before. He has it in his power to solve quite easily the problems of material existence. He has conquered the wild beasts and has even conquered the insects and microbes. There lies before him, if he wishes, a golden age of peace and progress. All is in his hand. He has only to conquer his last and worst enemy—himself.
Winston Churchill

A society without dreams would be like an individual sleeper without dreams to fill his night; it would die.
Tom Nairn

145 This, too, shall pass

It is only at the tree loaded with fruit that people throw stones.
John Buchan

Not only around our infancy
Doth heaven with all its splendors lie;
Daily, with lives that cringe and plot,
We Sinais climb and know it not.
James Russell Lowell

Adopt the pace of nature; her secret is patience.
Ralph Waldo Emerson

Not forever can one enjoy stillness and peace. But misfortune and destruction are not final. When the grass has been burnt by the fire of the steppe, it will grow anew in summer.
The Mongolian Steppe

I have always said that the way to deal with the pain of others is by sympathy, which in first-year Greek they taught me meant "suffering with," and that the way to deal with one's own pain is to put one foot after the other.
Wallace Stegner

Botanists say that trees need the powerful March winds to flex their trunks and main branches, so that the sap is drawn up to nourish the budding leaves. Perhaps we need the gales of life in the same way, though we dislike enduring them. A blustery period in our fortunes is often the prelude to a new spring of life and health, success and happiness, when we keep steadfast in faith and look to the good in spite of appearances.
Jane Truax

Today is the Tomorrow you worried about Yesterday.
   Margaret T. Applegarth

When the winter is severe
The pine trees in this ancient land
Stay green throughout the year,
Is it because the earth is warm and friendly?
No, it is because the pine tree has within itself
A life-restoring power.
   Old Chinese Poem

The dogs bark, but the caravan goes on.
   Indian Proverb

A gourd wound itself around the lofty palm and in a few weeks climbed to its very top. "How old may'st thou be?" asked the newcomer.

"About 100 years."

"About 100 years, and no taller! Only look, I have grown as tall as you in fewer days than you count years."

"I know that well," replied the palm. "Every summer of my life a gourd has climbed up around me as proud as thou art, and as short lived as thou wilt be."
   A. Purnell Bailey

Life is like being at the dentist. You always think that the worst is still to come, and yet it is over already.
   Otto von Bismarck

What really matters is what happens in us, not to us.
   James W. Kennedy

Cavemen probably suffered as much strain over the problem of choosing the right cave as businessmen suffer today over choosing the right stocks and shares.
   Richard Asher

The best way out of a difficulty is through it.
   Anonymous

Take a large amount of laughter,
And some teardrops mixed with sighs,
Add to this some sunshine,
And the smile of merry eyes.

Put in two cups of morning dew,
Diluting it with rain;
Stir it well with happiness,
But season it with pain.

Pour this in a golden cup
Buttered well with strife,
Wrap it 'round with problems,
And there, my friend, is life.
   Irene McKenney

When you get into a tight place and everything goes against you, till it seems as though you could not hold on a minute longer, never give up then, for that is just the place and time that the tide will turn.
   Harriet Beecher Stowe

A man ninety years old was asked to what he attributed his longevity.

"I reckon," he said, with a twinkle in his eye, "it's because most nights I went to bed and slept when I should have sat up and worried."
   Dorothea Kent

146 Mystery and wonder

Philosophy begins in wonder. And, at the end, when philosophic thought has done its best, the wonder remains. There has been added, however, some grasp of the immensity of things, some purification of emotion by understanding.
Alfred North Whitehead

Intelligence has been defined by the psychologists as the capacity to learn. That is nonsense. Intelligence is the capacity to wonder.
Hy Sherman

'Tis revelation satisfies all doubts
Explains all mysteries except her own.
William Cowper

One of the unanswered questions of life is: "When is old age?" My answer would be: "When we have ceased to wonder."
Source Unknown

Men live on the brink of mysteries and harmonies into which they never enter and with their hand on the door-latch they die outside.
Ralph Waldo Emerson

The most beautiful thing we can experience is the mysterious. It is the source of all true art and science. He to whom the emotion is a stranger, who can no longer pause to wonder and stand wrapped in awe, is as good as dead; his eyes are closed. The insight into the mystery of life, coupled though it be with fear, has also given rise to religion. To know what is impenetrable to us really exists, manifesting itself as the highest wisdom and the most radiant beauty, which our dull faculties can comprehend only in their most primitive forms—this knowledge, this feeling is at the center of true religiousness.
Albert Einstein

During a nature class the teacher began telling her third grade pupils about the chicken. "Isn't it wonderful," she exclaimed, "how little chickens get out of their shells?" One of her eight-year-old charges was moved to respond, "What beats me is how they get in."
About Face

The longer I live my mind gets to be more of a mystery to me.
Carl Sandburg

Why, who makes much of a miracle?
As to me I know of nothing else but miracles...
To me every hour of light and dark is a miracle,
Every cubic inch of space is a miracle.
Walt Whitman

We are all born with a gift of wonder. Some of us retain the child's belief that creation is fabulous. A lifetime commitment to the majestic abstractions of modern science has not weakened my sense of marvel at the seemingly miraculous appearance of commonplace happenings. The explosive emergence of a particular type of wild

mushroom at the appropriate time and place after a soaking rain still appears to me a phenomenal event.
Rene Dubos

Two things fill the mind with ever new and increasing wonder and awe—the starry heavens above me and within me the moral law.
Immanuel Kant

The most important things that grown-ups can do for children lie behind and beyond practical expedients. The best gift we can give is help in the development of a sense of wonder, not only at natural beauty but at all goodness and beauty—in buildings, in music, and above all in people.
Rosemary Haughton

To pray is to take notice of the wonder, to regain a sense of the mystery that animates all beings—the divine margin in all attainments. Prayer is our humble answer to the inconceivable surprise of living. It is all we can offer in return for the mystery by which we live.
Abraham Joshua Heschel

If Spring came but once in a century, instead of once a year, or burst forth with the sound of an earthquake and not in silence, what wonder and expectation there would be in all hearts to behold the miraculous change.
Henry Wadsworth Longfellow

A woman bounced into an art gallery and made a superficial tour of the exhibits.
"Are these the masterpieces I have heard so much about?" she asked, with a scornful tone of voice. "I don't see anything in them."
Quietly, the curator said, "Madam, don't you wish you could?"
Mrs. Paul Goodyear

---

147 The quest for meaning

Times that "try men's souls" are periods when men reflect upon the meaning of their existence and that of the nation which has given them sustenance and protection.
Edwin F. Klotz

A young man once asked, "What am I in this world for?"
The next day the Iroquois Theater burned. This young man carried several children from the third story of the flaming theater. That day he saved twenty-eight lives.
F. W. Gunsaulus

The purpose of life is not to be happy—but to matter, to be productive, to be useful, to have it make some difference that you lived at all.
Leo Rosten

Beware the terrible simplifier.
Jacob Burckhardt

A human being who has not a single hour for his own, each day, is not a human being.
Moshe Leib of Sassov

Primum vitare, deinde philosophare—first you just survive, and then you philosophize.
Thomas Aquinas

There is a nineteenth century parable which tells us: A man had been wandering about in a forest for several days, not knowing which was the right way out. Suddenly he saw a man approaching him. His heart was filled with joy. "Now I shall certainly find out which is the right way," he thought to himself. When they neared one another, he asked the man, "Brother, tell me which is the right way. I have been wandering about in this forest for several days."

Said the other to him, "Brother, I do not know the way out either. For I, too, have been wandering about here for many, many days. But this I can tell you: do not take the way I have been taking, for that will lead you astray. And now let us look for a new way together."
Hasidic Lore

Man's concern about a meaning in life is the truest expression of the state of being human. We can easily imagine highly developed animals or insects—bees or ants, say—which in many aspects of their social organization actually are superior to man. But we can never imagine any such creature raising the question of the meaning of his own existence. It is reserved for man alone to experience the whole dubiousness of being. More than such faculties as power of speech, conceptual thinking or walking erect, this factor of doubting the significance of his own existence is what sets man apart from animals.

Ultimately, man should not ask himself: what is the meaning of my life? He should realize, instead, that it is he who is questioned, questioned by life. It is he who has to answer—by answering for life.
Viktor E. Frankl

Albert Einstein was well-recognized at Princeton University as the original absentminded professor. One day on board a train, he was unable to find his ticket. Said the conductor: "Take it easy. You'll find it. I'll be back in ten minutes."

When the conductor returned, Einstein still couldn't find the ticket. Said the conductor, "No matter, Dr. Einstein. I'm sure you bought a ticket. Forget about it."

"You're very kind," Einstein said. "But I must find it—otherwise I won't know where I am going."
Source Unknown

The true meaning of a term is to be found by observing what a man does with it, not by what he says about it.
Percey Williams Bridgman

In good conversation parties don't speak to the words but to the meanings of each other.
Ralph Waldo Emerson

And this our life, exempt from public haunt, finds tongues in trees, books in running brooks, sermons in stones and good in everything.
William Shakespeare

Religion is an ultimate concern about the meaning of our existence and the destiny of mankind.
Paul Tillich

"He knew all the little answers, but he missed the large questions." He knew the little answers, how to become vice president of the bank, how to keep life upholstered. He missed the big questions, what is it all about, how do you put high meaning into life?
John P. Marquand

Rabbi Elijah, the Gaon of Vilna, once explained a verse of the Joseph story. He was thrown into a pit by his brothers. The Bible reports, "And they cast him into the pit. The pit was empty. There was no water in it." To explain the tautology, the saying of the same thing twice in different words, the commentators reflect "There was no water but there were serpents and scorpions in it." The sage explained that "If man's life is not filled with a life of meaning which comes from the study of the Torah, the emptiness will be filled with snakes and scorpions." Dostoevski has said that man must serve something; if he does not serve something, he will serve the idols.
Seymour J. Cohen

For each problem comes a moment of decision. The choice must be made before it is too late. Otherwise all is meaningless.
Ralph Perry

---

148 Be strong and of good courage

A man must calculate upon his powers of resistance before he goes into the arena.
George Gordon Byron

My knowledge is pessimistic but my willing and hoping are optimistic.
Albert Schweitzer

One of the most successful men I have ever known was asked by an admirer, "How do you always manage to act so bright and optimistic? It must be a natural gift. You must have been born with a great supply of optimism." "Not at all," the successful man replied, "I have no greater natural supply of optimism than anyone else. It's just that I use mine."
Robert J. Flint

Our fears do make us traitors.
William Shakespeare

The courage we desire and prize is not the courage to die decently but to live manfully.
Thomas Carlyle

There is a wide difference between true courage and mere contempt of life.
Marcus Porcius Cato

The strong man is not he who hides his own failings from himself, but he who knows them well.
Paul Tournier

Great novelists develop by swimming against the strong tides of their own time.
William E. Barrett

They do me wrong who say I come
  no more,
When once I knock and fail to find
  you in.
For every day I stand outside your
  door,
And bid you wake and rise and fight
  to win.

Weep not for precious chances
  passed away,
Weep not for golden ages on the
  wane.
Each night I burn the records of the
  day,
At sunrise every soul is born again.
Walter Malone

A letter from you calls up recollections very dear to my mind. It carries me back to the times when, beset with difficulties and dangers, we were fellow laborers in the same cause, struggling for what is most valuable to man, his right of self-government. Laboring always at the same oar, with some wave ever ahead, threatening to overwhelm us, and yet passing harmless under our bark, we knew not how we rode through the storm with heart and hand, and made a happy port.
Thomas Jefferson

Let him not quit his belief that a popgun is a popgun, though the ancient and honorable of the earth affirm that it be a crack of doom.
Ralph Waldo Emerson

Dr. Chester M. Pierce, research psychiatrist of the University of Oklahoma Medical Center, has studied the reason why husky men will practice Saturday and Sunday afternoon mayhem all season long start fall. "Men play football to master adversity," says Dr. Pierce. Once a man has had the privilege of testing himself against adversity, the doctor maintains, he will be able to operate more confidently in all areas of life. Happiness, too, may be nearer this man's reach, for Demetrius said 2,000 years ago, "No one is more unhappy in my judgment than a man who has never met adversity."
Flora Rheta Schreiber

Courage is a special kind of knowledge: the knowledge of how to fear what ought to be feared and how not to fear what ought not to be feared.
David Ben-Gurion

Someday I hope to enjoy enough of what the world calls success so that somebody will ask me, "What's the secret of it?" I shall say simply this: "I get up when I fall down."
Paul Harvey

Pay no attention to what critics say. There has never been set up a statue in honor of a critic.
Johan Julius Sibelius

149 Moving toward tomorrow

Today we are faced with the preeminent fact that, if civilization is to survive, we must cultivate the science of human relationships—the ability of all peoples, of all kinds, to live together in the same world, at peace.

. . . as we go forward toward the greatest contribution that any generation of human beings can make in this world—the contribution of lasting peace, I ask you to keep up your faith . . .

. . . to you, and to all Americans who dedicate themselves with us to the making of an abiding peace, I say:

The only limit to our realization of tomorrow will be our doubts of today. Let us move forward with strong and active faith.
Franklin Delano Roosevelt

All the world is heavy with the promise of greater things.
H. G. Wells

It does not pay to get sour as you get old. I pity a man who lives in the past. He lives on stale manna. He gets stunted.
Dwight L. Moody

Someone asked Thorvaldsen, the noted Danish sculptor: "Which is your greatest statue?"

He promptly replied, "The next one."
David T. Armstrong

I desire that death may find me planting my cabbages.
Montaigne

I am done with the years that were: I am quits:
I am done with the dead and old.
They are mines worked out: I've delved in their pits:
I have saved their grain of gold.

Now I turn to the future for wine and bread:
I have bidden the past adieu.
I laugh and lift hand to the years ahead:
"Come on: I am ready for you!"
Virgil Markham

You will always underestimate the future. With willing hands and open minds, the future will be greater than the most fantastic story you can write.
Charles F. Kettering

Face the future courageously. Exercise patience and good judgment in dealing with problems which may arise.
William Green

Who knows but what the dawn may bring
New sorrows, untold sadness sore,
To what the coming day shall cling
As it breaks upon life's melting shore.

But whatso'er the morrow sends
Must be met with armor on.
Defiant, striving toward our ends,
We bravely stand to meet the dawn.
John Harlan Dix

I want to be all that I am capable of becoming . . . a child of the sun.
Katherine Mansfield

A great historian of the Roman Empire, Samuel Dill, says that what overthrew the Roman Empire was "not sheer moral weakness, but an intellectual complacency that froze the life blood." That is a phrase to remember and pray about. Complacency and self-satisfaction are deadly things.
Halford E. Luccock

The future is bright with the hope of religious advance—if in the field of theology we are prepared to move ahead, drawing on the spirit of inquiry and the new knowledge available in this exciting era of history. Someone once asked Einstein how he discovered relativity. He replied, "I challenged an axiom." Theology in the space age could do with less appeal to orthodoxies and more challenging of axioms.
Harvey H. Potthoff

I do not pin my dream for the future to my country or even to my race. I think it probable that civilization somehow will last as long as I care to look ahead.
Oliver Wendell Holmes

---

150 A rendezvous with destiny

The future is something everyone reaches at the rate of sixty minutes an hour, whatever he does, whoever he is.
C. S. Lewis

We reject the religious heritage, first because to master it requires more effort than we are willing to make, and second because it creates issues that are too deep and too contentious to be faced with equanimity. We are afraid to face any longer the severe discipline and the deep disconcerting issues of the nature of the universe and of man's place in it and of his destiny.
Walter Lippmann

Little junior was traveling with his mother. As the train went through a dark tunnel, the boy looked puzzled and then relieved when they emerged again into the sunlight.

"Mother," he exclaimed, "did you see that? Instant tomorrow!"
Doris V. Mendes

Historic responsibilities must be performed with the fullest measure of devotion for such deeds are indelibly inscribed by God Himself.
The Midrash

Man is in danger of being made obsolete by his own progress.
Burton Hillis

It's an age of enormous contention and tension. You get the idea that something is going to be born. You don't know what; you only know it's going to be painful.
Theodore M. Hesburgh

Who is the wise man? Only he who knows the mission and destiny of his life.
Leo Tolstoy

We and God have business with each other. And in that business our highest destiny is fulfilled.
William James

The future is neither wholly ours nor wholly not ours.
Epicurus

Go placidly amid the noise and haste, and remember what peace there may be in silence. As far as possible without surrender, be on good terms with all persons. Speak your truth quietly and clearly; and listen to others, even the dull and ignorant: they, too, have their story. Avoid loud and aggressive persons, they are vexations to the spirit. If you compare yourself with others, you may become vain and bitter; for always there will be greater and lesser persons than yourself.

Enjoy your achievements as well as your plans. Keep interested in your own career, however humble; it is a real possession in the changing fortunes of time. Exercise caution in your business affairs; for the world is full of trickery. But let this not blind you to what virtue there is; many persons strive for high ideals; and everywhere life is full of heroism.

Be yourself. Especially, do not feign affection. Neither be cynical about love; for in the face of all aridity and disenchantment it is as perennial as the grass. Take kindly the counsel of the years, gracefully surrendering the things of youth.

Nurture strength of spirit to shield you in sudden misfortune. But do not distress yourself with imaginings. Many fears are born of fatigue and loneliness. Beyond a wholesome discipline, be gentle with yourself. You are a child of the universe, no less than the trees and the stars; you have a right to be here.

And whether or not it is clear to you, no doubt the universe is unfolding as it should. Therefore be at peace with God, whatever you conceive Him to be; and whatever your labors and aspirations, in the noisy confusion of life keep peace with your soul. With all its sham, drudgery, and broken dreams, it is still a beautiful world. Be careful. Strive to be happy.
Found in Old St. Paul's Church in Baltimore

With the future hold a truce,
If I live the life God gave me
He will turn it to His use.
Lucius Annaeus Seneca

Tomorrow's flowers come from the seeds of today.
Chinese Proverb

Come, my friends,
'Tis not too late to seek a newer world
For my purpose holds,
To sail beyond the sunset and the paths
Of all the western stars, until I die.
Alfred Tennyson